Living Blue
in the Red States

Edited by David Starkey

University of Nebraska Press

Lincoln and London

"How to Ruin a Perfectly Good Swamp
in South Carolina" by Gilbert Allen
© 2007 by Gilbert Allen
"Election Season" by Lee Martin
© 2007 by Lee Martin
"Red Politics and Blue in Wyoming" by David Romtvedt
© 2007 by David Romtvedt
"America, Where's Your Sense of Humor?" by Michael J. Rosen
© 2007 by Michael J. Rosen
"The World Loves New Orleans, but America
Has Not Come to Its Rescue" by Mona Lisa Saloy
© 2007 by Mona Lisa Saloy
© 2007 by the Board of Regents of the University of Nebraska
Manufactured in the United States of America

Library of Congress Cataloging-in-Publication Data
Living blue in the red states / edited by David Starkey.
p.   cm.
ISBN 978-0-8032-6008-5 (pbk.: alk. paper)
1. American prose literature—21st century.   2. Right and left
(Political science)—United States.   3. United States—Social
life and customs—1971–   4. United States—Politics and
government—2001–   5. United States—Description and
travel.   6. Political culture—United States.   7. Conservatism—
United States.   8. Liberalism—United States.
I. Starkey, David, 1962–
PS648.P6L58   2007
814'.6080358—dc22
2006039639
Set in Minion by Bob Reitz.
Designed by Ashley Johnston.

For my wife, Sandy,
and my children,
Elizabeth, Carly, Stephen,
and Miranda:
"blue bloods," one and all

Contents

Part 3. South

Acknowledgments

First and foremost, I want to thank my wife, Sandy, for her love, and for all the support and advice she provides for my many projects. I am, of course, deeply grateful to all the wonderful and enthusiastic contributors to this book, though I'm particularly in debt to those who embraced the living blue concept very early in the process, writing their essays "on spec," before I had a contract. Deb Olin Unferth, David Case, Lee Martin, Sidney Burris, and Jonis Agee: the five of you made it easier for the rest of us. And thanks to Ladette Randolph at the University of Nebraska Press, an ideal editor.

Living Blue in the Red States

Introduction

David Starkey

I.

On the evening of the 2004 Presidential election, I sat at the computer in my Santa Barbara home and *willed* the voters in the Cleveland-area precincts to carry Ohio into the blue, Democratic column. I poured all my mental energy into it. If Ohio went for John Kerry, there might be just enough Electoral College votes to tip the balance in his favor. But if Ohio voted Republican red, it was all over: Bush would be re-elected, this time with a majority of both the popular and the Electoral College votes.

I sat there for several hours—like someone praying for the safe return of a ship he inwardly knows has already foundered—but each time new counts came in, they were no help. Kerry needed a sharp upturn in the number of Democratic votes, but that didn't happen. Most of the Ohio precincts were favoring the Republican candidate. Even the "battleground" city of Columbus was drifting right. Finally, I went to bed, full of despair.

The next morning, like tens of millions of other progressive Americans, I woke up angry. *What the hell were those red voters thinking?* I wanted to know. The war in Iraq was going badly by almost everyone's account, and the weapons of mass destruction had never turned up. And what about Abu Ghraib? And Halliburton and Enron and Tom DeLay? Didn't any of those scandals matter to conservative hoi polloi? Was the president to be held accountable for *nothing*?

Sometimes I'd stare at the red and blue map I had taped to my wall and just seethe. It was easy, then, to lump everyone in the red states together as a bunch of Bible-thumping yahoos. I relished a map that began circulating on the Internet immediately after the election, which showed the blue states as part of The United States of Canada and the red states renamed Jesusland. In fact, my wife and I, like many liberals, talked briefly of moving to Canada, where there weren't so many bigots and morons. Compared to the indignity of suffering another term under Bush II, life in the Northwest Territories sounded pretty grand.

In the months that followed, there were plenty of explanations about why the election went the way it did. Some analysts argued that the many state amendments outlawing same-sex marriage brought out the Right in force. The numbers, at least, seemed to support the frequent assertion that Republicans had done a better job of getting out the vote. Writing in *The Washington Quarterly*, Charles Cook pointed out:

> The three-point gap in the popular vote between Bush and Kerry can be partially explained by a disparity in voter turnout increases between the Bush "red" base states and the Kerry "blue" base states. In the 12 "purple" swing states, voter turnout went up a whopping 17 percent over that of 2000. In the bright red states, those that were universally expected to vote Republican, turnout increased by 14 percent. In the bright blue states, those expected to go for Kerry, however, turnout went up by only 11 percent. It would be logical to assume, then, that, in those states that were not "in play," Bush supporters were more motivated than those voting against him. It's hard to find someone who was enthusiastically voting for Kerry, but not at all difficult to find someone who was passionately voting against the president.

Other pundits contended that the majority of people always find it easiest simply to support the status quo. I read somewhere that the soccer moms who'd voted for Clinton now backed Bush because they feared that terrorists threatened the safety of their children. Certainly, September 11, and the war in Iraq and the Patriot Act all played some role in the outcome of the election—just not in the way those of us on the blue side had been hoping. As William Chaloupka noted in a *Theory & Event* article entitled "What's the Matter With Us?": "There is a small group of infrequent voters (whose power was most important in states such as Ohio, Iowa, Nevada, New Mexico, and Colorado, and who are somewhat more often women than men) for whom disentangling the difficult knot of 'war and democracy' proved too daunting to do on their own. They voted the war on terror."

As Cook suggests, there *were* several maps that showed a slightly less either/or picture of the electorate. One "purple" map displayed the relative percentage of Democratic and Republican votes in each county. Outside a few Rocky Mountain and Midwestern states, dark red was rare, just as the deep blue pockets were largely limited to the coasts and a few large cities in between. Mostly America was purple—a reddish purple, granted, but purple nonetheless. Analysts looking to strike an optimistic note seized on the idea that we weren't so far apart after all. In his book *Culture War? The Myth of a Polarized America*, Morris Fiorina argues that "the hatreds and battles [of the political classes] are not shared by the great mass of the American people . . . who are for the most part moderate in their views and tolerant in their manner."

But I didn't remember experiencing that sense of moderation and tolerance when I'd been living in the Deep South. Quite the contrary. For me, the most telling map—and the one that inspired this book—showed red and blue majorities by county. Again, there was significantly more red than blue, especially if you counted the square miles, but there were many reminders that the red states contained areas of dissent. Great chunks of Colorado, Iowa, New Mexico, and even Arizona were blue. South Texas along the Rio Grande, and the Mississippi River Delta, and the beach counties of southeast Florida: all those places had favored Kerry over Bush. Not surprisingly, throughout the South and Midwest, counties with large universities had voted for the Democrat. And it wasn't simply that there were blue patches in the red; the reverse was also true. In supposedly liberal California, only two noncoastal counties went Democratic. Indeed, the counties to the north and south of my own—San Luis Obispo and Ventura—had both voted for George W.

Obviously, while it was convenient to revile the stupidity of one half of the country and laud the good sense of the other half, it was also profoundly naive. Even at the height of my righteous indignation, I knew I was oversimplifying the matter. It was relatively easy for my wife, who has lived her entire life in liberal Santa Barbara, to formulate a two-dimensional picture of the "fly-over states." But I was born and raised in the red Central Valley of California. I spent every summer of my life, from the time I was born until I turned sixteen, at my grandparents' homes in Beaumont, Texas, and Lake Charles, Louisiana. And I'd lived out there in America for thirteen years, seven of those years in the Deep South. No doubt about it, the political atmosphere is markedly different in Republican strongholds, but some of the bluest people I've ever met live in the red states.

In the following months, I began corresponding with those people—writers, most of them. What were they thinking? How were they dealing with the feeling of being outnumbered that I remembered so keenly? As I listened to their stories of depression and fury and bafflement, I came to believe that it was important to gather some of their voices together in a collection of essays. *Living Blue in the Red States* seemed an obvious title for the book, and I began soliciting work that would reflect on the experience of being deeply committed to regions of the country where the majority of the citizens don't share many of the writer's core values. "It seems to me the best art is political," Toni Morrison has written, "and you ought to make it unquestionably political and irrevocably beautiful at the same time." That became precisely my aim in gathering a collection of new essays that I hoped would shed some light on nothing less than the past and future of America.

Granted, the self-critique I heard most often from those on the Left was that we were too fair-minded, too willing to look at both sides of an issue. Still, I wanted to put together a book that, while pointedly and unapologetically progressive, would gather the work of essayists who were able to look beyond the passions of the moment. And this was to be a work of *literature* above all—"irrevocably beautiful"—so it was essential that every essay succeed first of all as a piece of creative nonfiction. I planned to shy away from one-sided rants (unless they were truly brilliant) and remain wary of highly topical allusions that would quickly fade from public memory. Yes, many of the essays might take the Iraq war and the reelection of George W. Bush as their starting points, but my project was to collect essays that would be just as readable and relevant fifty years from now as they were the day the book was published.

I hoped, therefore, that my contributors would grapple with big questions. How exactly *does* one live blue in a red state? What compromises are required? What unexpected benefits result from the inevitable friction between liberal and conservative values? What accounts for the current gulf between red and blue states? Over the years, has it gotten worse, or better? Is there something in the American character that's been leading to this schism all along? Is the gap likely to widen or narrow? What are the "duties" of essayists who live in a democracy they believe is headed in the wrong direction? What, if anything, might bring our country together again?

The book I most admire on the current Great American Divide is Thomas Frank's *What's the Matter with Kansas?* Frank squarely addresses the central conundrum for those of us on the Left: why do so many middle- and working-class Americans vote against the Democrats, the party that would seem to have their best interests at heart? The answer, according to Frank, is that Republicans have convincingly buried economic issues beneath cultural populism. As long as the Right can effectively present the Left as a clique of all-powerful Ivy League, Volvo-driving, latté-drinking, church-hating snobs, most working Americans will turn their wrath in that direction rather than at the corporations that Frank claims are doing the real damage. The irony, as he points out, is that by pledging allegiance to Values rather than Economic Opportunity, the people who were once the backbone of the Democratic Party now support the very people who exploit them.

Whether or not Frank's thesis adequately explains the great red swaths in some very poor parts of these United States, his book deftly weaves autobiography and argument. It is political reporting, yes, but it's also an eminently readable work of creative nonfiction. *What's the Matter with Kansas?* quickly became my model for integrating personal experience and social analysis, although I imagined that in my book, narrative and memoir and description would be even more crucial to every chapter's overall argument. Generally, that turned out to be the case.

Of course once the essays began arriving, I had to find something to do with them. Having edited and coedited a number of books already, I knew I had the savvy to put a collection together and get it to press, but what of the fact that I was no longer a red-stater? I worried over that for a week or so until I realized that if I still lived in Louisiana or South Carolina, it would probably have never occurred to me to make this book. Drowning in a sea of red, it was all I could do to keep my head above water. Now, from my tiny blue island on the edge of the country, I could catch my breath and call out to my friends in that great red sea who are stronger swimmers than I ever was.

Ultimately, though, I did not want the book to be a festival of red state bashing, so I decided to seek a publisher not from New York or Chicago or Seattle or San Francisco, but from the red states themselves. I reasoned that many of the buyers of humanities books published by red state university presses are as blue as anyone living on the coasts, and therefore there might be a blue editor or two among those publishers. My hunch turned out to be correct. Many of the editors of the red state university presses I queried responded enthusiastically to my proposal. It only remained to poll contributors and learn which one they favored, and the University of Nebraska Press emerged early as the clear favorite. Somehow that seemed fitting, if ironic. After all, Nebraska is one of the three states (Oklahoma and Utah are the other two) where the Democratic candidate for president in 2004 didn't carry a single county.

II.

Living Blue in the Red States is divided into three parts—West, Midwest, and South—to reflect the major geographic divisions of the red states. While discussions of the misunderstandings and resentments between people on opposite sides of the political fence carry over from essay to essay, there are distinct differences between the three sections. Again and again in the four West essays, we have a sense of the expansiveness of the land, the physical presence of mountains and trees and animals. Yes, every square inch may be owned, surveyed, and coveted, but there is still the sense that something unknown and wonderful may yet lie over the next ridge. Even more than the land, weather itself helps shape the outlook of the essayists living in the Midwest. But neighbors are a greater presence here; the weight of contrary human opinion from those living nearby figures vividly in this part of the book. In the section on the South, the pressure to conform to family and community standards, especially in the sphere of religious doctrine, comes to the forefront. According to *Living Blue*'s contributors, thinking differently in the South has clear and immediate consequences.

The book begins with Sherry Simpson's magisterial analysis of bear hunting in Alaska. For thirty years, the McNeil River State Game Sanctuary on the Alaska Peninsula has cultivated the ecotourist activity of bear watching. With the bears now thriving, hunters have put increasing pressure on the state government to ease restrictions on where bears may be shot; even the land adjacent to the sanctuary is now in play. Simpson's essay addresses the inevitable conflict between environmentalists and sport hunters, a recurring blue-red battle. As she says, "The history of wildlife management in Alaska is the history of Alaska, which is an inevitable extension of the history of the West, the United States, the New World. Which is another way of saying that the way we talk about bears—and wolves and squirrels and moose and forests and land—is the way we think of ourselves and our place in the world."

Another Alaskan, Frank Soos, furthers the discussion of his state's unique opportunities and the shortsighted self-interest that too often threatens the very resources that support its citizenry. For Soos, hauling one's own water from the local spring becomes a metaphor for both the value of and the restrictions imposed by self-reliance. Soos believes Alaskans' insatiable desire for "more than is necessary"—selling the state's resources in exchange for "the mountains of wasteful by-products of our getting and spending"—is, ironically, putting "Alaska on a course that will make it more like the Lower 48, that place most of us came here to escape."

David Romtvedt, Wyoming's Poet Laureate, argues that "the coding of our states as red or blue according to whether they have given their vote to a Republican or Democratic Party candidate tells us very little about the people with whom we are passing our lives." He believes this way of thinking not only "isolates us from one another and forces us to lead lives that are intellectually and emotionally impoverished," it is an "early symptom" of the mindset that leads to ethnic cleansing. Instead, Romtvedt values "the strange beauty of each person" in a state where cowboy poets read their work to lesbian feminists and people leave their keys in the ignitions of their unlocked trucks in case someone else has an emergency and needs "to get somewhere— the hospital, or something."

Unlike Romtvedt, Jennifer Sinor feels far from comfortable in the Utah-Idaho border area where she works and lives, despite its great natural beauty. She wonders if her difficulties "come from living in a rural area rather than a red one. Perhaps my problem . . . has nothing to do with the number of Republicans living in Idaho and more to do with the number of cows." However, she adds sardonically, "it is a hard distinction to draw." "Running in the Red" is both wry and sad, the journal of an outsider, a young mother who is also an avid jogger trying to pound her daily worries and conflicts "into a manageable size by the end of a long run."

The Midwest section begins with Lee Martin's lyrical "Election Season," which contrasts the all-for-one work ethic of his boyhood life in southern Illinois with the presidential election in suburban Columbus, Ohio, where he now lives. Martin considers himself relatively apolitical, but the antigay fervor of his neighbors forces him to reconsider everything from his political activity to whether or not he should withhold the bountiful crop of tomatoes from his backyard. This isn't a trivial consideration, for unlike election season, the earth's seasons really matter: "Then the killing frost comes, and then winter's snow and ice, and we wait again for spring and the thawed earth and the chance once more to put our trust in the sunlight and the rain and the plants that grow. How small we are—how insignificant in the light of all this."

Jonis Agee's "Trapping" is a meditation on death and honor. After all the trouble she's had with raccoons, allowing a trapper onto her rural property in Nebraska seems like a good idea. But the sudden death of her brother, both of whose sons are headed to the war in Iraq, causes her to rethink her decision: "Because you see what I had done. I had drawn myself into a trap and now there was hardly anything I could do or forget." She ends the essay by quoting Lucretius: "So each man flees himself, or tries to."

Steve Heller balances his decades of living in Oklahoma and Kansas against his new life in southern California. Cutting back and forth from Clay Center, Kansas, to his apartment in Marina Del Rey, which looks out on the yacht of Midwest native Johnny Carson, Heller tries to answer the question, "When did the civil conversation, the one we used to have with our buddies and our families, whether they were red or blue, bigots or progressives, whether it was face-to-face or by emissary, when did it end?"

Michael J. Rosen's "America, Where's Your Sense of Humor?" is certainly the lightest piece in this collection. With blithe disregard for "the work of statistics experts, political pundits, or well-credentialed analysts in the given field," Rosen attempts to surmise the political leanings of those who submitted work to the most recent version of his humor anthology *May Contain Nuts*. Drawing on data that may, or may not, be accurate, Rosen nevertheless concludes that humor in America, "always the province of minorities and underdogs" is, not surprisingly, "pretty darned blue."

While Robin Hemley's "Control Issues" contains a number of somber moments, it does go some way toward answering Rosen's question about what happened to America's sense of humor. With a dark, scathing, sometimes absurdist wit, Hemley compares the illegal annexation of Hawai'i and the Philippines with the recent invasion of Iraq. He is boggled not only by the similarities but also by "how often we have no control over the way others perceive us, how often the viewpoint of others is in conflict with the way we see ourselves."

The Midwest section is bookended by another election story. Deb Olin Unferth's "A Campaign That Failed" narrates her disastrous turn as a MoveOn political coordinator in the Kansas City suburb of Independence. Like Hemley, Olin Unferth writes prose that is both acidic and droll. "I had thought that once I got through the messy parts, the planning parts, the boring parts, and despite the difficult prelude, that in the end the experience would be a good one. But now, as I peered through the screen into the cool apartment beyond, I understood that no part of this was going to be fun, and it wasn't." Despite fully acknowledging "the heavy weight of things I did not understand," Olin Unferth manages to see the farcical aspects of her unsuccessful crusade.

The Southern section is the longest in the book not only because my own roots are in the South, but also because I think this region has the most powerful influence on how the rest of us define just what it means to be red. While most of the essayists make an effort to see both sides of the red-blue divide, David Case is having none of that. "Playing Debussy in the Heart of Dixie," which begins this grouping, is an unapologetic screed against the racism, sexism, xenophobia, homophobia, and general small-mindedness of his native Alabama. The essay is scornful and poignant and, frankly, without hope that anything very blue will ever take root in the Heart of Dixie. In Case's words: "As far as I can tell, being 'progressive' among Alabama whites means reaching out to Catholics, learning to dislike African Americans a bit less, and reserving most of their current hatred for feminists, Hispanic immigrants, and gays."

Like David Case, Jim Peterson finds his attitude toward the South has been deeply affected by childhood, but unlike Case, who only thinks of escape, Peterson's way of battling his dominating and "truly libertine" father was to embrace the evangelical Christianity that Case disparages. Peterson uses "The Amazing Kreskin," a hypnotist capable of convincing people to do all manner of silly things, as his central metaphor. He argues that withstanding "the Kreskin Effect" is the key to avoiding the blue-red dichotomy: "Living blue in a red state, or living red in a blue state for that matter, may well be a continuing process of resisting the powerful attractions of conformity and acceptance."

John Lane's chapter, like Peterson's, focuses on the role of Christianity in Southern life. Having faced in a short span the deaths of three people close to him—a colleague, his mother, and his aunt—Lane considers the complications, contradictions, and possible consolations offered by faith: "all these deaths made me think of my own mortality. It also made me realize how similar we all are—fragile, human, puny—and how little the political and social issues really matter at the very end. No matter how painful, these three deaths made me better, made me hang onto every detail of life rushing past."

Where Sherry Simpson and Frank Soos discuss the fate of vast tracts of land in Alaska, Gilbert Allen simply wants to turn less than five acres of small-town wasteland into a park. "How to Ruin a Perfectly Good Swamp in South Carolina" chronicles the years-long efforts of Allen and his wife to do things "the Red State Way": "We watched the remnants of a perfectly good swamp ruined, in the name of Free Enterprise. When what was ruined was about to become even worse, we and our neighbors decided to protect ourselves. We had no local park, and we made one, while our government watched—and, at the end, smiled for the camera."

In "Rescue the Drowning, Tie Your Shoe Strings"—the title is Thoreau's advice to would-be philanthropists—Sidney Burris compares the political leanings of his own generation with those of his red state students. He finds that, unlike in the '60s and early '70s, when being a young person in college meant being a de facto liberal, today's students at least *believe* that their political choice begins by looking inward. Still, Burris is wary: "I wonder if they aren't finding their community of friends first, and then internalizing the group's way of doing things; I wonder if they aren't adopting their politics after they've found their friends." Ultimately, Burris concludes: "Our political opinions are dear to our hearts because it is our hearts, and not the national interest, that we are tending to when we utter those opinions."

The letter "P" stands for both "Poetry" and "Pacifism" in Stephen Corey's "*P* Is For . . ." A native of Jamestown, New York, Corey has spent more than thirty years in the Deep South, a perennial "visitor/observer/interloper," always searching for ways "to explore the possibilities of life and language in a distinctive, individualized way, [which] is *ipso facto* diametrically opposed to notions of doing intentional harm and of allowing others (whether individuals or political organizations) to make one's moral decisions."

In "Minority within Minority: Dynamics of Race and Culture in the New South," Anthony Kellman is befriended by a white real estate agent named Gordon, but there are many stresses on an interracial friendship in the Deep South. Kellman, from Barbados, finds that while Southern whites show less prejudice toward Caribbean blacks than toward African Americans, the same racial pigeonholing nevertheless eventually occurs: "And the results are the same. Always the same. Every crab in his own hole."

Like so many other contributors to this volume, Donald Morrill resents the "misleading binary" of blue state–red state, which he believes is "imposed for its high-contrast tele-value." Yet Morrill's essay is among the angriest in the book. He "dangle[s] over the spike of contempt for George W., a man who's never accomplished a thing on his own and has the blankness of his arrogance to prove it." Postmodern in the very best sense of the word, "Theater of Operations" is a fusion of quotations, journal entries, dialogue, poetry, and personal observations.

The title of Crescent City native Mona Lisa Saloy's "The World Loves New Orleans, but America Has Not Come to Its Rescue" sums up her frustration with the federal government's response to Hurricane Katrina and its aftermath. In a warm and lively voice, Saloy remembers living through Hurricane Betsy, then gives a detailed account of her exodus following Katrina. At the center of her essay is a description of the complex network of friends and family that has helped so many evacuees survive the tragedy.

Angus Woodward, current resident of Baton Rouge, former resident of New Orleans, takes a broader look at "Louisiana's New Political Landscape" in the wake of Katrina. With impressive lucidity, Woodward unpacks the complex situation before and after the natural disaster that turned New Orleans "into a brutal testing ground for Bush, Chertoff, Brown, Blanco, Landrieu, Nagin, and dozens of other politicians on the local, state, and national levels."

"Summertime," my own contribution to the book, juxtaposes my childhood summers in Texas and Louisiana with my adult life in Louisiana and South Carolina. The essay is my attempt to "reconcile the different parts of myself—the red and the blue, the bold and the meek, the agitated and the peaceable, the optimistic and the cynical, summer and winter—just as this country is trying to hold itself together, to see its many conflicting impulses not as a weakness, but as a source of strength."

The book closes with an afterword in which I reflect, with the generous help of my contributors, on the various characteristics—the pleasures and challenges and peculiarities—of the "subspecies" of creative nonfiction that this anthology brings together.

III.

During the early stages of the book's evolution, a cartoon appeared in *The New Yorker* showing a uniformed repairman talking to a female office worker as she feeds a piece of paper into a copier. Elbow on her file cabinet, the mustached repairman tells the woman: "You Democrats will never win back the red states if you keep refusing to go out with me." These essays have a different message. I think it is something like what I imagine the woman's response might be: "I'll never go out with you if you don't change the way you see the world."

In her essay "Small Wonder," Barbara Kingsolver writes:

One problem with democracy as it plays in our country is that the majority rules so hard; we seem bent on dividing all things into a contest of Win and Lose, and declaring that the Losers are losers. Nearly half of us are routinely asked to disappear while the slim majority works its will. But the playing field is the planet earth, and I for one have no place else to go.

Most of the contributors to *Living Blue in the Red States*—deeply rooted in their homes and communities—share Kingsolver's sense that there's no place else to go. They would, at any rate, prefer honestly and articulately to discuss their issues and concerns rather than pack up and move to more cerulean pastures. If you live in a blue state, they are your largely unheard comrades in arms. If you are a red-stater, they are your teachers and your neighbors, your family and your friends.

Part One
West

1. Another Way of Saying

Sherry Simpson

The first time I saw the bear known as Fred, he was pacing along the far bank of McNeil River toward two other brown bears that were consorting. "Consorting" is the lyrical word wildlife biologists use to describe the way bears shadow each other when they're not quite ready to mate. When the female paused, the male caught up. He drew her to him with one shaggy foreleg, then mounted her. None of the fourteen bears around them paid much attention. They slumped in repose or gazed at the river, enraptured by the prospect of a passing salmon. A dozen of us watched from gravel viewing pads across the river, a human principality in a suzerainty of bears.

Later I would learn the copulating bears were called Dolly and Weird. The wildlife biologists at McNeil River State Game Sanctuary on the Alaska Peninsula didn't usually volunteer a bear's name. We visitors would pester them, or maybe overhear their comments to each other. They could identify maybe 60 or 70 local bears by physical features and disposition, and they could speak of matriarchal lineages: the Melody clan, the Holdermann clan, the Rolli clan. In years past, when more bears came to the river drainage to feed, the staff recognized as many as 120 bears. Most visitors, though, couldn't distinguish Teddy from Dolly, Albert from Earl, Dusty from Dallas. We just liked saying their names.

But anybody would know Fred from every other bear inhabiting the river that July. For one thing, he was a colossus. Almost any brown bear automatically counts as "big" when it's inhabiting the same plane of existence as you—standing fifteen or thirty or even two hundred feet away, with nothing between you but soft green sheaves of grass and whatever attitude the bear holds toward people at that moment. This bear, though, was a Denali among bears, not just bulky but distinctive. He had shed his pelt, as bears do, so that tattered fur partially caped his face and shoulders. A punk-ish bristle ridged his spine. Countless brawls had tattooed pale scars across the dark skin of his face, neck, and flanks. The muscles surging along his broad frame seemed less like flesh than marble. He walked deliberately, head lowered, his hind legs swinging wide.

The female clasped in mating swung her head around and glimpsed Fred advancing behind the pair. She struggled to free herself from the oblivious male covering her. Finally she succeeded, and her partner, suddenly aware of the larger male's approach, sidled into the brush and out of Fred's path. Thus began a slow-motion pursuit that continued for hours as Fred relentlessly trailed the female. She moved just shy of a lope, trying to outlast his interest while occasionally snatching a fish or pausing to look back.

Once during this circuit from one side of the river to the other, she crossed several yards below the lower viewing pad where four of us, wildlife biologist Polly Hessing and three visitors, sat in camp chairs beside a bluff. Everyone else sat above us on a platform topping the promontory. We saw the bears coming and stood to assert our collective presence. It was a way of saying, "Hey, remember us? Over here in people land?" Fred strode by twenty feet away, pursuing the female with that untiring interest that wavered just an instant. I felt rather than calculated his overwhelming size, the way he muscled through space. But it was the intensity of his sidelong glance that caused me to flinch, as if the force of his gaze had delivered a blow.

Not for a second did I consider raising my camera, but I know I jerked backward. The woman beside me, a backcountry ranger from Katmai National Park, half-turned away. The man at the far end muttered, "Whoa." Polly, standing impassively beside our group, said in a low voice, "When a big one comes by, you want to move slowly. Your heart can move quickly."

We knew that. But Freddy was not just any bear. When he appeared on the river, all other bears shifted out of his way. Sometimes they disappeared into the brush or veered up the bluffs. This made me feel a little better about my own visceral reaction. To encounter a bear that large anywhere else but here . . . the half-formed thought unsettled me every time I saw his dark shape looming during the next three days. My next thought would be deliberate and rational: chances are I'd never see such a bear anywhere else, because most bears don't tolerate humans as easily as McNeil's bears do. Finally, I would dwell for a moment on my good fortune, that I should have lived to see such a creature walking the same earth, passing for just a moment through a shared existence.

"It's hard to tell, but that's the biggest bear in the world," said sanctuary manager Larry Aumiller the next day, as Fred followed a female in another of his tireless loops along the river. (Was it Dolly? Don't ask me.) Larry was only half-joking about Fred's claim on world dominance. Once, researchers tagged a male bear at the river that weighed a thousand pounds. Fred was at least a third bigger, Larry said. Any trophy hunter would covet him. His pelt would wallpaper somebody's den. His reconstituted carcass would dominate any hotel lobby or airport, and everyone who paused to stare would say, "Now *that's* a big bear," as if once taxidermied and posed into some stiff approximation of alertness or even mock aggression, the hollowed bear could ever convey the same magnitude of being.

Polly always called that bear "Fred," and it was a little while before she acknowledged that other wildlife biologists had named him "Freddy Krueger" after the horror movie icon. Polly believed it was unfair to label a bear with shorthand for mayhem and death. But most of us called him Freddy after that, too.

The practice of naming bears is always touchy. Before he was killed and partially eaten by a brown bear in 2003 on the Katmai Coast not far south of McNeil, Timothy Treadwell, the subject of Werner Herzog's documentary film *Grizzly Man*, gave bears names like Cupcake, Booble, Snowball, and Mr. Chocolate. Many people considered this gesture mawkish and disrespectful, including me. Giving human names to bears said more about our desires and needs than anything true or real about the bear, I believed, and often the name itself seemed to obscure the actual animal.

Hunting advocates despise naming bears because it seems annoyingly Disneyesque, a symptom of the tender-hearted and fuzzy-headed emotions displayed by animal rights activists. Many Alaska hunters regard McNeil Sanctuary as a tourist playground that panders shamelessly to these inclinations. "When I think of wildlife, I don't think of them in my anthropomorphic views of how they relate to my world," said bear guide Rod Arno to a reporter. "When I hunt, I think of relating to their world." Arno, one of Alaska's most politically active hunting advocates, was speaking in favor of proposals to open more bear hunting near McNeil River.

After thirty seasons at the sanctuary, Larry Aumiller himself had begun questioning the principle of naming these bears. Larry spoke as we leaned back in camp chairs on the upper platform, warming in the sun. Below us, anywhere from eighteen to twenty-five bears worked the river. They waited for a trigger: a lustrous flash, a slicing fin, a promising ripple. Every bear had developed its own fishing technique. There were belly floppers, divers, snorkelers, submariners, snatchers, waders, plungers, bullies, thieves, scavengers. I saw one chum salmon change custody three times. This was a lean year for salmon in a string of poorly years. The bears yawned, pissed, erupted into brief battles, dozed, soaked in cool eddies, stripped skin from struggling fish, coupled, scratched themselves, snapped at gulls, nosed each other, ignored each other, shat, emerged from grass that covered the land like a thick green pelt, disappeared into a world larger than any of us could know in one minute, one day, four days, thirty years.

Larry has spent more time at McNeil than anyone, and that morning in his cabin he'd done some figuring as a way of accounting for his life here. During at least 3,140 days spent here—that's 8.6 years—he'd made more than 60,000 bear sightings. Seen 150 different bears during a single day. Counted 72 bears at one time. Taken 95,400 photographs. Hiked at least 1,130 times the two-mile trail from camp across the tidal lagoon, up the bluff and through the meadows to the falls. Seen uncountable variations of bear behaviors bold and subtle during the transactions of life common to us all—mating, fighting, eating, playing, traveling, resting, raising young, killing, aging, dying. Learned to recognize a nuanced multiplicity of gestures, vocalizations, stances, decisions, reactions, glances, comportment, inclinations, tendencies, and cues. And he would be the first to say that all that was not enough to comprehend the full mystery and complication of a bear's daily life, because even 8.6 years of witnessing could not account for all the other months, all the other places where bears dwell.

Plenty of reasons justify naming bears individually, Larry said. For one, sanctuary bears are rarely collared, tagged, or tampered with scientifically, so for safety and research reasons, biologists need an easy way to identify and discuss particular animals. And naming McNeil bears acknowledges that these creatures are individual beings, animals different from each other, not just coffeemakers, as he put it. "The more you know about something the more you can appreciate it, whether it's modern art or a bear," he said.

But lately he'd started to believe that naming a bear something like Freddy Krueger or Teddy implied some false understanding, as if Freddy were intrinsically evil and Teddy as familiar and cuddly as a childhood plaything, as if people had actually established some kind of intimate relationship with them.

"The most simplistic way to put that is that we care a lot about them, we're involved in their lives, we name them, we think about them, we study them, we spend time with them," he said. "But I think from their point of view, they couldn't care less. As long as we stay out of their way, don't hassle them, they're not connected. All of these names—that's part of that superficial connection. 'Teddy's an old friend of ours, blah blah blah.' When in fact, I don't think she gives a rip."

He sounded perhaps harsher than his usual good nature allowed. A few months earlier, the Alaska Board of Game had made several decisions that eroded protections for McNeil River bears. Though hunting is not allowed here, the board voted to consider opening hunting seasons in adjacent areas in 2007, knowing that McNeil bears range beyond the two hundred square miles that define the sanctuary. Though numerous long-time Alaskans had testified that bear-viewing in the area was economically important and intrinsically valuable, there was no way to argue that the death of a few more bears anywhere would ever damage the entire population of bears in Alaska, where it's thought as many as thirty-five thousand brown bears (also called grizzly) exist.

"There is no mutually exclusive conflict between viewing of bears and hunting if you consider them as a population," said one of the board's most influential members. "That's been brought up in the testimony here. There is no conflict until you start identifying that the loss of one viewable bear at McNeil River is some mortal sin."

The board, seven citizens appointed by the governor and approved by the legislature, had made a similar decision about the brown bear sanctuary at Pack Creek in Southeast Alaska. It was all part of their philosophical shift, a new landscape of policies created to manage bears as predators now that it's clear that bears as well as wolves can eat lots of moose and caribou calves. So in certain areas of the state where heavy predation is thought responsible for suppressing ungulate populations, hunters are encouraged to bait and kill brown bears and are allowed to sell those hides as economic incentive. It was an unprecedented way of managing wildlife but a very old way of thinking.

The controversy over the McNeil decisions embodied the very definition of "user conflicts." At McNeil, people who enjoyed watching bears (known as "nonconsumptive" users) thought it unfair and unethical that hunters (defined as "consumptive" users) should be allowed to kill bears that had become habituated to people. Habituation is a behavioral term often mistaken for "tame." (I defy anyone to see Fred up close and think of him as tame.) Its simple meaning is that the presence of humans doesn't change bear behavior, either by displacing them from their normal activities or conditioning them to food. At McNeil, the concentration of bears sharing the salmon run is unusually high, and it's believed that their ability to tolerate each other for the sake of food also allows them to ignore people, who are restricted to groups no larger than ten. (A similar behavioral dynamic operates elsewhere on the Katmai Coast, which is one reason why Timothy Treadwell managed to live as long as he did.)

The board's decisions meant, Larry said, that perhaps a third of McNeil's bears were in danger of being shot when they travel beyond sanctuary boundaries—an invisible border within an hour's walk for a bear. Bears aren't territorial; they occupy overlapping ranges, often traveling goodly distances in search of fish runs, dens, tender grasses, nourishing roots, berry patches, mates. The biologists believed a combination of low salmon runs and increased hunting in nearby areas was responsible for severely reducing the number of bears returning to McNeil River to feed in recent years.

For the first time, Larry confessed, he'd avoided thinking of the bears as individuals. "On a personal level it's really painful knowing that they're going to die," he said, his eyes hidden behind sunglasses. "And it's even more painful to know that I'm, more than any other human, responsible for that." By this he meant that for thirty years he'd taken the sanctuary's mission to heart: to protect the world's largest concentration of bears. He and the sanctuary staff had helped these bears feel comfortable around humans by teaching people how to behave calmly, predictably, without fear or aggression. It had worked. Bears nursed their young within view, ambled past people, even napped beside the platform. We ourselves had watched bears mating twenty feet from us, or eating fish within our reach. Staff biologists have never once fired their shotguns at McNeil.

Away from the river, some bears would flee the moment they spotted a person—but some would not. Larry had seen this himself on hikes throughout the sanctuary, when the tense posture of a startled bear would instantly relax as soon as it recognized a human form. That pause would be plenty long enough for a hunter to steady his breath and sharpen his aim as he sighted through a riflescope a hundred or two hundred yards from the bear, somehow pretending that with his shot, he was relating to the bear's world.

Much later I would realize how rare it is for one person—any person—to accept any personal responsibility for what happens to Alaska's wildlife. In a state that operates through brawling rather than consensus—forget compromise—it becomes fine sport to identify wrongdoers and wrong-thinkers. "Them"—that's who the bad guys are. Not us. Them.

Sometimes them is a him—the guy who earned the most votes, the guy now dancing so frantically with those who brought him to the party. So it made sense that Larry Aumiller, feeling responsible more than any other person for the bears of McNeil, thought his last chance of changing things would be to talk to the guy who *could* be most responsible for McNeil's bears.

And because Larry Aumiller is a man so patient and observant he could watch bears for hours, days, months, and never grow bored or complacent, a man who is not physically large and yet is so self-assured and vital that he can change a bear's intentions by shifting his stance, altering his voice, or tipping his hat at the right moment, a man who measures the future by weighing what's best for his little girl and for these big bears—well, it made sense that his last hope lay in somehow collapsing the distance between us and them, between the governor of Alaska and the bears of McNeil River.

There are many ways to kill bears, and many reasons to do so. In 1810, a Russian naval officer named G. I. Davydov described how the Alutiiq people of the Alaska Peninsula killed brown bears. First, they sent their best hunter to wait by a known bear trail. He carried a bow and two stone-tipped arrows. If a bear appeared, he shot it once at "absolutely point-blank range," Davydov wrote. The hunter then dropped his parka and darted away. If the first arrow failed to slay the animal immediately, the parka was meant to draw its attack, giving the hunter one more chance with his remaining arrow.

Today, contemporary Alutiiqs live in several villages on the Alaska Peninsula. In the late 1980s and early 1990s, villagers from three such communities described for subsistence researchers how they killed, ate, and used brown bears in ways they had learned over time. In modern Alaska, the term "subsistence" is a legally defined notion that describes the "customary and traditional" use of wild fish, game, and other natural resources as food, clothing, handicrafts, shelter, tools, transportation, and so on. Subsistence is eating what you killed, gathering eggs, collecting berries, making parkas, mitts and hats from fur. The means of gathering food have changed—snowmachines, rifles, explosive harpoons, boats with engines—but the meaning of gathering food has not. It means sustenance. It means life.

The Alutiiq people reported to researchers that they ate almost every part of the brown bear, except the hide, head, entrails, and heart. Hanging the meat softens the powerful flavor after several weeks.

Rendered bear fat is especially valuable. You can eat it with dried seal or halibut, make soap with it, bake pies and bread.

Usually an Alutiiq bear hunter kills for the community, not for himself or herself (a few women have been trained to kill bears). One young hunter said, "We pretty much share most of the bear. That's the way we were brought up. You've got to feed the elders first because they took care of us. Without the elders we wouldn't know nothing."

As in the old days, a bear hunt was not to be undertaken as a whim. It was a practice drawing on customs, some half-remembered, negotiated during a long relationship with bears, which is another way to say that humans and animals once shared an understanding, a reciprocity. Hunters knew not to joke about the hunt, not to refer to a bear by name, not to act with disrespect. "What my grandma told me [was] that the brown bear was our ancestor," a hunter said. "That when you take one, it was a prayer."

Pete Buist of Fairbanks knows a lot about killing bears, too. He'd come to Alaska with the Army in the 1970s and stayed, hoping to live as a trapper in winter, a hunting guide in spring and fall, and a wildlands firefighter in summer. The arrival of a child forced him to earn paychecks at a desk, though he hunted and trapped for fun and made firefighting his work. A former president of the Alaska Trappers Association, he's been involved for years in hunting and resource politics, and the governor had appointed him to the game board that considered the most recent McNeil proposals.

Over the phone, he told me that although he'd been a bear guide for years, he'd only ever killed one trophy brown bear himself, in the Revelation Mountains near McGrath. "At the time I was upset because you could only shoot one every four years," he said. "But as I matured and my brain caught up with me I have never killed another grizzly." Now its tanned hide hangs on his wall. "And when I look up at it I can see myself sleeping in a slimy little tent with the wind blowing and climbing through butt-deep snow and just having a great time," he said. He'd guided many bear hunts, always enjoyed them, appreciated the way they demand more skill than shooting pheasant or rabbits.

"Quite frankly, the idea that you're hunting something that's bigger and badder than you are is appealing," he said.

People who kill bears react in different ways, he said. "Most people that I have guided are kind of in awe of a big brown bear. They didn't realize how big it was. And they are in awe of it, to the point where some of it is just backslapping. I've seen hunters cry about it." Is that regret or emotional release? I asked. "Probably a mixture. Not that they regretted going bear hunting but maybe that it was over."

(Later I wished I'd asked him if talking about bears as the bigger, badder predators that lend meaning to a hunter's existence wasn't anthropomorphizing them as much as any softie who speaks about loving bears and touching their souls.)

The governor had decided not to reappoint Pete to the board when he'd refused to change his "yes" vote on a politically sensitive proposal to allow bear hunting on the same day hunters flew. Some people were surprised that the governor would ditch him, because Pete is hardcore pro-hunting, like almost everyone else on the board. But Pete prides himself on speaking his mind, no matter whom he angers.

Still, he was pretty careful about the words he chose during our conversation, because he knows better than to speak with a writer the way he'd talk to a buddy, no matter how friendly we were. As we discussed the nitty-gritty of recent bear management decisions, our discussion would politely grind down to me saying something feeble like, "What we're really talking about is a question of values, then," and him agreeing. At the end of two hours, we were reduced to tossing fuzzy scenarios at each other, like battered tennis balls we could never hit back but only deflect. Our conversational gambits went something like this:

ME: Ethically speaking, and completely aside from the legal requirements (of which there are many), why is it OK for sport hunters to take only hides and skulls of bears, but a Native Alaskan who recently killed a walrus for its tusks was sentenced to six years in federal prison for wanton waste?

PETE: So, ask yourself, why is it bad to take only the claws of a bear and leave everything else to decompose, when if you leave the entire animal there in the forest, you're returning everything back to the ecosystem?

ME: Why does it matter to hunters that they have the chance to kill a bear from the McNeil area when bear hunting is available in so many areas of Alaska, and especially when bear hunting everywhere is less restrictive than it's been in decades?

PETE: (His exact words matter here) "To demand that this population of bears, or that this individual bear, not ever be hunted, is not a reasonable request. And in fact it's a rather selfish request. When you get right down to it, you have millions and millions of acres in Alaska where only nonconsumptive use is allowed. There are very few places where nonconsumptive uses are limited or even regulated in any way. And I think it's selfish of those people to demand even more places to be closed when they're not utilizing the places that are already closed and set aside for them."

By this, he meant Alaska's 55 million acres of national parklands, 32 million of them designated as wilderness—a bitter statistic for consumptive users who think of wilderness as a land grab. Several key members of the game board helped make land use decisions during the contentious creation of the Alaska National Interest Lands Conservation Act of 1980, an event that drives many of their responses today.

ME: Why would an ethical hunter want to shoot a bear habituated to people?

PETE: "A hunter who wants to hunt a wild brown bear, he has no interest in hunting a bear who's been used to fishing next to tourists all summer. Now that's not to say every hunter, because there are hunters who just want a three-dimensional bear to be two-dimensional and live in their houses."

ME: Are you saying we have an obligation to accommodate that kind of hunter?

PETE: "Sure. Sure."

And when we hung up, neither of us was exactly arguing—because to argue openly would be to relinquish the high ground of reason and right that each of us secretly claimed—and yet we remained unyielding in the way we see our mutual home. I was exhausted by words and their maddening plasticity, the halting way they semaphored their way toward meaning and yet never once collaborated in a single truth we could agree upon.

Which is another way of saying you can never know what it's like to watch a bear lie against a meadow so her cub, born that winter beneath the cold earth, can climb onto her broad belly and suckle life from her, that you will never understand until you stand nearby, as quiet and open as you have ever been in your life, and see it for yourself. And even then, it may mean less to you than the two-dimensional bear forever stalking your wall, because all we're really talking about is values.

The history of wildlife management in Alaska is the history of Alaska, which is an inevitable extension of the history of the West, the United States, the New World. Which is another way of saying that the way we talk about bears—and wolves and squirrels and moose and forests and land—is the way we think of ourselves and our place in the world. It's possible to sort this relationship out simply by responding to questions as narrowly channeled as something like McNeil. To wit:

- Are the bears of McNeil River (or the wolves of Denali or the caribou of the 1002 area in the Arctic National Wildlife Refuge or the wolverines of Game Management Unit 13) individuals or a population?

- If they are individuals, is that because people recognize them and photograph them and make calendars and postcards out of them and sometimes name them, or is it because every creature is an individual unto itself?

- If they are a population, do you group them as part of a valley, a drainage, a game management unit, a species, a state, a nation, a continent, a planet, an epoch?

- Do you count bears in harvest classes or life spans?

- Are bears predators, furbearers, big game, charismatic mega-fauna, apex species, consumptive uses, competitors, friends, foes, all of the above, or none of the above?

- Is hunting is a privilege or a right? A necessity or a sport? Or does it matter why you kill something, rather than what you kill?

- If hunting is a necessity, must you eat up every bit of what you kill?

- If it's a sport, who gets to have the most fun?

- If you hunt for subsistence, does it make a difference if you live in downtown Anchorage, in the Athabascan village of Huslia, or in Iowa?

- If bears are better off in parks and sanctuaries, are they fair game (no pun intended) if they leave the park?

- If people are better off in wilderness, is it still wilderness if they're there?

- Do you think of people as individuals or populations? Do they have values or rights? Who decides?

- Should the board that regulates Alaska's wildlife be known as the Board of Game or the Board of Wildlife, and will a simple name change make a difference?

- If your dream is to see a bear, where did that dream come from? The movies? Timothy Treadwell? Some old, dark place? Some vague longing? And what do you suppose the bear gains from fulfilling your dream?

- If you see a bear, will you freeze, run away, scream, reach out as if to touch it, name it, or shoot it?

- If you answered "shoot," did you mean with a rifle or a camera or both?

- When hunting advocate Rod Arno said allowing bear hunting near McNeil is "not going to hurt a bit," to whom do you think he was referring?

When I was a kid in Juneau, we learned the state flag song so we could sing it during the centennial celebration of the 1867 purchase of Alaska from Russia. Seventh-grader Benny Benson, born to a Russian Aleut mother, created the flag's eloquent design by spreading the constellation of Ursa Major across a blue background. The tune begins confidently: "Eight stars of gold on a field of blue . . ." It's one of those impossibly constructed melodies that requires operatic training to conquer the higher registers, so most Alaskans finish by squeaking it out, our voices cracking and then plummeting to safer octaves by the time we reach the soaring conclusion: "the 'Bear,'—the 'Dipper'—and shining high, the great north star with its steady light, o'er land and sea, a beacon bright, Alaska's flag—to Alaskans dear, the simple flag of the Last Frontier." People sometimes cry at that last bit. (A later, second verse meant to acknowledge Alaska Natives has never passed both houses of the legislature.)

Our legal north star is a constitution written in 1956 by a gathering of the territory's most faithful, hopeful citizens. (One of the fifty-five drafters was a Native.) They drew on their own knowledge of living in a colony established on the wholesale extraction of gold, fish, fur, timber, coal, oil—anything that could be cut down, canned, dredged, tanned, or churned from earth and sea. The extraction wasn't the galling part. What outraged territorial residents was the sluicing of this stolen wealth to Outside interests.

It's true the delegates loved wilderness, too. Few people survive in Alaska if they don't. But wilderness for them was not a state of being or an act of personal aspiration. It was a livelihood, an appendage to identity, the means and not the end.

The constitution's article addressing national resources makes plain those good citizens' intentions—our continuing intentions—in what may be the last spasm of Manifest Destiny in American history: "It is the policy of the State to encourage the settlement of its land and the development of its resources by making them available for maximum use consistent with the public interest."

Listen to how this mandate sounds so authoritative and yet so abstract as it elaborates upon the "utilization, development, and conservation of all natural resources . . . for the maximum benefit of the people . . . on the sustained yield principle, subject to preferences among beneficial uses."

And ever since, Alaskans have wrangled over the multiple meanings of these brittle words, splintering them into thin definitions of what it means to live on the Last Frontier, in this wilderness, in this land. From this bounty, so much bewilderment: How are we to live? What sustains us? What do we deserve? What do we surrender? Who gets what? Who says so? Who are they? Who are we?

It's not even the words that elude us but their shadow meanings. Thus, from *beneficial, sustained, utilization,* somehow we arrived at *intensive management,* a statute that requires the game board to *restore the abundance or productivity of identified big game prey populations as necessary to achieve human consumptive use.* (Some people call this "game farming.") Phrases that began in wildlife management migrated to politics: *Consumptive use. Nonconsumptive use. Adaptive management. Predator control.*

And we indulge in these phrases as if we all shared their meaning, as if it doesn't matter that such vague concepts have cascaded into policies that nobody ever voted for, exactly. That includes *recognized and prudent active management techniques* such as shooting wolves from airplanes, snowmachines, boats, and all-terrain vehicles, and shooting brown bears over bait. This doesn't happen everywhere in Alaska, just in intensive management areas identified through science skewed by politics.

Because no one can credibly claim the healthy populations of wolves and bears in Alaska are endangered by such actions, any protests become the mewlings of those crazy animal rights activists interfering from Outside. This is true even if you're a retired wildlife biologist, a lifelong Alaskan with a view beyond the next hunting season, or somebody as knowledgeable as Jack Reakoff of Wiseman (population 14), a hunter and trapper who continues testifying and criticizing and writing proposals for a game board he considers woefully biased and scientifically ignorant. "I live here," he explained to me once. "Nobody's talking for the animals. Somebody's got to stick up for the game, you know."

Yet even when Alaskans stick up for the game, twice voting down the practice of shooting wolves from airplanes, it didn't matter because the legislature ignored the results, reasoning that "ballot box biology" is not truly the people's will because it is vulnerable to inaccurate ad campaigns, the fiscal corruption of those Outside groups, and emotional blackmail. Some people will say that Alaska's system of game management is the most democratic in the world, because the game board is a citizen group appointed by an elected leader, guided by recommendations of citizen advisory councils, and beholden to consider any proposal submitted by any resident. The right to speak up, however, has yet to obligate anyone in power to listen.

Which is why Larry and other bear experts and wildlife advocates sigh heavily whenever you ask them about the Board of Game. For example, the board received something like 7,500 public comments about the McNeil proposals. Fewer than 15 people supported further hunting in the area. Pete Buist didn't mention anything about the overwhelming public testimony in favor of more protection. He did, however, talk about 6,000 anti-hunting messages that became the source of much snickering and head-shaking among board members. The electronic form letters were generated by the Defenders of Wildlife in a well-meaning attempt to rally national support for the bears of McNeil River and against wolf control. The local organizer printed and delivered boxes and boxes of printouts to the board because electronic messages aren't accepted.

Pete sent me a booklet he'd compiled from these printouts because he thought I'd get a kick out of it. He titled it "The Best of the 6,000" and helpfully highlighted in yellow some of his favorite lines. The first message read simply "stop killing wolves asshole." Another began, "The Wolves and bears of Alaska are endangered species due to their treatment by humans. Both species are omnivors [sic], and principally eat fish and rodents." This is incorrect, of course; neither wolves nor bears are endangered in Alaska, and neither eat principally fish and rodents.

"I am hoping that one of you elected officials who voted on this ARE accidentally SHOT, JUST LIKE YOU ARE SHOOTING THE WOLVES," wrote another concerned citizen. Somebody else suggested, "Dude, you must somewhere in there realize how sick it is to hunt wolves from an airplane—don't give me that—how dumb—just stop it; now." The message that made me laugh aloud used the boilerplate paragraphs expressing opposition but failed to omit the form letter's prompt to "[INSERT PERSONAL OPINION HERE]."

Such messages are passionate but worse than useless, and they make me angry, because the damage they do is tangible and lasting. You can hear their effect every time someone derides "those animal rights activists" or "those wacko greenies," which has become code for "everyone who disagrees with me." You will recognize the harm of such careless invective in the way it infuses rhetoric over Alaska's biggest land issues. The result is language that functions like Styrofoam, lightweight and uniform and insubstantial, yet capable of filling every bit of space and squeezing out thought.

It happened with wolf control, and it's happening with the perpetual wrangle over drilling in the Arctic National Wildlife Refuge. I confess to being bludgeoned senseless by this battle just when attention was most necessary. One example: the National Petroleum Reserve–Alaska is a northwestern plain of 23 million acres of public lands bordering the Prudhoe Bay oil fields. It also supports some of the continent's most ecologically productive lands, including a calving caribou herd, critical nesting grounds for huge flocks of migratory waterfowl, and many Inupiat who feed themselves with meat, fish, berries, eggs. Oil companies are lots more excited about NPR-A than they are about ANWR, because the reserve offers promising deposits of oil and gas beneath public lands long intended for development. No troublesome words like "wildlife" or "refuge" interfere; no congressional permission is required.

But while environmentalists were transfixed by the political pyrotechnics surrounding ANWR, the Bureau of Land Management quietly broke long-standing promises to the Inupiat not to lease tracts in NPR-A's most sensitive areas, notably around Teshekpuk Lake. Even the Reagan administration favored protecting that area. "It's the beating heart," said an Inupiat leader in one of few news articles published about the NPR-A's imminent development. "It's one of the last completely undisturbed areas. It's God's country."

You won't hear much about Teshekpuk Lake, and anyway, it's too late now. Words fooled us, words that declared one place a petroleum reserve, and the other a pristine refuge, though your feet and your beating heart could never tell the difference between the two if ever you looked with your own eyes.

One evening at McNeil, Larry Aumiller invited me to share dinner in his cabin with the other biologists. We ate fresh greens just arrived by floatplane, along with rice, and broiled salmon Larry had caught in the bay. They talked about research into salmon-spawning patterns and Freddy and similar topics that make for news in these parts. After the others left, Larry showed me the season's journal. For the first time, he'd begun writing from a personal perspective rather than as a business-like accounting of daily events. The journal began, "I am an emotional person." He'd been writing it for his daughter, and for himself, trying to examine more deeply what he believed about McNeil.

He'd also practiced what to say when the governor visited the camp later in the summer. It was a governor, after all, who'd visited the sanctuary one day in 1995 and then directed the state to recommend closing the adjoining refuge to bear hunting. That game board had agreed, mostly because non-hunters had flooded the permit lottery and won seven of eight permits. They never used them, effectively shutting down the season. The public had spoken; the governor had listened; the board had acted. But that was then. The current board had made a philosophical stand to such "extremism" by reopening hunting on adjacent land. They made the decision sound provisional and subject to public comment. It's not.

So Larry outlined what he would tell the governor, and it was a fine speech. He'd explain that the sanctuary was like no other place in the world. He'd emphasize how Alaska had the immense responsibility and pride of acting as its steward. He'd say, "We're not dealing with a population at all. We're dealing with an experience." Then he would look the former banker right in the eye and ask, "What do you say, Governor? Would you help us?" And the governor's answer would tell him everything he needed to know, about the sanctuary's future and his own.

I knew how tenuous Larry's plan was. The current administration had always made vodka-clear its notions of how to manage land and resources and wildlife in Alaska, and those convictions had little dalliance with public opinion or further conservation. Still, relying on political labels in a place where voters registered as "nonpartisan" or "undeclared" far outnumber the traditional parties—that's often a good way to fool yourself, in the same way that naming bears Freddy Krueger or Teddy persuades you such monikers carry any actual meaning beyond perception.

At eighteen, I voted for my first governor, a Republican who had been a bush pilot, a trapper, and a wolf bounty-hunter who later renounced predator control. He was also an honest and capable visionary who'd guided Alaska through the most turbulent years of pipeline development, land claims, and Native rights. Alaska's last Democratic governor, for whom I also voted, was a businessman who disappointed every environmentalist thrilling to the possibility that at last a liberal would control the oil companies that pump Alaska's living from the ground. He's the one who encouraged further exploration in the NPR-A. The governor who served once as a Republican and another time as an Independent was famous for uttering the divinely ridiculous aphorism, "You can't just let nature run wild." (I didn't vote for him either time.) He also signed the original legislation that created the McNeil sanctuary.

That night, in the dimness of my tent, I listened to bears making their strange and primal sounds across the lagoon and thought hopefully about Larry's speech. A man who'd learned how to read the body language of bears, who knew how to remain calm and confident around animals and people—surely he'd convince the governor that McNeil mattered. If Larry couldn't, then who would?

As it turned out, the governor never visited McNeil. Something more important interfered. In his place he sent two top officials, his new commissioner of the Department of Fish and Game, and his deputy chief of staff, who is also a taxidermist specializing in bear hides and mounts. Whatever Larry read in their body language or heard in their responses was not enough to prevent him from retiring from the Alaska Department of Fish and Game after the season ended.

He wrote a newspaper commentary explaining why: "To purposely and knowingly kill these habituated animals for trophies is beyond any definition of reasonable ethics or fair chase, and, I believe, is morally wrong. I've always envisioned that I'd be at McNeil River until I couldn't physically do it anymore. But I can't continue to remove the bears' only protection—their natural wariness—knowing that even more of them will soon be exposed to hunting." I didn't have the heart to call and hear the details of his decision. Over and over, in his own way, he'd been saying good-bye to McNeil all summer.

A few months later, I had a chance to talk with the governor's men about wildlife policy. The commissioner said the kinds of things new commissioners say; he was articulate, careful, and vague. He said he wasn't really sure why Larry Aumiller had retired. The director of wildlife conservation said he was surprised, too, and that he should probably ask Larry about it some time. The deputy chief of staff, the taxidermist who advises the governor on wildlife issues, said almost nothing during the two-hour discussion.

Finally I asked him how he had liked his visit to McNeil. He shrugged. He'd been close to bears many times before, he said. (I admit that I thought, "Yeah, *dead* bears.") But one thing really impressed him, he added. That was when the dominant male bear showed up and all of the other bears cleared out of his way. The men laughed appreciatively. Leaving the governor's office, I thought about how the taxidermist had enjoyed most the display of domination and power, not the long cultivation of humility and tolerance, and not the possibility of some new way of seeing bears. The way we talk about bears is the way we see ourselves.

Every morning as we crested the grassy ridge and the waterfall's thrumming enveloped us, all those brown bears gathered beside the river suddenly came into view, and the moment jolted through me as if I had just shuddered into being.

It wasn't simply the presence of so many bears at once—twelve, seventeen, twenty-five. Those are merely numbers. Glimpsing a single bear in the wild can make your legs weak and heart shivery, too. And it wasn't only the nearness of bears as they lumbered within a few yards, sometimes glancing at us and then away as they moved past, disinterested and preoccupied with their own business. It doesn't matter to bears whether you come and look at them, what names you give them, whether you believe in them as individuals, whether you believe in yourself as an individual. Those things matter only to you.

What seized me was understanding for the first time that always bears are out there, somewhere, whether or not you see them or think of them or understand them. Every moment of your life, bears exist in this world, the same world to which you belong. They are thrashing after fish, nursing their young, scrabbling roots and lapping up insects, dreaming their way through winter, tearing open hot flesh, searching for mates, dozing in the sweet grass. Like you, they are living their lives moment to moment, summer to summer, year by year.

This understanding was beyond words, but of course we could not help but utter words all day long as we watched bears conduct their lives in the open. In fact, we could not shut up, not even just this once. The need to define, to describe, to react, to share, to separate the world into us and them, to name out loud—this imperative is something that makes us human.

And being helplessly human, I thought into the winter about all the ways we name our way through life, how calling a people's guiding document a *constitution* is another way of saying *compact*, which is another word for *covenant*, which is a promise to ourselves and to the future, even if the promise no longer fits the future, even if we no longer have faith in the past. Somehow *wilderness* figures in there, too (though you'll never find that word in Alaska's constitution), but although it should be large enough to hold other words like *wildlife* and *subsistence* and *living*, it seemed too vague, too pallid, too used up, to endow those ideas with all the meaning they deserve. *Sanctuary, refuge, reserve*—those I'm still worrying over.

I wondered what prayers we are making when we kill (no matter who pulls the trigger or writes the statute). What language becomes our default? What names do we choose for each other and ourselves, and how much do they limit us and narrow our vision? I thought about how identifying myself as "nonpartisan" has too often meant "noninvolved," no matter how faithfully I vote.

I read long and prickly debates among Alaska hunters on a Web-based outdoor forum, and this made me feel more optimistic than anything I've seen, because a subsistence hunter named "Bushrat" constantly but respectfully challenged his fellow hunters with intelligent, articulate, and thorough criticisms of the game board's decisions. He understood more than any of us how intimately our lives are yoked with the ethos of wildlife management. He talked about bears as if they mattered, even the ones he'd eaten. He made the others think, even when they disagreed with him. And I wondered if I could struggle that hard for a new language beyond what others force on me, beneath the language I myself hide behind.

When finally words exhaust me, I remember that last day at McNeil River, when the waters of Kamishak Bay filled the lagoon and separated us from camp, and so we crowded into a skiff and motored back. Beneath the shallow, clear waters of the flooding tide, I could see thousands of bear tracks pressed deeply into black mud. They pointed in every direction, planted one upon the other, every step deliberate and purposeful, every paw print left by a particular, individual animal, every track the mark of some nameless bear making its way through the world.

2. Hauling Water
Frank Soos

For five years, I lived in the cedar-sided hip-roof cabin at the top of Old Wood Way. As Alaskan cabins go, it was pretty deluxe. It was maybe sixteen by thirty feet and had a big deck that faced south and almost a full second-story loft up the steep stairs. At the end of the cabin that was my kitchen, I had a small white table and three chairs. A full-spectrum light sat right on the table; it kept my spirits up on the darkest days. All the storage space was covered by red-checked curtains—lots of storage, enough for my food and cooking stuff and my tools and ski waxes, too. In the living area there were two big couches, one a little broken down, a coffee table made from an old wire spool, and hooks I'd screwed into the exposed rafters for my skis and bikes and extra wheels. Up in the loft I had my bed, my writing desk, and my fly-tying desk.

Because it was a cabin, I hauled water, hauled it in six-gallon jugs from the spring in Fox every couple of weeks or so. And because it was a cabin, it had an outhouse, just down the hill. Enclosed on only three sides, its open side, too, faced south. Sitting in there, a person could look down on the hardtop road that ran below. Maybe in the winter, people driving along the hardtop could look up and see me, too, but I didn't think they'd bother, and if they did I didn't care.

I thought my cabin contained everything a person could want.

Except: up on the east side of Chena Ridge, the side that tapers down into Fairbanks near the university, a guy had built a four-story house complete with a Victorian turret running up one side, all that house, so they say, built just for his wife and him. Probably this was the first house to go up in Fairbanks that cost over half a million dollars. Now, given the escalating real estate market, it may very well bring a million and a half or two million. Just about anybody in town could tell you the story behind that house. How the guy started building it, and as it went up and up, his neighbor behind him sued because the house would block his view of the Alaska Range. So for over a year, the house sat unfinished, covered in blue tarps and plywood. And then the neighbor lost the suit. The house was finished, the view was blocked, and the two households have lived locked in a certain enmity ever since, I suppose.

When I first came to Fairbanks almost twenty years ago, there were still old pickup trucks banging around with bumper stickers that proclaimed, "We don't care how they do it in the Lower 48." There was something stubborn and pig-headed in that slogan that I had to admire. It's part of what brought me here. Alaska was a different place and it would require different ways of thinking.

The pipeline changed all that. The old timers, the true Sourdoughs, will tell you everything was better before the pipeline came in. People took care of themselves and looked out for others, too. They learned how to be frugal and inventive. You'll know the old Sourdoughs from their yards. A near neighbor on Old Wood had a yard full of vintage Land Rovers, another a yard full of old Rambler American station wagons, and each had his share of fifty-five-gallon barrels, chain and cable and pipe. The Land Rovers seemed the better choice, but who could know? You never know what you'll need or when you'll need it.

Who can say what a person might need? Or want? Or ought to want? Jesus tells the Rich Young Ruler to sell all his belongings and give the money to the poor. Only then would he be a fit disciple. I used to like to pester a graduate student of mine, a former seminarian, over this very question. And he owned up to the issue as it was applied in seminary bull sessions. Was it OK to have a nice stereo when a boom box might do? Could a person rightfully have a big CD collection, a smallish collection, or would the radio have to serve? Among his fellows, these were weighty questions.

Where would such inquiries end? I ask because when the pipeline was being built, money ran through Fairbanks, through all of Alaska like spring run-off.

I ask because the spring at Fox is only a few hundred yards up the road from the intersection of the Steese and Elliott Highways. Looking north from that intersection, looking if you could all the way to the Yukon River, you would see a giant pie-shaped piece of public land, land we all own together. A person can hike on it, fish its creeks, ski or snowmachine to its cabins. Or a person could mine it or timber it even, though the timber is nothing to speak of.

I ask because the powerful engine that drives our wants and needs requires constant fueling, and that fuel has to come from somewhere.

Here in Alaska, you'll hear people talk of "locking up the land." What they mean is that acres and acres of land in this state are held by the federal government, by the Bureau of Land Management, by the National Park Service, as National Forest, and as Wildlife Refuge. Locked up because for all the walking and fishing and skiing a person might do on this land, that would not be enough.

I cannot begin to explain where we get all our ideas of how we might value the land, but I can say that none of these ideas is fresh with us in our time. We inherited them all. When Europeans encountered Native Americans, they met people who believed leisure mattered more than material goods. In other words, time to them was worth more than money. They believed land was too sacred a commodity ever to be owned by a single person.

For a while, I believed that, too. I thought private ownership of land was a pretty bad idea. All around Fairbanks, you can see the cost of private ownership dating back to the Gold Rush, piles of tailings, piles of rusted junk that mined those tailings, and newer piles of junk on top of the old junk. Like drawn to like, I suppose. Land carelessly used and nearly ruined for good.

The trouble with collective ownership of land as practiced by a group of nearly 300 million American people is that few people feel especially responsible for this corner or that. So it was that in our state the old Atomic Energy Commission performed underground tests out in the Aleutian Islands and would have nuked an artificial harbor at Point Hope had the Natives not pulled together and stopped them.

What is the purpose of the land? It's an oddly occidental question. It's a question that implies what very nearly all of us think, that land just sitting there minding its own business, running its ecosystems independent of any of our wishes, has no value or use.

Thanks to the Romantics, we have inherited a sense of beauty that insists on the sublime. The Alps, for the longest time just an impediment to commerce, suddenly became beautiful once the Romantics got our attention. Once we absorb them, we carry those notions along with us. That's why places such as Yellowstone and Yosemite, endowed with such startling beauty, have been declared National Parks. In Alaska, we have plenty of such sublime beauty—the Alaska Range, the Brooks, the Wrangells, the Chugach.

And this may be why people who have never set foot in the Arctic National Wildlife Refuge can blissfully declare it a wasteland. The land on the Arctic Coastal plain is marshy and flat in the summertime, so infested by mosquitoes that a caribou calf might die of anemia as a result of their bites. In the winter, it is an icy, wind-blasted sheet a person, or just about any animal for that matter, would just as soon avoid. It is land that belongs to all of us, but land that most will never set foot on. It is hard country and not particularly welcoming. So it is easy to think of it as expendable. I've even heard representatives of our own state government say, "There's nothing up there."

As it happens, I have been to the Refuge. When our Cessna broke through the clouds above Schrader Lake, I could not quite make out what I was seeing. There seemed to be clumps of bushes scattered all around the lake. I knew enough to understand they could not be trees. We'd left trees behind on the other side of the Brooks Range. As we dropped closer to the lake, I could see they were caribou. Hundreds right at that moment, and before we left a day and a half later, thousands more. They came in clots of as few as five or six to as many as twenty down to the outlet of the lake, paced nervously up and down and then plunged into the river and swam across.

Schrader Lake is backed into the Brooks Range enough so that on a sunny day a person might feel the presence of the surrounding mountains. But in the brief time I was there, I saw only the nearby hills, the brush scrub that scarcely came to my knees. If beauty is to be found there, a person has to look down through the scrub to see the delicate arctic flowers. A person needs to look across the horizon line at the constantly flowing patterns made by the caribou as they walk and feed. The Refuge offers more beauty than a person could ever take in. Provided he knew how to look.

When you haul your own water, you learn to be careful with it. I used to hate it when a jug tipped over in the back of my truck and I lost a gallon or two. You learn to wash with very little, you learn that a little grease never hurt anybody. And once you begin to economize on water, other economies tend to follow. You have less trash, and what you have you put in recycled grocery bags. You keep your place on the cool side so the fuel truck only has to visit once a year to fill the tank. You plan your routes to town, stringing errands together, the gym for showers, the Laundromat.

In the best old-fashioned sense, that's what's meant by conservation: thrift, care, an awareness of our place in the larger world. Still, "people got to eat," my friend Knut, a wildlife biologist who specializes in arctic fox, tells me. That's what he says whenever I rave on about the huge modern open pit gold mines at the top of Cleary Summit or the old-fashioned inefficient mines in the Forty Mile Country, whenever I get going on proposed clear-cutting operations along the upper Chena River.

In the Kuskokwim villages upriver from Bethel, gasoline is already $4.75 a gallon and winter has barely set in. Fuel oil is nearly as much; already some villages are worried they may come up short on money to keep their generators running. Yes, the price and the shortages it has created are terrible things. Yes, it is ironic that this could be happening where hot oil runs through the pipeline right down the middle of the state every day. But irony is often best appreciated from a distance. What it means is that the tipping point for opening ANWR for oil exploration and drilling may have been reached. The hurricanes in the Gulf of Mexico, the howls of indignation at high fuel prices, and our inabilities to curb our own appetites have brought us to this sorry pass. Yes, people have got to eat, but how much?

Just now we Alaskans are all over the Lower-48 papers for making pigs of ourselves.

The so-called Bridge to Nowhere will cost over $230 million just to get it started, considerably more to finish. It will link the town of Ketchikan to its airport on the other side of the Tongass Narrows. The Bridge to Nowhere is not the only expensive construction project that our lone U.S. representative, Don Young, has stuffed into the bill coming out of the House Transportation Committee, which he chairs.

When a senator from another state suggested that Don Young turn the money back so it might be used to repair the damaged levies around New Orleans, he said, "He can kiss my ear, if you know what I mean." I thought I knew.

Though it is harder to know *why*. When the pipeline started flowing with oil, money ran through Alaska again, ran like summer glacial run-off, ran so hard that they say the state accountants in Juneau could hardly keep up with it all. We, through the good offices of our politicians, decided to forgo any form of state taxation and to give ourselves an annual dividend from the accumulated oil royalties. And although we Alaskans have paid virtually no state taxes since, and per capita receive a most generous return from our tax dollars paid to the federal government, most of us will tell you we want the government to get off our backs. Right in the middle, hollering the loudest, would be Don Young.

Don Young: it may be impossible to consider Alaska without writing about Don Young. Say his name in the right bunch of people and everybody laughs out loud. In another group, there are just knowing half smiles. The first time he stood for the office, he lost to a dead man. The next time he beat a guy who made the mistake of admitting that some form of gun control wouldn't be altogether bad. Don Young has been our representative for over thirty years now, and most likely the job is his until he dies. We Alaskans keep sending him back to Congress because he knows what we stand for—our right to own as much land as we can get a hold of, our right to use our resources as profligately as we want, our right to make messes and not worry a whole lot about cleaning them up. Alaskans love Don Young and he loves us back. Lately, thanks to his seniority and the Republican majority, he's made it his business to bring home as much bacon as he can: more money for roads, for development. I am trying hard to understand Don Young because I believe he does love Alaska; he loves Alaska as much as I do.

There is no evidence the Rich Young Ruler ever got back to Jesus on his proposition. It's hard, I'll be the first to admit, to do with less when you don't have to. It's harder still when we live in a world that is so insistent on measuring not just our worth but our happiness by the number of things we own. It may be time to ask another question: not how much we need or want, but how much we think we deserve. This may be the hardest question.

At the Fox spring, the question hardly seems to come into play. The water springs miraculously out of the ground, and we can all have our fill if we're only willing to wait our turn. And the water is free. Most of the time, this arrangement works out fine.

But here is something that happened to me at the Fox springs a couple of winters back. When I pulled into the spring, there was an older couple getting water and another couple sitting in a great big Ford pickup listening to the radio and waiting. I pulled in behind the Ford and listened to my radio, too. It was a Sunday afternoon; KSUA had on the Grateful Dead show; I had the Sunday paper to keep me company, and besides it was cold, maybe minus twenty or thirty. The old folks were taking forever to fill their bazillion jugs ranging from surplus army jerrycans all the way down to crates of gallon milk jugs. So we kept waiting. After a while another couple of cars pulled up. A guy got out of one car and began to line up his jugs. In fact, this is the way it's usually done; you get out and line up your jugs just outside the small boardwalk that leads to the water taps.

I waited a while for the folks in the big Ford to get out and line up their jugs, too. When they didn't, and the other new arrivals started to get out of their car, I jumped out and grabbed a couple of my jugs to claim my spot before I got any farther behind.

The guy in the Ford got out. He was pretty big, maybe six-two or -three and had black hair down to his shoulders and wraparound sunglasses. His parka was thrown open over a sizeable belly. "All right," he hollered, "we're leaving and coming back after a while. But I want you people to know you're all assholes."

The guy who was first in line—clean-shaven, good posture, I had him pegged for career military, retired—said, "Everybody knows this is how it works. You get in line, you claim your place."

The big guy—a Native guy, I'm thinking—said, "Who says? Who says that?"

And the retired military guy smugly said back, "Anybody who's lived here any time at all."

"Oh yeah? Well, I was born here." Then he got in his truck and drove off in a spray of gravel.

Standing out at Fox, standing there waiting by running water, both the spring and the little creek that flows year-round under the taps, can make a person inclined to run some water, too. People would race into the woods just beyond the spring and pee. They just couldn't help it. The state had to put up a fence to stop them. Otherwise, there would be all this pee going into the ground right there above the water table that fed the spring. Nobody wanted that, but they had not been able to control themselves.

Whether we asked for it or not, the government (in this case, you might call government a wiser and more thoughtful version of ourselves) stepped in and made a fence. And the government, too, had channeled the water into pipes that fed the two water taps and made a pipe for the excess to flow safely into the creek. And every now and then, the government shows up to test the water to make sure it's still safe for all of us to drink. Sometime in later winter or early spring, when the excess splash has built big icy glaciers around the water taps, the government comes along and steams it away so none of us breaks a leg.

A few years back, a group of Scandinavian social planners came to Fairbanks. Since we had invited them, we should not have been outraged by what they had to say, but we were. They told us we were urban people. They told us to face it, most all of us spent well over twenty-two hours of each day indoors in the winter months and very nearly as many in the summer. We lived in houses with central heat; we relied on conveniences like supermarkets and mini-malls. We lived in an elaborately constructed, if highly inefficient, social structure. We were not wild and fearless frontierspeople willing to stave off bears with our Leatherman tools. But we still insist on acting that way.

As a result, many Alaskans see government differently than I do. The federal government is, more often than not, a remote, controlling enemy. So it's OK for the rugged individual to pull down as much federal money as he can get. In this version of our lives, it is possible to see Don Young as somehow akin to John Wesley Harding. The state government could be a troublesome impediment, too, if allowed to get out of hand. The prevailing view is that government does well when it just stands back and lets citizens have at it. It does best when it clears the way.

What I wish for my government is that it be a wiser, more thoughtful version of my neighbors and me.

When we flew out of Schrader Lake, we went west to Deadhorse to refuel. Along the way, we saw musk oxen doing their musk oxen thing—at the sound of our engine, the adults formed a circle with the calves in the middle. It was a good strategy to fend off wolves and even people with spears. But it was a deadly strategy once guns were introduced on the North Slope. One day, somebody killed the last Alaskan musk ox. How could he have known? He probably assumed there was another bunch over the next hill or the next. It seems like early people on this continent may have successfully hunted other large mammals, mammoths and mastodons especially, to extinction. Once again, who could know?

The musk oxen story takes a happy turn. People went to Greenland and acquired a herd of those musk oxen, raised them first in captivity on a university farm, then released them onto Nunivak Island. They thrived, and when the herd grew big enough, some of the animals were put on the North Slope. There they thrived as well and have repopulated the costal plain.

These days we can know or at least make a good educated guess about the viability of a species. These days we recognize we can completely deplete any of our resources. These days, we handle our musk oxen with care and only allow a few to be hunted each year.

You could say that with the musk oxen we got lucky. Here was a simple problem with a simple solution. People have been able to restore some of the shorter salmon runs damaged by mining or timbering in much the same way. Sometimes we are able to fix what we break.

But the problem we face with our addiction to oil, the effect that addiction is having on our environment, will require a much more complicated fix, a fix our state and national governments both seem uninterested in tackling. This is what I meant about peeing in the woods and the fence it caused to be built. This is when government as a wiser and more thoughtful version of a single self should come into play.

The other night on the *News Hour*, a Native man and a white woman representing an environmental group were invited to have at it over the Refuge. The woman, in her Jones New York outfit, made the usual arguments about alternatives and conservation. The man, dressed in an anorak, said that his village of Kaktovik was just now getting electricity, running water, and a sewage system. These basic services, he said, are the benefits of drilling for oil. I agree: Kaktovik and all the other villages in Alaska ought to have such basics. The trap lies in thinking that there is only one choice, the choice that equates drilling with electricity.

I admit, I am just like the Rich Young Ruler. I cannot say that gas running up over $3.00 a gallon here in town has caused me to alter my driving habits in any significant way. I still have my truck, a little truck, a fairly fuel efficient truck, a truck I own because I never know when I might need it to load up a bunch of gear and go camping, or haul a load of good dirt or sand or gravel, or just haul my human refuse to the dumpster site where it will pass out of sight and out of mind.

When I left the cedar-sided cabin on Old Wood Road, I left with some regret. Yes, plumbing is nice and so is the giant blue storage tank in the house that holds 2,500 gallons of water. A truck comes every other month to fill it, but I still get my water for tea at Fox. The spring has been promoted from a necessity to a luxury. The regret comes from a recognition that once such a step is taken, it is rarely taken back by choice.

So we all have made such steps. The people along the Kuskokwim River who lived for centuries without benefit of any petroleum products would have a hard time going back. Those of us who live nearer in to town would, too. The short drive to the grocery store and the post office is just part of the way we live here in wilderburb. The gas we use every day has slipped without anybody's being too conscious of it from a want to a need in our way of living. Stuck out on this limb, how can we crawl back?

My falling away from my younger self when I thought I was a socialist or a communist or something like that was a fall from faith, faith in others or even myself that left to our own devices we would do the right thing, that we could really love our neighbors as ourselves. People would kill the last caribou just as we killed the last woolly mammoth to feed our own faces. Pushed far enough into a corner, we would kill one another as well.

Maybe we do care how they do it in the Lower 48, after all. We Alaskans will take all the federal dollars Don Young can get for us and spend them on big roads that will only invite more big cars and trucks, though we will not tax ourselves to maintain the roads we already have. We will build more roads even when the people in their paths don't want those roads to come.

You would think a guy like Don Young, who has had to live in the Washington DC area for these past three decades, would have seen enough automotive congestion by now. You would think he would see that in bringing home the bacon, that he is setting Alaska on a course that will make it more like the Lower 48, that place most of us came here to escape.

Because I believe Don Young would like to be hunting and fishing and tramping out in the woods as much as any of us, I have to wonder why he persists in doing deals that will wipe out the very thing he loves. It's a devil's bargain. To get the goods, Don and the rest of us have to deliver the goods—the ANWR oil, the Tongass timber, the gold, the fish.

And once we have our goods, then what? I believe it's possible to become "stuff-poor," to reach the point of being over-burdened by the ownership of things. When the Gold Rush prospectors came into the country through Skagway, they had to climb the Chilkoot Pass, the Golden Stairs. For many, the burden of their gear was too great to carry up the steep climb; they sloughed it off or collapsed under its weight. That could happen to us, both as individuals and to the whole lot of us.

It may be time to ask, so if I'm so smart, what's my solution?

In my time living in Alaska, the spring at Fox has only failed a time or two. People were annoyed at having to drive all the way to Fox and get no water, annoyed because they expected the state to come along and fix it. Sooner or later, the state did. In the interval, nobody suffered much; there are plenty of places around Fairbanks to get water, the Laundromats, the Water Wagon sites, the power plant, but that water isn't free and it doesn't taste as good. When the spring started running again, we had good water. But what would happen if the spring did fail, if it ran dry?

I don't have an answer for that one. The puny efforts I make at recycling grocery store bags, bottles, and cans, at keeping the thermostat low and the unnecessary lights turned out are laughable in the face of the problem we're looking at—it's not just the Fox water, but our oil, our air, the mountains of wasteful by-products of our getting and spending. And the way I choose to live, luxuriously really, in light of the way most of the rest of the world must live, is part of that problem. It may be time to admit the problem is beyond my (or any individual's) skill or scope.

There's a kind of collective American mindset that believes our ingenuity will come to the rescue just in time. Just when we are either out of oil or it is priced beyond our reach, just before coastal cities drop into the ocean, we'll think of something different, something better. Trust the invisible hand of supply and demand, blindly put our faith in progress, wherever that may be.

Of all the arguments for opening the Artic National Wildlife Refuge, only one compels me. It suggests that there is no oil left to be had that is not in some environmentally sensitive area, so given all the scrutiny surrounding the Refuge, it stands the best chance of being developed with care. I might buy this argument if I believed the oil taken from the ground there would be used thoughtfully, conservatively.

What do I have to offer, though, as arguments for keeping the Refuge as it is? Only these: that there should be, always be, places where animals—human animals, too—come and go largely unmolested. That beauty must be preserved at all costs, beauty in all its unexpected forms. Two abstractions that won't make your car go or heat your house.

Of the thousands of caribou that swam the creek during those two days I was in the Refuge, one slipped on a rock coming up out of the water. She broke her leg and struggled dozens of times to get herself up and go on. Though we weren't supposed to, one of my friends had brought a gun for bear protection. Now he thought we should shoot the caribou and put her out of her misery. Our pilot talked him out of it. First, he said, it would get us all in a world of trouble. But, he also said, the caribou would have fallen had we not been there. Like time travelers, we could not intervene in its fate. When we flew away, it was still struggling against drowning or hypothermia.

The trouble is we have already intervened in the caribou's fate in a web of complicated ways. Now, we cannot simply fly away. Being the only animal capable of foreseeing what might be over the next hill, what might happen in the next season, we're stuck. We're the only responsible party. This thought does not hearten me. So far, we've done a poor job as stewards of the earth.

We find ourselves running out of oil even as the world's economies demand more and more. We are running out of oil at the same time that oil and other fossil fuels are our biggest pollution problem. In all likelihood, there is no oil left to be pumped out where the pumping itself will not create additional environmental problems. So where does that leave us now?

Here are two ways of thinking about it:

In Jack London's chestnut, "Love of Life," two prospectors are walking out of the gold country. They've struck it rich; a ship is waiting to carry them back to the Lower 48; all they have to do is reach the coast. But one man trips, sprains his ankle, and when he looks up, his partner has gone on down the trail. He picks himself up and goes painfully on. Out of necessity, he begins to drop his gear little by little until he finally must begin dropping the contents of his poke of gold. Within sight of the ship, the gimp comes on his ex-partner dead in the trail with his full pack still on his back. To his karmic credit, the gimp leaves his partner's pack and gold intact. We might think he has freed himself from wanting as a result of his ordeal. After killing a weak and starving wolf with his hands, and drinking its blood (this is Jack London, after all), the surviving man crawls on to the ship. There, safely surrounded by the crew, bound for home, he can do nothing but stay in his bunk and hoard the hardtack the sailors give him. Maybe we can never be fully free from wanting.

Or it could be like the Miracle of the Loaves and Fishes. Jesus, after a hard day's preaching, finds his audience has grown hungry. After instructing his disciples to gather from among the crowd what food there is, a few loaves and fishes, Jesus feeds them all, feeds the multitude. It's important to remember that Jesus does not do this by magic. It's not like raising the dead or giving eyesight to the blind. It's not a miracle at all but something any of us could do. Not by pulling more fish and bread out of the sleeves of his robe, but by dividing the food that those who thought to bring snacks have freely given, Jesus somehow gets the food, shared equitably, to go around. This may be Jesus at his best, the turn the other cheek Jesus, the Jesus who recommends giving to others whatever they may ask of you, the Jesus who leads by example. And I would like to think it's people at their best as well, those with a lot willing to give so those who have nothing might eat.

No kidding, these two examples really are representative of our choices. We can go it alone, split ourselves off as rugged individuals or ingrown bands of fellow economic travelers. Or we can find ways to solve our problems together and equitably. We could stop thinking about government as a system of winning big and cashing in and think of it as a means of solving the hard problems that face us. Instead of spending money on more things we don't really need, we could spend it on things we do. We could share our wealth, not hoard it. We could recognize that we are animals, too, and that we live in a fragile ecosystem that does not have borders or boundaries. We could try it this way for a change just to see what happens.

3. Red Politics and Blue in Wyoming

David Romtvedt

1. An Introduction to the State

I've spent many years repairing windmills with my father-in-law at his Four Mile Ranch. There are nineteen of these windmills on the broken land that looks west to the Bighorn Mountains and east to Powder River. It's mostly grunt and sweat labor, though we've got an old rig truck that we use to pull the galvanized pipe out of the deep wells. At the top of each well tower there's a platform where a person can stand to work. The two-by-six boards of these platforms are saturated with oil and grease, and they're so small that I have to twist around like a contortionist to get at some of the parts. In high winds the fantail brakes on some of the mills slip, and the assembly swings around to hit me. I wear a heavy belt clipped to the tower so that when I'm hit I can't be knocked into space, though I still get pushed off the platform once in a while and dangle there for a few moments before I can scramble back up along the belt line. Sometimes when it's calm and I'm changing the oil in a wellhead, there's time to stare out into space and think while the oil quietly flows into the gearbox reservoir. After a day of work, I'm worn out and, early in the evening, I fall into bed. I close my eyes and, for a few moments before I drift off into what I think of as practice for dying, I'm inexplicably happy.

This happiness is with me when I awake and look at the blue sky as it stretches down to touch the mountain peaks. There's another blue in the cold water of Meadowlark Lake just west of Powder River Pass. And there's the blue of a shirt my mother-in-law gave me for my birthday. In the brief Wyoming summer, we sit in the shade of an apple tree that I planted too close to the deck. We've got an outdoor table made from the cover to the old coal chute. We don't heat with coal anymore, instead using natural gas and wood. The wood comes from cottonwood trees along the banks of Four Mile Creek. We go there in September and set up a thirty-six-inch circular saw blade driven by the power take-off of our ancient tractor. We spend the day dragging storm-downed branches over to the saw where we cut them. We throw the cut wood into a horse trailer and haul it to town. Once there, we throw the wood back out of the horse trailer and stack it in our garage and shed. Then we sweep the trailer clean so that a horse will find it comfortable. When the work's finished, I pull two apples off the tree beside the deck. This early in the fall, the apples are just starting to turn red and are still a little sour. I give one apple to the horse and eat the other one myself.

On an October morning I was shoveling wet deep snow off the deck. The trees still hadn't dropped all their leaves and the snow hung so heavily in the branches that some gave up and snapped off. One tree split in two and the broken half nearly filled the yard. I was in a hurry to clear the snow and somehow cut my left hand while shoveling. When I came back in and the hand warmed up, the cut throbbed, and when I took off my glove the blood was smeared over my skin.

Here is the great empty square of Wyoming shown on a map following an election. It takes its place among the other states lined up in front of the television cameras with some states washed blue and some red. Here are the cars darting along the interstate highways. Natural gas flows through pipelines that sometimes follow the highways and sometimes cross them. Coal is carried away in long trains—undulating serpents hauling the inside of the earth outside of it. In the distance a small light on a narrow pole flashes—a cellular telephone tower. Everywhere the phones are ringing, playing their little electronic four-bar excerpts from famous symphonies or popular songs of the day. Now one of the automobiles slips across the lanes on ice, tumbles into the snow, and rolls. It comes to rest upside down, the engine off, the wheels quietly spinning. In this near silence, the phone rings, the jaunty electronic recitation begins, and a bird flying past lands and cocks its head as if it were listening to an important lecture on politics.

When I first moved to Wyoming, I was invited to participate in a statewide literary conference. This was way before I'd ever worked on a windmill. The conference included an open mike poetry reading. Anyone could sign up to read aloud for five minutes before an audience of fellow writers.

The first reader was a white woman in her seventies. When her name was announced she stood and walked slowly toward the front of the hall. Her bearing was upright and dignified. She explained that she was the reincarnation of an eighteenth-century Indian maiden whose spirit had given her the poems she was about to read. She turned in a circle, showing off the buckskin fringe on her dress then she closed her eyes and began to chant.

When she finished, a young woman dressed completely in black approached the lectern. This second reader had short spiked hair coated with gel and streaks of green. Her jewelry appeared to be made of extruded aluminum. She announced that she was a feminist activist lesbian poet. She paused then read a poem of social outrage during which she regularly lunged forward as if she might leap into the audience. Now and again, she pushed her glasses up her nose.

When she stepped away from the lectern, a middle-aged man came forward. He wore blue jeans, a cowboy hat, hand-tooled boots, and a belt buckle that was, as we say in Wyoming, as big as a dinner plate. He read a rhymed cowboy poem concerning stock tanks, coffee-drinking on winter mornings, and the good old days when people took care of each other.

The open mike session went on for two hours. People listened respectfully and, it seemed to me, happily to poems they must have mostly detested. Or did they like the poems? It was beautiful being together in that room full of difference. In the cities where I'd been before, the cowboy poets would have had their cowboy poetry gathering and the angry young feminist lesbian poets their angry young feminist lesbian poetry event. The reincarnated Indians would have planned to meet at a private weekend workshop. In the cities, you'd need free drinks to get these people into the same room at the same time, and then you'd need a cop to do crowd control. The congeniality the poets showed at that reading is the best and most representative feature of Wyoming.

Here's my point: the coding of our states as red or blue according to whether they have given their vote to a Republican or Democratic Party candidate tells us very little about the people with whom we are passing our lives. This kind of simpleminded labeling is degrading. It isolates us from one another and forces us to lead lives that are intellectually and emotionally impoverished. Worse, it is an early symptom of the thinking that led to ethnic cleansing in the Balkans and to the restructuring of Baghdad neighborhoods such that Sunnis and Shiites no longer live in physical proximity.

Still, there are large observable trends among groups and, this being the case, I can see why people try to generalize about other people's values. I'm impatient with the tendency because my experience in Wyoming brings me back to seeing the strange beauty of each person. There are so few of us that it's to our advantage to think this way.

2. A Short Excursion into Nothing

In *The Globalization of Nothing*, George Ritzer argues that we live in a world increasingly shaped by the concept of nothing. He defines nothing as "generally centrally conceived and controlled social forms that are comparatively devoid of distinctive substantive content." Nothing is something without a personality and life of its own. This nothing is a demented mirror image of the Zen concept of no-thing in which nothing is as real and present as something. If in Zen we turn nothing into some-thing, then in modern corporate American life, we turn something into nothing. Ritzer describes four types of nothing—non-things, non-people, non-services, and non-places.

Non-things are Old Navy T-shirts, Arizona blue jeans, and Nike athletic shoes. They are exactly the same no matter which mall you find them in, no matter whether the mall is in a red state or a blue one. Republican and Democratic voters are each asked to pay the same price. From a corporate perspective, that's about all there is to say about the red-blue difference. It's the same with the windmills—red state or blue, windmill repair is pretty much the same.

The next category of nothing is non-people—counter workers at Burger King, for example, and telemarketers who call at dinnertime. These are real people who become non-people when they enact scripted encounters with other people who become non-people by participating in the script. Somebody created these non-jobs and so created non-people. This makes me think about the relationship between God and humanity. God is God and we are non-God. We look and act like God but we don't have God's distinctive and substantive content. What happens when we turn God into non-God?

There are non-services, too—ATMs and Internet Web sites.

Finally, there are non-places. These are represented by shopping malls and Las Vegas casinos. Gertrude Stein described her hometown of Oakland, California, by saying, "There's no there there." That's how malls and casinos are. But, to tell the truth, I like Oakland and have friends there who are real people. (One is Alison Luterman, a poet and playwright with a beautiful kindhearted smile.)

Now imagine a hypothetical casino on the Wind River Nation in Wyoming. This casino would have a real presence—it would be a building. It would sit atop land that is saturated with the history of the Arapahos and Shoshones, with the bloody arrival of the Europeans, and their drive to end the native way of life and eradicate the native people. On this land, the ghosts of sixty million buffalo paw at the earth, making the dust rise. And in the distant boarding schools chalk dust hovers in the air above the desks where Indian children sit mute, forbidden to speak their own languages. Scraps of paper—torn up treaties or lost food stamp coupons—blow in the wind. Back at the casino, a white rancher who owns a chunk of the reservation drives by in a late model pick-up.

Were this casino to be built, it would be surrounded by dry sage grasslands at the foot of the Wind River Mountains. In the distance a little dust devil might blow across the sun dance site, the place where men honor forces larger than themselves. They swing on the ends of tethers hooked into their chests. They pull harder and harder until the hooks pull out and tear small chunks of flesh with them.

Then there's the casino—it would be like a casino in Detroit or Reno or Monte Carlo. Not Indian, even if the cocktail waitresses were enrolled tribal members and dressed in beaded moccasins with their hair braided into shining black strands. When the workers at the casino punch out, do they return to being people? Does each of us live a portion of life as a person and another portion as a non-person? Have people always done this? Is more time spent being a non-person in 2005 than was the case in 1905 or 1805?

If we look at people from inside their lives, we find that the non-person group gets smaller and smaller. At the same time, I know what it means to have a scripted encounter with another person. I've caught myself playing a part—saying and being what my institutional role allows.

The non-thing is distant and abstract. It shies away from human feeling and connection. To be non is to live in a world where we all become things and so can be manipulated by the advocates of global uniformity. In the non-world, we are apt to end up with our heads bowed in a church whose appearance is eerily similar to that of a corporate headquarters building or a model state prison.

These are universal features of the society in which we live and, as I've said already, they are about equally dispersed in red and blue states. When the television cameras roll, it doesn't matter how you vote. Maybe we all just want to be on TV.

When I first started working with my father-in-law on the windmills, I'd often misdiagnose a problem and so have the wrong part for repairs. Just as often, I'd forget an essential tool. These two characteristics of mine meant that we'd end up having to go back to the barn or even into town to get what we needed. My father-in-law, a lifelong Republican, would come with me, both because there was little work he could do on the mills alone and because he liked to talk. I loved listening to him tell the history of the ranch and the early Basque settlers in northern Wyoming.

One day when we had to go to town, my father-in-law did something I'd seen him do many times before though I'd never said anything about it. He parked the pickup and when he got out, he left the doors unlocked, the windows down, and the keys in the ignition. "Do you want to take the keys?" I asked.

"No. What if somebody had an emergency and needed to get somewhere—the hospital or something? This way, they could take the pickup if they needed."

Not a day has gone by during which I haven't thought of that question and answer. What if somebody needed the pickup? This way they could use it in an emergency.

The last car I bought was a Volkswagen Beetle with a diesel engine. For the first few months I had it, the battery kept going dead. The local mechanics couldn't find anything wrong and recharged the battery. They did this a number of times. Finally, I went to the dealer a hundred and sixty-five miles away. I learned that when you turn the car off, you have to lock it or the electrical system keeps running and the battery goes dead. No amount of explanation from the congenial vw service representatives helped me to understand why it was to my advantage to have a car that I had to lock whenever I got out of it. Every time I go to the garage to get something out of the car, or put something in it, I forget that I have to have the keys. Back to the house I go. What kind of society won't allow the owner of a car to decide whether or not to lock it?

3. More Introduction to the State

Wyoming has been a place that people passed through. This was as true for American Indians as it was for the late arriving Europeans. Two kinds of people have lived in Wyoming—those who can afford to live here and those who can't afford to leave.

The first European immigrants to Wyoming died in great numbers. They died of cholera, malaria, hepatitis, bad food, bad water, no food, no water, too much heat, too much cold, violent encounters with other travelers, fear. The dead left behind them the marks of their passage—the deepening ruts in the earth, the long lists kept in churches and county record books of names and dates, the now nearly unreadable lists of other names and dates that were etched into stone along cutbanks and cliff faces.

The travelers left a lot of stuff in their wake: pieces of oak and pine planking, wagon wheels and frames, fractured pianos and organs that, when the wind blows, still wheeze out songs though with no melody. There are wooden trunks that were tossed off wagons that starving oxen could no longer pull. The trunks sprang open and out fell silk dresses and scarves, woolen suit jackets and stiff collars.

Wyoming is the tenth largest state in the United States and the one with the lowest population. We vote Republican and so we are assumed to be anti-abortion, anti-gay rights, anti-taxes. While being anti-taxes, we're supposed to be pro-military spending increases, pro-prison building, and pro-increased numbers of policemen. We're anti-big government and pro-government incursion into people's personal and private behavior.

Even though I imagine some single person does believe all these things and knows one other person with the same beliefs, for most of us life is not so clear. The black and white, red and blue fantasy ignores parents whose philosophies are at odds with those of other parents but who are happy to see each other at their children's school band concerts. It ignores fundraising events for the library. It ignores dinner parties. It ignores most of what matters to most of us most of the time. It's a non-story.

Wyoming is known as both the Cowboy State and the Equality State. The territorial legislature granted equal rights to women in 1869. The state constitution, approved by the people of Wyoming in 1889, includes in Article Six, Section One this statement: "The rights of citizens of the State of Wyoming to vote and hold office shall not be denied or abridged on account of sex. Both male and female citizens of this state shall equally enjoy all civil, political, and religious rights and privileges." The state seal shows a woman holding a banner that proclaims "Equal Rights."

In 1920, Jackson, Wyoming's municipal elections were swept by women—the newly elected mayor, every council member, and the sheriff. Rose Crabtree defeated her husband, the incumbent, for her seat on the council.

Now gay citizens are struggling for equal rights. The current mayor of Casper is both the youngest man to serve in the post and the first openly gay mayor of the city. Following his election, the mayor expressed gratitude that he lived in a place where one is judged for the work and not for the label.

When the United States was preparing to invade Iraq, I put a sign in my front yard that read NO IRAQ WAR. It was red, white, and blue with some stars and a stripe. I was a little nervous about publicly expressing an antiwar sentiment and within a few days of putting the sign out, three strangers had knocked on my door.

But it wasn't what I'd expected. The first visitor said he too opposed the American invasion of Iraq but he couldn't speak out because he had kids in school and he worried that they would be punished in some way. "I don't mean anything overt, you know. It'd be more subtle than that." He said, "You have a lot of courage to put that sign up."

The second visitor owned a shop downtown—I knew her and her shop. She thought the U.S. invasion was terrible but she was afraid that if she expressed an antiwar view, people would refuse to shop in her store. She said, "I wish I had your courage."

The last visitor arrived at dinnertime. I was eating pasta with pesto and pine nuts, a piece of hard bread, and a green salad with a dressing of olive oil and balsamic vinegar. The visitor said, "I was just walking by and thinking, geez, look at that, a sign like that, I'd be afraid somebody'd come and bust my windows out. You have a lot of guts."

When I told a gay friend about the three visitors, he said, "Those people were right to worry. That kind of stuff does happen. You're kind of protected—a straight white male, married into an old family. You can be weird without being shunned. It's annoying."

As a poet, I've faced criticism for gender disloyalty but it's nothing like what gay men face. And somehow for people who hold antigay sentiments, gay males are "worse" than lesbians. Wyoming has a long history of independent women ranchers. Women couples have often done the same work men do and if they do it well, that's what counts, not their private lives. I can stand by this philosophy, except that I'd let the gay males in with everyone else. And by the way, anybody who wants to get married to anybody they like, bully for them. It's a long hard winter here and we could do with a few more parties.

4. A Meeting

In a state with as few people as Wyoming, it's pretty common for us to have personal relationships with our elected officials, or at least to have met and be on speaking terms with them. When you've spent the day fixing a windmill and late in the afternoon you finally get to watch the water spill out of the ground and into the stock tank, somebody might say, "I saw the Governor the other day and asked him what the hell the state's doing about coal bed methane water discharge." This is not a form of name dropping or bragging about one's connections to important people. We really are a small state.

With this in mind I want to report on a meeting I had a few months ago. I serve as the state's poet laureate and was in the Governor's office to discuss budget initiatives related to cultural programming. Before I could start my pitch for increased arts funding, the Governor leaned back in his chair and threw his legs up on his desk, revealing a pair of sturdy cowboy boots beneath dark gubernatorial slacks. He waved away budget talk and asked me about a poem that was included in a new book of mine. I'd sent a manuscript copy of the book to him because there were some poems that I thought might be controversial and I didn't want the Governor to be blindsided if anyone standing around the stock tank wondered out loud, "What the hell is the state poet doing? And who the hell appointed him anyway?"

The poem in question included the F word and a critique of patriotism. The narrator of the poem was opposed to the American invasion of Iraq and the now several years long war waged by the US in that country. He needed to express his feelings but he worried that he would be shunned by his community for those feelings. He felt outrage and despair, believing that the course of public policy was all wrong, and yet he was unable to have any influence on that public policy. He saw patriotism as the cause of much bad behavior. He ended up having an outburst and there was the F word. But then he wanted to apologize for his outburst. He wanted to be understood and even liked. He was torn between his belief that the poet has a responsibility to be a part of the political life around him and his equally strong belief that the great power of poetry is its intimacy. Poetry is a single human voice speaking to a single human listener. In this view the greatest poem is the one that can relieve the suffering of the world and make another person happy, even if only for a moment.

When the Governor brought the poem up, I thought he might be upset about my attack on patriotism. But he was more interested in the use of the F word. "Why," he asked, "must the poem include obscenity? When a poet uses obscenity, has he not admitted to being a mediocre poet for his inability to express his views without the obscenity?" He looked at me and said, "David, I've never heard you talk like this so why write a poem this way?" Poetry, in the Governor's view, should inspire us to be better than we thought we could be, to do more good than we thought we could do. It should lift us into a higher moral realm. Why write in a way that will only offend some readers? They're not going to get the point you think you're trying to make if they just get turned off by your language.

Sitting there in the Governor's office looking out the window at the Wyoming state flag whipping in a heavy breeze, I thought about how to respond. It has been said that in the end the writer's problems are not ones of technique but of character. I knew that the whole of life must appear in literature. The forbidden must be welcomed and the inexcusable excused. What defense could I give for these beliefs?

There is a level of despair or shame or anger or loss or excitement or happiness when obscenity is the appropriate vehicle given to us by language. I suggested that in these circumstances, a human being will utter what is unutterable.

For a few minutes we talked about other things—the upcoming legislative budget session, the state's mineral excise tax, environmental protection in the face of the current coal bed methane boom, Wyoming's lawsuit with the federal government over wolf management. We talked as though I might have something to say about these things.

I remembered an editorial I'd read by Ann Coulter. Coulter criticized Laura Bush for being overly active as First Lady, for trying to influence policy that was none of her business. Coulter asked, "Why can't the First Lady confine herself to her legitimate role—selecting the White House china pattern and naming the poet laureate?"

Since poets often think analogically, the White House china pattern reminded me of the poets of ancient China who lived in a period when applicants for government jobs were required to take examinations covering classical poetry. Yang Wan-li was a poet who spent his youth studying for the government exams. After passing them, Yang's first job was as administrator of finances of Kan Chou Prefecture. That's like me being appointed Finance Director for the state of Wyoming.

We came circling back to the obscene word. There is something we want to say but can't. There are forbidden issues we don't bring up in polite company but which we want to understand. We wonder about the edges of human experience. In literature we have some opportunity to go to those edges. We see through the eyes of others and we extrapolate.

I sit down alone and open a book. The writer is far from me, perhaps long dead and only the words remain—words that are witness to experience and feeling. It's just between the two of us, and what I think or the writer thinks needn't go beyond the walls of the book. There is a great net of privacy and calm surrounding us. Literature offers a freedom that is not granted in material life. Some of that freedom can be brought back and it can change the lives we lead outside of books. I discover after many years as a writer that I actually believe this.

The flag was still whipping in the breeze. Far away, the windmill blades were spinning, the sharp steel edges slicing the air, chopping it to pieces and turning it into water lifted to the surface of the earth. There was a moment of quiet in the room.

One of the Governor's aides stepped in and said, "Five minutes— you've got a proclamation to deliver at the Hathaway Building." The Governor waved the aide away and asked me again why it is necessary to use obscenity in a poem. I said all the things I've said here. He smiled and we shook hands as our meeting ended.

A few months later, I was scheduled to read a poem at the Governor's Arts Awards ceremony. The Governor himself was to deliver the annual state of the arts address. In his address he mentioned the poem we'd talked about in our meeting. He said that as a lawyer he had a clear sense of how language was to be used. He knew how to construct an argument, how to sway a listener. He claimed not to understand literature and made a joke about the fact that his wife had a pile of books on her nightstand that he couldn't imagine anyone ever reading. He went back to the poem and the speaker's expletive. "For thirty years," he said, "My wife has been trying to get me to open my mind a little and I've been resisting all the way." He said a few words about the role of language in art and how that is different from the role of language in politics and the law. Then he went on to other topics—the state's permanent cultural endowment fund, the role of art in keeping children at risk in school, the pride that a community can develop through public art. Notwithstanding his commitment to narrow-mindedness, his comments revealed flexibility and openness.

These are the features that I love about Wyoming—generosity and reticence. Both the place and the people will often withhold information about themselves so as not to impose. The great expanse of high plains punctuated by arid mountains, the land stripped nearly bare of vegetation by winter's wind and cold, summer's wind and heat—all this demands patience. And the people are like this, too. If, as a writer, I say something that disturbs people, they are as likely to hear me out and ask questions as they are to shut me up. Generous reticence is not the refusal to speak out but the willingness to listen to others. There is a beauty that arises from withholding judgment and evading comparison. Live and let live. Everybody has both an opinion and a right to a certain degree of privacy. There is grace in not demanding consensus. Nobody tells you what to think. Forget red state blue state. Think on your own and good luck to us all.

Note

"Red Politics and Blue," by David Romtvedt, originally appeared in *The Sun*, June 2006.

4. Running in the Red

Jennifer Sinor

For five years I have been running the roads of southeastern Idaho, always in the morning, often before sun up, every season of the year. Usually the only others I meet on my route are the dairy farmers calling to their cows with low "hoo-yahs" and the occasional car driven by young men returning from a graveyard shift at one of the nearby factories. Red-tailed hawks, possums, and snakes that slither from the alfalfa fields and onto the road in anticipation of a warming sun also accompany me, though they usually flee long before I pass them.

One morning, a few months after the start of the second Gulf War and a day right on the brink of summer, I was startled by a skunk scurrying about on the side of the road. In this rural area, skunks are not uncommon, and there are places on my route and times of the year when I expect to meet them. This skunk, however, was acting quite strange. Rather than dart back into the long grasses, he rambled along the edge of the road, taking in the morning light with little show of leaving.

Entranced by his odd behavior, I was busy thinking about how lucky I was to live in a place where wild things emerge from the grasses to scuttle at my feet, when a small truck pulled up alongside me. If it had been darker or if I were living somewhere besides Whitney, Idaho, I might have worried that a vehicle was slowing down. In this case, though, I just kept running, leaving the skunk and the truck, wondering if others were surprised at the friendliness of this skunk and had stopped to look.

I was a hundred yards away when I heard the gunshots: four of them, shattering the morning stillness. Though I could see little in the weak light of dawn, I stopped and turned. Two men had gotten out of the truck and were on the side of the road, but the truck's headlights prevented me from seeing anything else.

I debated about what to do. Tired and with only a mile and a half to go, I realized I wasn't sure I wanted to know what was happening back at the truck. It seemed easier just to ignore the situation, mind my own business, pretend that gunshots punctuated all my runs. Perhaps because I had only moments ago been thinking how happy that skunk made me or perhaps because the skunk reminded me of what I love about living here, I ran back.

By the time I got back to the truck, the two men were already inside the cab and starting to drive away. I stood in the middle of the road, hoping they would stop. In my running shorts and T-shirt, I felt small and exposed and for a moment second-guessed my decision.

What are you doing? I asked when the truck slowed to a stop.

Did you know a skunk was chasing you? the driver said, laughing as he wiped his hand across the brow of his mouth. They were large men, barely fitting the cab. I looked around for the gun.

He wasn't chasing me, I said, angered by the way he implied I needed help. *Did you shoot it?*

Yeah, we killed it, the passenger said, speaking for the first time and grinning madly.

The driver, though, knew I was angry and threw his friend a look to silence him. *No,* he said. *We just scared it away.*

Was the skunk harming anyone?

Those people, he answered, and pointed to the two still-dark houses down the road. *If we didn't shoot it, a car would have hit it, and then it would have smelled. Do you know how bad they smell?* He paused, a smug look on his face, and then continued, *We saved it from getting hit by a car.*

By killing it, I thought. You saved it by killing it.

In the 2004 election, I cast three votes: one for Kerry, one for Edwards, and one for a woman who was running as an independent for the job of county clerk. It wasn't that I didn't care more about local politics or that I was too uninformed to vote. Rather, those three candidates were the only three on my entire ballot who were not Republicans. To abstain, my only voice.

When we moved to southeastern Idaho five years ago I had expected to feel like an outsider. After all, we were used to living in cities, not farm country, and we were pagans living in what, for Mormons, is the Promised Land. My husband, Michael, looked forward to being on the fringe. Growing up in the South as both a Catholic and a Democrat, he knew the kind of community that forms as part of a minority, and he relished building those coalitions. But things were harder for me. We were only here a matter of days before I noticed how waitstaff and clerical workers only looked at Michael when they talked. And within weeks, I had become tired of justifying the absence of children. Plus there were so many battles to fight. Standing in line at the auto parts store, I listened to a customer tell a racist joke to the manager and stood silent as those around me laughed. In the grocery store, I peeked behind the plastic shields guarding magazines with bare bellies on their covers, as if skin were sin and women the devil. At the public library, my mouth dropped as the librarian read stories about Jesus during the story hour. And then there was the local video store.

On our first visit to Adventure Video, Michael and I learned that movies were categorized by actor, a fact that was mildly annoying for someone like me who can never remember who has starred in which films. We would spend ten minutes debating about whether a movie like *The English Patient* would be filed under Fiennes, Thomas, or Binoche. After a few visits, though, I realized that some actors were in special categories, grouped together and not allowed to mingle with the other videos. To the point, the actors of color—Bruce Lee, Morgan Freeman, Wesley Snipes—occupied a ghetto, two rows of films held in the middle of the store as if hostages. In retrospect, I suppose, I should not have been surprised at such a division, one that was apparently both natural and accepted. It is little different than the division that is played out in the geography of the town where the Latino community gathers in pockets and patches, railroad tracks marking the boundary between brown and white. Still, I was amazed when the video store owner seemed unable to comprehend another way of categorizing film, angered by his reluctance to see the layout of his store as racist.

What is the response, I wondered, to these potentially ignorant but painfully damaging examples of racism and sexism? Boycott Adventure Video? Picket? Take the plastic guards off the magazines and hide them under the candy bar rack? Write letters? Or move.

As a former military brat, I have moved more than I have remained. Up until this point in my life, the longest I have ever lived in one place is five years. Two years, my father always told me, two years before you feel comfortable in a new place, two years before a place feels like home. Like a shield, I would carry these words of my father's into my new elementary school, wrap them around me like a cloak when no one chose me for their team, pack them in my lunchbox as I sat by myself and watched the other kids play basketball. It was OK that I felt lonely, scared, and unwanted. After all, it hadn't yet been two years.

Two weeks ago this valley became the longest place I have ever lived in my life and I cannot say that I am home. Length of time in a place, I have come to understand, has nothing to do with whether you feel a part of things. My father simply wanted to fix the fact that every few years he uprooted his family, wanted to make his daughter less sad. After all, two years is a lifetime to an eight-year-old. Perhaps he was banking on the fact that by the end of two years I would have forgotten what it felt like to eat lunch alone. Perhaps he was hoping that within two years another military family would have moved into the neighborhood making me no longer the newest. Perhaps he knew in two years we would be moving again.

Sometimes I find myself wondering if my difficulties in living and working on the Utah/Idaho border come from living in a rural area rather than a red one. Perhaps my problem at the video store has nothing to do with the number of Republicans living in Idaho and more to do with the number of cows. But it is a hard distinction to draw. As the 2004 election map reveals, rural and red are often synonymous. The belly of the country, in fact a broad swath that runs from Canada to Texas and almost to the coasts, contains less than half the population. The population of New York City is three times that of Wyoming, Montana, and Idaho combined. In some states, North Dakota maybe, I have been told the cattle outnumber the people. And those living amidst all that space are predominately Republican, so much so that Democrats don't even appear on the ballots.

My classroom at Utah State University is a microcosm of Cache Valley. I study my students to understand decisions made about rezoning, gravel quarries, and open space initiatives. And I learn a lot. Two years ago I was teaching a course on gender and literature, and we had come to a unit on zines. For a week we had looked at girl zines, underground self-publications by adolescents, and now I wanted my students to consider the gap between how young women represented themselves and how the media represented them. I asked each student to bring in a magazine, like *YM* or *Sassy*, that targeted young women. In small groups, they looked at the glossy magazines, paying attention to advertisements and articles and making notes of recurring images or ideas. As I walked about the room, I was feeling happy about the way class was going. The chatter in the room suggested the students were engaged. Then I came to Ed's group.

Ed's magazine was at the center of the discussion. He held it in his hands while the other three students in his group leaned over their desks to look. For a group of four, they were very quiet. At another school, another environment, perhaps, such attention might have meant naked bodies, an article on orgasms or, at the very least, a group off task, but with these students I couldn't imagine anything even mildly transgressive. What I found was a magazine covered with black marker.

Ed, what happened to your magazine? I asked.

He looked at me. *What do you mean?*

Well, there's marker all over these pages.

My wife did that, he replied. *She wanted to make it OK for me to look at.*

It turns out Ed's *Seventeen* had been censored by his wife. She had gone through the entire magazine with a black marker and filled in every bit of "immodest" dress from the advertisements to the comic strips. Plunging V necklines had been carefully changed to rounded ones. Skirts were lengthened perfectly to the knees. Tank tops and cap sleeves were replaced by longer sleeves, and bare backs and midriffs were concealed beneath shiny black curtains of ink. She had done painstaking work. Rather than just scratching over the models, scribbling out offending faces and body parts, Ed's wife had redrawn them fashionably—sometimes with such success that it was hard for me to tell if the model's clothes had been adjusted at all. His wife, in fact, had concealed all that offended her with the care of an artist.

I work at a university heavily populated—somewhere between 80 and 90 percent—by students who share a common religion. In general, they are politically and socially conservative. In the 2001 freshman survey, close to 20 percent of the incoming class indicated that they had selected this school because of its "religious affiliation." It is a state school.

Primarily because of stories like Ed's I remain an avid runner. I find that the events of the day that trouble me at night get pounded into a manageable size by the end of a long run. Running has also always been a way for me to connect with a landscape. I pride myself on the fact that I have run on several continents and in a majority of the states. Even if I am only somewhere overnight, I like to run, like to feel how the land responds to my footfall, breathe the air, know the turns and folds of the place I am staying. The beach, the desert, the mountains, or the city streets, it doesn't matter where, I just like to take the pace of the land.

Running in Idaho has, for the most part, been wonderful. There are no sidewalks, so I am forced to run in the street, but I am surrounded by mountains that seem to grow higher in the winter when blanketed by snow. Although not the case, I feel anonymous when running, no longer marked as someone who is not from here, who is not Mormon, someone who is not married to a local farmer. Few things have made me feel more powerful in body than when running through my pregnancy, the northern lights winking red as my unborn son and I crested a hill, shooting stars falling along our path.

In pictures I drew during that part of my pregnancy, my son, Aidan, ran in my belly, his legs keeping time with mine, his arms swimming through amniotic air.

My faith in running as the religion that will save me has been shaken though. Some days I return home and realize that I have not outrun my worries. Ed and students like him remain with me. No amount of miles can negate the number of plastic covers that need to be removed at my local grocery. And then there are the dogs.

We have no leash law in Franklin County, though dogs must remain in the yard. In practice, however, they roam the area, sometimes congregating in bands that tear through the fields and corner cats against the barns. During my runs, I am apt to meet with four or five dogs a day, most of them friendly, some of them not. Sometimes their angry barks make me turn around, sometimes I wobble in the dark as I try to jump from their snapping teeth, and sometimes I call the police.

As is true for most runners, I find small dogs the most worrisome. They snap at my ankles and cause me to stumble over their tiny backs. I have only ever been bitten by one dog, and that was a small one who lives up the street from me. He bit my calf when I was six months pregnant. Bleeding and angry, I banged on the door of the house until the owner came out. She insisted her dog didn't bite people. I showed her the tear in my leg.

When the police officer came to my house to make the report, it turned out to be the same officer who had answered my call the year before when I was being chased by two large black labs. At that time, he had suggested I purchase an enormous can of mace; now he only looked at my belly and shook his head in dismay. I knew the story he would tell, the one where I should not have been running in the first place, in the dark, in the country, and pregnant. What kind of mother makes such decisions?

In five years of teaching, I have been told among other things that Toni Morrison writes filth, that the rainbow sticker on my door suggests that I am intolerant because it means I am against those who are homophobic, and that I hate men. I have had students walk out of class because we were discussing sex, and I have had students accuse me of abusing other students (to the point of sending them into a depression) for having them read works by writers like Michael Dorris and Amy Tan. I have received poor evaluations because I "have an agenda," and I have watched many smart and talented women get married at the age of twenty and drop out of school. Some days it exhausts me. Many days.

The other night Michael and I were watching a movie in our living room. Our couch faces a giant plate glass window and allows us to see across the valley floor and over to the Bear Mountains. On summer mornings, when I walk into the living room from our still-darkened bedroom I am blinded by the rising sun that streams across the valley bottom and pours into the house. Sometimes, I have to shield my eyes. On this particular night, early in the fall, we were focused on the television when all of a sudden we noticed a white glow at the ridgeline of the mountains, simmering silver light, as though a shooting star had landed. Within seconds, an enormous Harvest Moon literally burst from the mountains. We had never seen a moon rise so quickly, climbing into the night sky as if on fire. How can this be, we asked each other? How is it possible that the moon can fly so quickly, that our world can spin so deftly, that we can all be careening so madly through the universe? How had we not noticed before? And where else would we be so fortunate to watch such a display from the comfort of our living room couch?

The reach of the Mormon church is both long and complete. Whether I am at home in Whitney, Idaho, or teaching in Logan, Utah, I am "on the grid." The address for my house and the address for my office, like almost all addresses in this part of the country, indicate their distance from a central location: the church. Everything in Logan is measured by its distance or proximity to the Logan temple. Borders is ten blocks north, Sam's Club is thirteen, a new Hampton's Inn is close to twenty. I cannot name my place in space—I cannot say where I am or where I want to go—without indirectly naming my relationship to a towering building that I am not allowed to enter.

Unlike other parts of the country where someone's religion is incidental—akin, say, to being a pet owner or a voter or a soccer mom—here religion is the culture. Because Mormons have a rather strict set of practices and because the population is so heavily Mormon, these beliefs shape institutions, shape the classroom, shape my life. Michael once heard an elder in the church say that the reason they built institutes and seminaries within one hundred yards of all public schools from junior highs to universities was to give their members a "refuge from the world of ideas." They seek the same refuge by shielding magazine covers, prohibiting R-rated movies, banning the sale of alcohol, and encouraging women to stay home and raise children. When we first moved here, there was only one restaurant in town that served wine. Only a few years before that, you had to register your name whenever you purchased a drink. Until just recently, Viagra was covered by our university insurance but not birth control. On Sundays, everything is closed.

It can feel very lonely.

People ask me how I do it, how I stand having to censor myself in the classroom, how I put up with prayers at the water board meetings, how I can live in a place that doesn't mind storing the nuclear waste from the rest of the country even as cancer rates soar. Typically, I point to the natural beauty of Cache Valley, the fact that we can hike on trails that rival parts of the Rockies in numbers of wildflowers, that we are only hours from Canyonlands and even fewer from the Tetons. But lately, perhaps because the already long winters have been made more unbearable by the pollution that causes an inversion in the valley most residents euphemistically call "fog," I am wondering if the natural world can save me, save us. How long am I willing to barter the destructive decisions being made around me for the fact that I can be in the mountains within minutes. What does it say about my politics if I am able to bear racism or sexism in exchange for a view?

Oh, but it is beautiful. And our son, Aidan, has seen that beauty from the first day he was born. When nothing else would comfort him, no amount of walking, cooing, or rubbing could calm him, all we had to do was walk outside and stand beneath the giant spruce trees in our yard that are a hundred years old and at least that many feet high, where thousands of sparrows gabble and caper throughout the day, and he would immediately quiet. Those first few months of his life when he suffered from colic and writhed in pain, we spent entire days outside, walking our yard, the trails, the road by the river. He has grown up thinking that towering trees and stretches of sky and moose that appear suddenly while cresting a hill are as much a part of this world as his morning oatmeal and two parents who love him. We often wonder what kinds of bone-deep memories Aidan will have of being carried by his father over the tops of mountains and through rivers of snow and imagine that certain slants of light or stream sounds will bring him feelings of inexplicable warmth when he has long moved away from us and started his own home.

Just recently I was running with Aidan and our dog. Aidan sat in the baby jogger and pointed to the cows and horses as we passed, laughing at the tractors making giant bales of hay in the nearby fields. In the middle of a mile-long street, two dogs came running at us barking and growling at the wheels of the stroller. For years, I had yelled at these two dogs, hoping to scare them back into their garage with the strength of my voice and wondering why the owner never appeared amid the fuss. This time, though, they gathered around my dog, and all three stood staring at each other, the air no longer disturbed by tails or barks. Then one of the dogs attacked my dog, lunged at his throat. I yelled and ran toward them, leaving Aidan in the stroller crying and scared.

Once the dogs ran off, I made my way with stroller and dog to the front door where I banged several times. No one answered. I banged again. Only when I turned to leave did the door open to reveal a skinny man without a shirt evidently angry at being disturbed.

When I told him that his dog had attacked my dog, he said his dog doesn't attack other dogs. When I said I had been dealing with his dogs for years, he replied that no on else had trouble. When I said I would call the police, he said I had a problem with everyone on the block. Then he told me what he would do to my dog if he ever came into his yard.

Aidan is just learning to talk. While he either can't or refuses to say mama, he will point to the animals in our neighborhood and call out their names: horse, cow, goat, pig. When I take him running with me, he waves to the farmers on their tractors calling out *truck, truck*. Moo, says the cow. Neigh, says the horse. This boy of mine, not even a year and a half, can tell you the sound a barn owl makes.

When he began to name the world around him, he focused on the animals that brush their bodies against our fence and call softly to him while he sleeps. I am not sure what the value of such a vocabulary is. In some way, the fact that Aidan lives in a place where there is more open space than concrete, where mountains change with the season, complicates my attitudes toward the valley, softens them. Yes, it is true that when he was born we had to fight with the state to have his last name hyphenated and yes, his pediatrician is conservative and traditional, but the stars, the stars at night fill our sky like confetti and when he was only a few months old he raised his hand to the moon in an effort to turn it off.

Hiking on a trail, last year's snow still clinging to the undersides of cliffs even in August, wildflowers as thick as a quilt, and Aidan on his father's back pointing to the trees while he eats a peach fresh from the farmer's market, my world is neither red or blue. Such words fail when faced with the variety of the natural world. They are mocked. Here is a mountain that has been here for millions of years, and here, an ancient seabed. What do politics have to say in a conversation that has been happening over eons. I lift my head and see the sky. I look to my feet and reconsider the path I am taking.

On January 6, 2005, I was hit by a car while running. The night before a thick blanket of snow had fallen and, either because it had cooled quickly or warmed quickly or failed to cool or warm, the snow was especially slippery and wet. I have run in blizzards, as well as torrents of rain and caustic heat. Part of my pride in running comes from the fact that I am not deterred by weather. It never occurred to me not to leave Michael and Aidan sitting on a couch in the living room while I went out for a run.

Toward the end of my route and running down a long and sloping hill, I saw a truck approaching me. In order to yield as much of the road as possible, I crossed to the other side and ran along the edge of the road where the snow had somewhat recently been plowed. When I fell, I was only embarrassed. It was a rather spectacular fall, I imagine, one that landed me on my back, like an overturned turtle, after my feet flew out from under me. I sat there for a second, rubbing the back of my head and looking around to see if anyone had seen my fall. I can only think it was the Universe that caused me to look behind me. When I did, I saw a white van bearing down on me, so close that I could not see above the tire.

I knew I would be hit. I knew I could not make it out from under the van. Scrambling on my hands and knees to the side of the road, my only thought was that I had to try and live for Aidan. When the van hit me, I found myself narrating the impact. I am being hit, I thought. The van is hitting me.

That I am not dead is a miracle. Had I not turned around, the car would have struck my back. As it happened, I only suffered deep contusions and a general misalignment of my pelvis. The headlights of the van came after me every time I closed my eyes for weeks. And I have felt cracked in two ever since.

My department is having a discussion right now about whether we should accommodate students who object to the material we present in the classroom, material that conflicts with their beliefs. It is no small matter. The University of Utah was sued by a student last year because a teacher in the theater department made a young woman say "fuck" in a play. The case was settled outside the court system, but it is only a matter of time before universities will have to name their position on the continuum between academic freedom versus student rights.

The discussion has been, at times, quite heated. Most of the faculty in our department are not Mormon but most of the graduate students who teach first-year composition are. Faculty are arguing for complete academic freedom, while people from the community are suggesting that the university is trying to change the culture here.

As someone who teaches the very material that students most often object to—books where unmarried people have sex, children are born out of wedlock, and authors use profanity, books about gays and lesbians, books by gays and lesbians, clips from R-rated films—I am invested in the position the university eventually adopts. I worry that if we begin to accommodate one student, we will have to accommodate all. And I am wary of phrases like "deeply held beliefs." But mostly I am surprised by the response from the community, those graduate students in our department who accuse teachers of trying to change the local population. And I think of the work I do in the classroom every single day, the reasons I went into education, my desire for nothing less than social transformation. The fact that I believe reading and writing can change the way people think and act is not limited to a particular religion, a physical boundary, or a class of voters. I am hoping to change the world.

After the accident, we were overwhelmed by the generosity of the people in Whitney. We know only a few of our neighbors and none of them well. Though the church, which is right across the street from our house, has invited us to numerous events, we have never gone. When we first lived here, people tried to convert us with such tenacity that we now duck and hide whenever someone knocks on our door. Even though we have kept to ourselves, mingled little, and only wave hello from the relative safety of the car, the day the accident occurred, Holly, a woman down the street, came to the hospital and offered to watch Aidan. A woman up the street brought us dinner that night. And every day for the next week, someone was at our door with food for every meal. Every meal. The people who live across from us sent flowers that same day, even though they were on vacation in New Orleans at the time. Someone who doesn't live anywhere near us brought us a plant. Even having grown up in a military community where the women bake pies for those who are just arriving and have phone trees that allow them to contact everyone on the submarine, the ship, or the office within minutes, I have never seen such generosity or organization. I could not send thank-you notes because I had no idea who these people were that fed my family for a week.

I am sure that every single person who helped us out that week is

Mormon and fairly sure they are equally Republican. They censor the books their children read, they believe that women were meant to be mothers only, and they hope their sons are chosen to be missionaries and will notch the numbers of converted like other twenty-year-old men track the women they have slept with. But they are also incredibly kind and thoughtful, and at a moment when my family needed help, they came with plastic containers full of soup and dinner rolls warmed in the oven.

This semester I am teaching Multicultural American Literature. Most faculty who have taught the course swear they will never teach it again. The students, they say, are too conservative; the evaluations they have received too poor. But something Michael said to me years ago has stayed with me, shaping what I do in the classroom as well as how I respond in the community. He told me that if I want to change the way the world works, the values in which it trades, the language it chooses to use, I need to find a path my students can walk down.

Recently I asked a friend who taught at another school if he could recommend a book that addressed homosexuality without much sex or language. As a gay man who has fought his entire life against the homophobia that grips this nation, he was enraged. How could I make my curriculum palatable for those whose beliefs are so unjust? Why would I support stereotypes? How could I be so weak? But having taught these students, having talked with them in my office, having listened to the stories that they tell, read the papers they have written, seen the family photos they carry with them, I know that the only way I can get them to even think about the topic of homosexuality is to provide a path that seems possible for them to walk. I cannot make them read material that they find offensive. They will simply choose not to read, drop the class, or rant on my evaluations. But I can begin the conversation about social justice with novels and essays that ask them to shift and move a little at a time. I teach for ten years down the road, giving them a path that allows for the possibility that at some point, maybe years from now, when their brother or their daughter or their neighbor has the courage to come out to them, they will remember my class and the safety of our discussions, and maybe consider how much more alike we are than different. Small steps are all I can ask of them.

And all I can ask of myself. Maybe this is what I have come to learn in what recently became six years of living blue in this red state. Change is both slow and local. When I wrote a letter to Adventure Video, the manager called to talk with me and rearranged the store within the week. When I wrote a letter to the auto parts store, the manager contacted me and said he would be more vigilant about racist jokes in the future. And when I brought a gay and lesbian student panel into my class and had a frank discussion of what it means to grow up gay in Cache Valley, I had students say that the experience changed their lives. One student wrote, "I am truly grateful that there are professors like you who are willing to take the chance of being unpopular and still step out in front to try and broaden the horizons of students who have seen too little of the world."

It doesn't always work. The librarian at the public library will not admit that the fact they carry only five books by Toni Morrison, one by Alice Walker, and none by Louise Erdrich or Sandra Cisneros while providing forty-two by Mormon author Jack Weyland and shelves of videos about Jesus and the early church is symptomatic of their refusal to separate church and state. No amount of protesting will change the fact that faculty at Utah State are charged the same amount for health insurance regardless of whether they have zero dependents or twelve. And in 2008, I imagine I will only cast a handful of votes.

Fall has come to Cache Valley and when I run in the morning I look at the mountains where snow competes with yellow Aspen for my attention. In the afternoon, the sky is blue, a shocking clear blue, and I can imagine no other place I want to live. But there are no easy answers. We have stopped receiving the local paper. It left me in a rage too many mornings. And we have no idea what we will do once Aidan is school-aged. Running in the red every morning, though, watching for falling stars as thick as crayons, I consider each footfall and the path I have chosen, realizing that every step I take is one forward and that I can never be sure what will appear on the other side of the hill.

Part Two
Midwest

5. Election Season
Lee Martin

The man on the corner, Ed, has a snowblower, and all winter, whenever we get a fresh accumulation, he cleans out his driveway and then the sidewalk as far as my own drive, three houses down the cul-de-sac. I don't know him very well, but when I watch him clearing my sidewalk, I think of my father who taught me the kind gestures between neighbors that take so little effort and make everyone a bit more cozy.

Summers, my wife and I return the favor of the snowblowing by sharing tomatoes from our garden with Ed and his wife, Cindy. We live with only one house between us, and yet we know so little about one another. They know I teach at Ohio State, that we grow heirloom tomatoes in our garden; we know that Ed has a snowblower, and he's happy to put it to use so we'll have a clean sidewalk. When I see him out in the cold, doing something he doesn't have to for people he barely knows, I think, there goes a good neighbor.

Then, one glorious Sunday in early autumn, he knocks on our front door. He has a clipboard in his hand, a big smile on his meaty face.

"Hot for this time of year, isn't it?" he says to my wife. "Darned hot." He hands Deb a small sandwich bag with a few Brach's candies inside—cinnamon, peppermint, butterscotch, toffee—and a slip of paper that says, *Bless the Family: Save the Nation.* "Election Day's coming," he says. "You've heard about Issue 1?"

Issue 1 is the proposed amendment to the Ohio state constitution that, if passed, will make marriage between a man and a woman the only union that the state will legally recognize. It's the "anti-gay" amendment, and Ed is at our house to get our signatures on a petition to put Issue 1 on the November ballot.

"I'm sorry," Deb tells him. "I can't sign."

Ed's confused. His eyebrows go up. He gives Deb a tentative grin. "But you're married, aren't you?"

"My husband and I have an open mind about this sort of thing."

Ed pulls his head back. His eyes narrow. "Oh," he says. "I see. Well, that's too bad."

It isn't long before almost every front lawn in our neighborhood sports a Bush/Cheney sign. Only one or two Kerrey/Edwards signs interrupt the Republican majority. Then there are lawns like ours that announce nothing at all. Let 'em wonder, I think. Or better yet, let 'em ask Ed.

When it comes to politics, I'm my father's son, through and through— a Democrat—but even that affiliation makes me uneasy since, as my father said of most politicians, whether Democrat or Republican, "I wouldn't trust any of the bastards as far as I could throw 'em."

I pretty much feel the same. In fact, I don't even think of myself as a political person. Every four years, I threaten not to vote. Then, when it comes time, and the thought of a Republican in the White House presents itself, I knuckle down and do my duty. I march into that voting booth and vote for every Dem on the ballot.

My father was a Democrat because he was a child of the Depression who grew up on a farm in southern Illinois and blamed Herbert Hoover for everything. Hoobert Heever, he called him. Don't ask me why.

A Roosevelt Democrat, that was my father. He was working class. He was the little guy. Republicans were out to protect the fat cats, he said, and he was never one of those.

Still, I suspect that if he were alive today, he'd agree with Ed. He'd sign that petition in a whipstitch because toward the end of his life he was a Christian man who believed strongly in morality and was quite willing to let his church, the fundamentalist Church of Christ, define for him exactly what was moral and what wasn't. He objected to single men and women "shacking up." I'm fairly certain he never would have approved of a gay or lesbian marriage.

My mother was a timid, discreet woman who never discussed her politics. We all knew, though, that she voted Republican as her parents and her siblings had as long as memory could recall. That fact flummoxes me every time I think about it because my mother's family, the Reads, were little people just like the Martins. In fact, they may have been just a tad worse off than my father's family. My Grandfather Read tried to make a living farming and ended up losing his land when the bank foreclosed. He tried to make a go of it in small business, operating more than one general store, and failed at that as well. The theory that people always vote their pocketbooks—the wealthy voting Republican and the poor voting Democratic—goes right out the window when it comes to the Reads. I have no idea how it came to be that they cast their lot with the Republicans, and I can't bring myself to ask my one surviving uncle since I fear it would lead to dissension the way it did a few years back during the Clinton/Dole election when his daughter confessed that she'd voted for Clinton and my uncle said to her in a horrified voice, "Why, Melanie Ann. Your mother and I thought we raised you better than that."

From time to time now, my wife says to me, "I couldn't have married you if you'd been a Republican." She wonders how partners of different political affiliations sustain a relationship.

"My mother and father did," I remind her.

"Your mother never talked about politics. She just let your dad blow."

That's true. I can recall my father and my Uncle Bill Heath, who was married to my dad's sister, sitting on porches and around kitchen tables complaining about crop prices and farm subsidy programs and grain embargoes, and kicking the Republicans all to hell. My mother never said a word. She refilled iced tea glasses, served chiffon cakes, and kept everything she believed to herself.

In many ways, I'm like my mother, unwilling to make my political beliefs public. How unfair, it is then, for me to spy a Republican sign on a neighbor's lawn and immediately feel a distaste for that person I may have only previously known as the driver of the Acura suv, or the one who has the ChemLawn service, or who relies on Merry Maids for housecleaning (gee, it strikes me now that even those details are political—we carry our politics with us in the things we own, the services we engage, the stores we frequent; nothing is pure, not even the organic fertilizer I spread on our lawn). Who am I to pass judgment on these neighbors who profess their support for Bush/Cheney when I don't have the conviction to make my own pronouncement? I'm the guy who on late night walks is tempted to rip out those Bush/Cheney signs, every last one of them. That's who I am. That guy.

When someone speaks of the Midwest, I think of small towns and farming communities like the ones in southern Illinois where I grew up, and not the cities like Columbus where I now live. To me the Midwest will always mean the countryside and the people who inhabit it. When I'm back in southern Illinois, as I am each summer, I like nothing more than to drive out into the country through the township where my father's farm now belongs to another man. I like to watch the fields of timothy grass ripple out toward a distant tree line when the wind comes up. I like the way the land is marked off into square sections, the gravel roads running at right angles. The straight rows of corn and soybeans, so neat and orderly, are beautiful. I can pull off the road at one of the graveyards where my ancestors are buried and for a while hear nothing but the wind moving through the trees, a squirrel scrabbling through the grass, a crow calling from overhead, a bobwhite's two-note whistle. I like the farmhouses with their neatly tended gardens and their lawn ornaments—shiny gazing balls, carved wooden ducks with wings that circle with the wind, statues of deer and geese. Sometimes I'll see a collection of metal lawn chairs under the shade trees, or a glider in a breezeway, and I'll know that come evening folks will gather there and for an hour or so their lives will be that simple—the gentle motion of the glider, the easy rock of the lawn chairs, the sun setting on another day of labor. Maybe someone will talk of the war in Iraq, or what Bush is doing to squeeze the farmer, or the price of gasoline, but eventually the voices will fade away and the world will exist the way it did before politics. Twilight will give way to dusk, and the fireflies will come out. Bullfrogs will croak from the pond in the pasture. The bright stars will twinkle overhead, and the earth will keep turning over, despite our own stupidity and everything we do to threaten it.

My first political memory is the 1960 Kennedy/Nixon election. I was five years old, and I remember being in our car along a gravel road outside a church that was the polling place for my parents. A man came up to the car and offered me an apple. It was a yellow delicious—firm and sweet—and I remember how good it tasted on that sunny November day. Indian Summer was lingering that year, and everything seemed to have a golden tone: the apple, the dried cornstalks, the yellow leaves on the hickory trees. How wonderful, I thought, this thing my parents called an election.

My father was in the car with me—babysitting, I suppose, while my mother was in the church casting her vote. He knew the man who gave me the apple. I remember that much. "Tell him thank you," my father said, and I did.

Of course, everyone knew everyone else in Lukin Township, and once the election was done, they went back to their ordinary lives—the farmers and the schoolteachers and the oil field workers and the shop clerks. Summers, they helped each other bring in the hay; winters, they gathered around the radio at the Berryville General Store to listen to high school basketball games, or went to each other's houses to play Euchre or Pitch. They might disagree about Kennedy, but in the end they were still these people in this township finding a way to get on with the living that had to be done there.

From time to time at harvest season, a farmer got down on his luck—maybe he got hurt in an accident or maybe he got sick and was laid up in bed—and then the other farmers in the township pulled together and brought in that man's crop. They brought their machinery and they got the job done, no matter what their politics were. The season and the wheat or corn or beans in the fields didn't care about politics and these men couldn't afford to either. At such times it didn't matter a whit who was a Republican and who was a Democrat.

I like to think, then, that there are certain things we hold in common here in the Midwest—a sense of fairness, a work ethic, a responsibility to our neighbors—but I have to admit that after Ed makes his appearance with his petition and the election season begins to percolate, I start to get testy.

"Republicans," I mutter when Deb and I are out for a walk and we pass the lawns with their Bush/Cheney signs on display.

Deb is even more agitated, vowing to withhold tomatoes from our Republican neighbors.

That'll teach 'em, I think. No Moonglows or Lemon Boys or Black Russians for you or you or you.

It turns out that the young man who lives in the house between ours and Ed's puts a Bush/Cheney sign in his yard. If he's on his porch or in his driveway as we go past in our car, Deb keeps her eyes straight ahead. "Don't wave at that Republican," she says.

A part of me wants to say that none of this matters—that politics don't matter, that one person in the White House or the Congress or the Governor's Mansion, doesn't make a speck of difference since he or she occupies only one place in a larger political machinery that despite its best intentions ends up doing the world more harm than good.

Still, certain things persist, independent of our politics. In present-day Peru, for example, the place of the tomato's origin, eight species still grow wild in the Andes Mountains. Over centuries, people have saved seeds from these tomatoes, domesticated them, transported them across the globe. Today, I can grow the same tomato as people did well over one hundred years ago—the Brandywine, an Amish heirloom from 1885—and from all parts of the world—the Galinas from Siberia, the Marmande from France, the Plum Lemon from Moscow, the Principe Borghese from Italy, the Thai Pink Egg, Aunt Ruby's German Green.

But even the tomato, at one time, couldn't escape being touched by politics. In 1883, Congress passed a tariff act that levied a 10 percent tax on imported vegetables. A few years later, a tomato importer challenged the law on the claim that the tomato was a fruit instead of a vegetable and should, therefore, be free from taxation. The Supreme Court heard the case in 1893 and considered the distinction between "vegetable" and "fruit." The plaintiff's counsel, after reading definitions of the two words from Webster's Dictionary, Worcester's Dictionary, and the Imperial Dictionary, called two witnesses who had long been fruit and vegetable sellers. One of the witnesses said it was his understanding that the term "fruit" referred to "plants or parts of plants as contain the seeds." The other witness said, "I don't think the term 'fruit' or the term 'vegetables' had, in March, 1883, and prior thereto, any special meaning in trade and commerce in this country different from that which I have read here from the dictionaries." The plaintiff's counsel then read the definition of the word "tomato." The defense countered by reading the definitions of the words "pea," "egg plant," "cucumber," "squash," and "pepper." The plaintiff then read the definitions of "potato," "turnip," "parsnip," "cauliflower," "cabbage," "carrot," and "bean." Neither party presented any other evidence.

In offering the court's ruling, Justice Gray wrote:

Botanically speaking, tomatoes are fruits of a vine, just as are cucumbers, squashes, beans, and peas. But in the common language of the people . . . all these are vegetables, which are grown in kitchen gardens, and which, whether eaten cooked or raw, are, like potatoes, carrots, parsnips, turnips, beets, cauliflower, cabbage, celery and lettuce, usually served at dinner in, with or after the soup, fish or meats which constitute the principal part of the repast, and not, like fruits generally, as dessert.

The botanical truth that the tomato is indeed a fruit, actually a large berry, held no weight with the court. All the while, those eight species of the tomato continued to grow in the Andes, flowering and setting fruit.

My father taught me to keep faith in the seasons, to know that winter gave way to spring, that the earth warmed, and seeds germinated, and plants grew. So it is year after year. I turn my garden over, work the soil to tilth, plant lettuce and radish seed, cucumbers and pole beans. I set out the tomato seedlings Deb starts in our greenhouse. The bare plot, as summer lengthens, becomes lush with the tall tomato plants, the tepees of pole beans twining up their stakes, the cages of cucumbers. Then the killing frost comes, and then winter's snow and ice, and we wait again for spring and the thawed earth and the chance once more to put our trust in the sunlight and the rain and the plants that grow. How small we are—how insignificant in the light of all this.

I choose to live here in the Midwest, in part, because of the way I feel connected to the land and the climate. The flat plains suit me. I listen to friends from the east or west coast talk about how boring it is to drive across all those "I" states—Indiana, Illinois, Iowa, and Ohio no less mind-numbing and banal—but to me there's something about the way the roads run straight and the farmland stretches out on all sides, plain and unassuming, that comforts me. Perhaps it's my Libra scales that always want to be in balance, but when I see the predictable landscape that some find lackluster, I feel at home, familiar with the right angles and squared corners. At the same time, I chafe against the fact that like the landscape the people here often hold fast to their conservative ways, feel threatened by anything that seems "liberal." They can fence themselves in, close their minds and hearts to the ever-expanding awareness of human rights that is often more accepted in other, more diverse parts of the country. No doubt there's a homogeneity here that numbs, that makes people like my good neighbor Ed believe he has a right to decide what threatens morality.

Sometimes our climate becomes dramatic, and, when it does, it flattens the ego, and maybe that's not a bad thing. Tornadoes, blizzards, droughts. When they come, we huddle in our basements, stay off our streets, ration our water. We feel small in the face of the planet's drama. It reminds us that we don't always stand at its center.

Still, we debate and legislate, sign or not sign petitions, express our political allegiance or remain silent. We pass Issue 1, in November 2004, and also elect George W. Bush to a second term, a fact that later stuns the Democrats who thought John Kerry had the election in the bag because he had a 356,000 vote advantage in Ohio's six largest cities. It's the rural counties and townships that make the difference for Bush. All those good country people I count as my kin turn out in droves to uphold what they consider the sanctity of marriage, and overwhelming numbers of them vote Republican.

So Ed wins, or at least he thinks he does. I really can't talk to him about it now because shortly after the election, his company, victims of an economy gone sour, downsizes and he loses his job. Then he sells his house, no longer able to pay the mortgage, and he and Cindy move into an apartment and I don't see them again. I don't feel happy about this. In all honesty, I don't feel anyway at all about it.

What I think is this, and I imagine I'll still be thinking it this coming winter when I'm left to shovel my own sidewalk, Ed no longer around to do me the favor: we can participate in a democratic society and think we're making the right choices. We can give leeway to one group while denying the rights of another. We can turn a blind eye to the fact that we're powerless when it comes to the earth turning over, summer's growing season giving way to winter's snows, one year becoming the next until so many have gone by we're stunned by the fact that we stand in the here and now, when it seems like only yesterday we couldn't see it coming to save our lives.

6. Trapping

Jonis Agee

It's Christmas Eve, 4:00 a.m., and my brother is dead. In some terrible way, it has taken his entire family. They will never think of December without that shiver of dread, like a pulled thread in a very expensive, rare cloth. It is a month, a holiday, that has been ruined forever, stained with the white ring of loss. His two grown boys in the military struggling like small children against the blizzard of the future, lean like the good soldiers they are—and are borne into the waste by the war in Iraq, which now seems like time without end.

My visiting daughter believes that politics do not matter—a distasteful subject avoided at the dinner table by polite company, but politics are all that matter now. Without the discussion, we lose everything—soon, even his two children who actually believe in all that warrior fineness, a gesture so beautifully nostalgic that it leaves me howling in the bitter night cold.

At my desk, I open Lucretius, *De Rerum Natura, The Nature of Things*, looking for some ancient truth, some words to take me past the end of the night here. "Men generally fall toward their wound," he writes, speaking of both love and war.

Tonight the moon is so bright, rising to fullness, that it lights the room and seems to heat it, though I know that even the new comet in the southeastern sky trails an icy tail. The coldest night of the year. Seven below at 8:00 p.m. and dropping, when the furnace's specific pitch, more a yowl than a grumble or hum, comes on it's so loud that it rattles the floor grates and we have to speak louder.

The land is down, quiet in this kind of cold, even the rabbit, usually scattering across the driveway, this evening stopped and blinked uncertainly, brown fur rumpled as if it had been tumbled from bed. It's been a week since the deer were around, when the coyotes' joyful chaos visited, howling and singing outside my bedroom window, just the other side of the fence, then chased down along the creek until they faded with the kill of the night. The cold has pressed them to the ground also. The hawk that waits in the trees hunting the fields for mice on the other side of the driveway hasn't been disturbed of late by our departures, rising pensively into the sky above us, massive wings in slow motion touching the invisible currents with the assurance of a boatman easing into a river. The redtail a spot behind the belly that has turned white in the past weeks to no avail. We are waterless, snowless, without winter except for the arctic cold that has made my eyelids sting the past two mornings walking the dogs.

Two weeks ago the furnace man came for the annual checkup and asked if he could trap the creek for raccoons. He seemed a nice young fellow, and something in his manner suggested that this supplement to his income was necessary for a young family. He was kind to the dogs who couldn't stop jumping on him, licking and nipping the toes of his boots, half in love and half protective. He said that he had dogs of his own at home, and so I said yes with that reasoning that occurs just a step ahead of your brain.

"I'll order some more dog-proof traps," he promised, his face devoid of guile, honest, open, almost handsome, just enough to have been trusted by the generation before him. Black hair and slightly amused eyes is all I can remember. Genial. His manner said you have nothing to fear from me, I fixed your furnace, for god's sake.

He appeared the following Saturday afternoon to survey the creek and confirm permission. Again, I said yes as he eyed the dogs, offering a hand to the youngest, who was using every ounce of will in his small taut body to keep from chomping down on the fingertips. Don't do it, I urged silently.

This time he drove a late model pickup truck, shiny maroon, four-door, and parked it in front of the yard gate as if he were visiting us. At first it only mildly bothered me. I kept thinking he would be more decorous in the future, park down the driveway on the shoulder where he could keep his business private. That's the way hunters who work the land in the fall do, as if they are half-ashamed to be taking advantage of my generosity, the ease with which they dispatch with deer, grouse, ducks, squirrels, turkeys, and rabbits, as if they half-fear that I might ask for a token of the bounty, like the Lord of the Manor. I grew up with hunters, I could tell them, had meat on the table for a large family because my father and brothers brought down the game. I thought everyone ate venison heart, roast haunch, deerburger, had wild goose and pheasant and duck. I spent part of every fall weekend plucking and peeling paraffin-dipped skin so the pinfeathers would ease up and out of their sheaths. We ate like kings and never knew it—so I don't have a problem when a nice young man asks to hunt my land. I judge them by their manners, their story.

Donnie, the only local permitted in the lower meadow and woods, lives a mile from me as the crow flies. Each fall he asks permission and deposits his story in exchange, the one about marrying his high school crush after all those years of a failed marriage. How they came to buy the horses, and the mare that was difficult in the beginning, and the barn that didn't get put up, and now she wants to move and if he'd known she was there in the middle of his future, he would have bought a doublewide.

The furnace-man trapper offered nothing except a self-deprecating smile and a gesture, which I now think I might have constructed in my mind, of spreading his arms and turning his palms out as if to say, see, I have nothing to hide, even your dogs are licking my pant cuffs.

I didn't actually see him set the traps. I took his word for it that a dog couldn't get them open—they'd need hands to spring them, he said, and mimed pulling down a heavy metal bar so I could substitute the tiny raccoon hand for a dog paw, which suddenly seemed clumsy, unuseful, and safe. It was about then that I began to wonder what it was that I had against raccoons and their big, roly-poly ways around the farm. It's true that last summer I was startled out of my sleep by a big raccoon walking the top of the fence, rattling the chain link as if he were a child banging it with a stick. I was convinced the neighborhood kids who partied up and down the dirt road had come after me, probably because I picked up the cans and bottles they heaved out the windows of their speeding cars and trucks—I was a nuisance, keeping them from making their statements, a kind of rural graffiti I went along and cleaned up as soon as they put it down. But no, it was a huge raccoon on the fence, in the midst of an invasion of the yard, coming to pluck the ripe tomatoes, the rosebuds, the tips of the forsythia. I yelled out the window and he paused, startled, then dropped down into the yard and galloped out of sight around the corner of the house.

What I didn't want to think about were the young twins the dogs treed in the front yard one night a few months ago. Dragging the dogs inside, I just assumed that the raccoons would shortly descend and take themselves away, and sure enough, by the next morning the fork of the tree was empty. It wasn't until the dogs went crazy again, throwing themselves at the fence closest to the spring house that I came out and realized something was trying to work its way in through the window.

As they scratched at the glass and tried to get a grip on the slick wood, the raccoons were groaning, not quite in fear of the fenced dogs whose size matched their own, as much as in frustration at the unyielding surfaces. They wanted in the small building that housed the pump for the sprinkler and my husband's study. Who knew what delicacies the raccoons could discover in such fertile ground. I fetched a large plastic leaf rake, certain that the mere sight of such an instrument would drive them back to the creek and woods.

My husband stayed inside the fence warning me to "stop what I was doing, back off, ignore them, they might be rabid."

They attacked instead, grabbing the plastic tines, clinging to them, threatening to bite or break the flimsy green plastic, as their bodies twisted and pushed toward me. I stood my ground and managed somehow to scrape and scoot one of the raccoons onto the wide part of the rake, and while my husband practically howled with disapproval, I hurried to the edge of the woods and turned the rake over in the deep grass. The raccoon clung to the rake and snarled loudly. I tried to rub him off on the ground, he started to climb toward the handle. I lifted the rake a foot high and banged it down, not wanting to hurt him, but not quite unable to avoid my husband's urgings to "run if he comes for you." The raccoon clung harder. Could I outrun a raccoon? I doubted it. Maybe make the spring house and lock myself in—held prisoner by raccoons. How would that look to my husband?

I raised the rake a little higher and shook it in midair and turned it over and over, like a fun ride at the fair, and finally, probably dizzy by now, the dang thing dropped off, landing catlike on all fours, snarled once more at me with those sharp little teeth showing, turned and sidled into the woods.

"You're lucky," my husband said as I came back for the second raccoon. "Just wait, he'll follow his brother. Do you want to have to go through those rabies shots? I hear they hurt like hell."

The raccoon was still searching the edges of the window with his long sharp claws, trying to find the way in. "It doesn't open," I muttered and scooped him up on the wide flat part of the rake, much handier now that I had a method. This raccoon rode facing me and snarling, poised for any funny business. This time I simply had to turn the rake over for the animal to drop off, although he didn't immediately hurry away. Instead, he stood his ground, eyeing the spring house, my legs, the dogs who were still barking wildly, and my husband who seemed to be measuring me for a stupid suit. I waited a moment, then gently pushed him with the rake, trying to scoot him along rather than push him since one thing I had already learned was that raccoons didn't like being pushed around. He grabbed at the tines and I jerked the rake up, brandishing it like a medieval weapon over his head. He glared, snarled, and reluctantly turned to follow his twin, walking slowly with a certain amount of swagger to his hind end. It left me with the definite feeling that they'd be back for revenge.

"I hope you're happy," my husband said.

For the rest of the summer they tore up a raised round flowerbed by the spring house. Every time I planted it with tomatoes, vinca, snapdragons, liatris, petunias, lilies, basil, it didn't matter what, they would eat, shred, tear into pieces, or simply uproot whole plants. I had it fenced against rabbits, but that meant nothing to the raccoons. They knew what I loved. When I looked out across the yard at the empty flowerbed, I remembered the way I felt every time they destroyed my work. Rather godlike to exact this kind of retribution on them, I guess, but I didn't care. Maybe they were already dead, coyote meat, maybe they wouldn't be trapped. The truth of the matter was, I wouldn't let myself care. They weren't the cute little cartoon faces of children's fantasies, nor the hungry little marauders peeking out at you from storm drains in urban residential areas, a vestige of the natural world that urbanites use to reassure themselves that they haven't really, really killed off everything so they can have the comfort and convenience of pavement and flush toilets. See, they always hasten to point out, we live side-by-side with nature, right here in the city! Really, I want to argue, when was the last time coyotes ate *your* housecat? How many snakes live in *your* basement?

I was prepared, you see. "The fiercer every breed, the more it tends to savage dreams," Lucretius observes.

"They've got something," I said to my husband, and we both stepped outside the house to listen. It was broad daylight, and the whole thing seemed wrong, though I can't say why. The dogs were killing for the joy of it, not for hunger. I imagined a deer, another, smaller dog like one of ours, some helpless creature torn to shreds by those two monsters.

"Should we go see?" my husband asked. Usually he's the sensible one, so I know he was as bothered as I was. I too had the urge to get the rifle down, the one we still didn't know for sure how to load. Something should be done, I know we both felt that way, watching the woods in the bright thin winter sunlight. You could see the straight tan trunks of the sapling hawthorn taking over the little paddock beside the old barn, and the red cedars turning rusty as they do this time of year, and beyond the dark thick corrugations of the bur oak, but that was only in my mind since the barn blocked their view, and the matted tan grasses flattened by the deer. I hoped it wasn't one of the fawns we'd seen a few months before, hoped one of the hunters hadn't tracked the doe and gotten her. Maybe a beaver, maybe one of the beavers who were forever damming up the creek to create all those thick brown water pools . . . I could see the soft belly ripped open, spilling bright red blood, the dogs gorging themselves on the fresh entrails, wearing their red masks proudly, eyes wild and full of joy you could hear in their voices.

"It's probably a raccoon. They found a trap," my husband said. There was no regret in his voice, he's not a sentimental man, but perhaps a tinge of sadness or resignation.

"I feel like shooting them," I said, surprising myself.

"Wait until they come home covered in gore, the owners will start keeping them penned."

"I hope they throw up all over their rugs then. I hope it makes them sick, as well, as dogs . . ."

My words seemed too small for what I was feeling. For the image of the raccoon, still alive perhaps, unable to free itself, ripped apart for sport. I wanted to believe he hadn't been frantically trying to gnaw his leg off, I wanted to see his inert body instead, neck broken cleanly, dead, when they found him. I'd never asked how that iron bar came down, how it took the animal.

"That poor sonofabitch is just trying to make some extra money for his family, you know. He has kids. Christmas is coming. He repairs furnaces, for chrissakes. Now some pampered house dogs come and take away his livelihood." I wanted to put the blame where it belonged, someplace else.

"We should warn him about the dobermans," my husband said.

That night the trapper was already returning from checking his traps to his truck parked by the gate by the time I ran outside, just in time to see him lift a large raccoon by the hind legs over the tailgate. I could tell by the stillness, the inertness, that it was dead when I told him about the dobermans.

"Something got one of the traps," he said. "Figured it was coyotes or dogs." He shook his head. "Guess I'll have to start carrying a gun."

I agreed, feeling bloodthirsty, wanting the dogs and the owners both punished for what had transpired. Yet later, I could not get the image of that body out of my mind. Really, it was only a dark shadow, backlit by the yard lights, but still it hung there, fat, bloodless, featureless, really, but full of death, full of the lingering form of life that made its death specific to it, to none other. I don't know why it bothered me, the author of the whole deal, but it did. It still does.

For the next week, the truck continued to creep up the drive after dark and park, and the trapper slipped out across the barnyard, disappearing into the woods without a word. In fact, I never saw him, even as a shadow, he was that unobtrusive, quiet. I would simply look out the windows later and the dark form of his truck would be absent again, as if he could coast in and out of the barnyard without even turning on his engine. One night I heard two shots from the woods, and I prayed that he was defending himself, or that he had to finish killing something in the trap or that coyotes had come too close. I couldn't even make myself complete the other thought about the possibility of those two dogs. I waited that night, to make sure he returned to his truck, checking the windows occasionally, and the last time I looked out it wasn't there. Then the next night my brother died, and we left town for the funeral, and by the time we returned, he was gone for good.

My brother's burial took place in a tiny Iowa town a few days after the funeral. It was one of the coldest days of the year, with a bitter gusting wind that dropped the air to well below zero although the sun was big and bright in the cloudless blue sky. The drive from my farm to Essex was across the Missouri River, then up into the Loess Hills on the other side of the Nebraska-Iowa border, lovely country, the narrow winding blacktop empty, trees clinging to the road, picturesque little farms snugged into the hillsides, surrounded by rolling pastures I was too numb to care about even when they were filled with horses. It took me three tries to find the cemetery well outside the little town. I finally had to stop at the lone cafe and ask the young man in the blue Air Force ROTC uniform if he was on the way to the burial also. Did he know the way? My brother's younger son is part of their program in college, you see, he wanted to pay for everything himself so he took the ROTC scholarship. The older boy is already active Air Force.

There were two van loads of uniformed kids, and I followed them at a distance, not wanting to seem clingy—college kids don't like that in adults, and besides, I was unsure about my rights as the sister of the deceased.

They led me out of town, turning finally onto a gravel road that gave a glimpse of what was to come, the three tall pines perched on a distant hillside surrounded by the treeless fields. We drove to the three-sided canvas shelter flapping wildly in the wind where the lead van paused, talked to someone, then continued on up a narrow crushed-rock road that made my truck tilt and lunge, across the top of the cemetery, finally stopped in a grassy area next to another truck. I pulled in facing away from the entrance, while all other vehicles pulled in facing out, as if they understood that you didn't want to stay any longer than necessary here.

By the time the hearse arrived and the area was filled with cars, we had to practically run to catch up before the service started. My brother's wife and children came in cars that parked right by the little tent, I realized, as the blue uniformed young men and women and I hurried down the road, twisting our ankles awkwardly on the crushed rock. They had no coats, only the thin wool of the uniforms to protect them, and by the time I arrived, they were huddled along one side of the tent's interior, only slightly sheltered from the wind and cold, shivering. I handed my gloves to a girl whose hands were already chaffed and red. I wanted to give her my coat. I had worn two against the cold, and I hardly deserved one.

The assistant funeral director had to hold the flat roof flap down to keep it from blowing away, and the minister hurried. The coffin sat like the sleek bright blue hull of a jet ski, something you could go fast and have fun in. My brother was not present though. I never felt him anywhere near it, not at the funeral home when his body was so life-like I kept thinking I saw his mouth smile, his eye wink, not here, and that was about the saddest thing of all—tears freezing on my cheeks, the minister a good man who said the right things and stopped to comfort the crying baby, my brother's sons, who were good young men, all those bright uniforms soon to be shipped away, like this body, never to see this world again. When the young woman tried to hand my gloves back, I made her keep them so her hands would stay warm for a few minutes longer, because we had done so little for each other, I discovered, so very little, and they didn't wear coats because they couldn't afford the official ones, they said, and what was unsaid, that they needed their uniforms to show for their brother soldier who had lost the person dearest to him in the world, and so never mind the cold, it never lasted that long, did it? "And heaven and earth will end, as certainly as ever they once began."

It was inevitable, my brother and these bright children who believed in what they were doing. The Pershing Rifles Brigade. They were honor cadets, the best and brightest, some of whom would die themselves within the year, living up to the honor of the chosen. This nephew, perhaps, among them, his brother soon to volunteer for duty in Iraq. How I wish my brother were alive to stop them, to beg them not to go. How I wish we did not teach our children so much that they learned to stand freezing to honor the dead. Someone should show some sense, someone should run screaming up that hill for the warm shelter of a car heater and a good shot of bourbon. Someone should stop being a good kid, a good soldier, a good father and mother, a good citizen. Someone should stop this.

"Change loosens things," Lucretius writes, "makes them dissolve and die, parts are transposed, can move from their positions, submit to dissolution, and succumb."

The day the furnace man asked if he could trap, I said, "Sure—and I'd really like to come along with you one time, just to see how it's done. I've always wondered about trapping, I come from a long line of hunters. I grew up eating wild game."

He smiled and nodded and agreed.

I meant it, too, intended to go out there with him, follow along, find out something about what I had set in motion. But after the dobermans got the first raccoon, and I saw him lifting the other one into the truck, I don't know. Then the shots, my brother's heart stopping so suddenly and irreversibly in the middle of the night. I don't think I wanted to go into those dark woods with that man, didn't want to disappear so completely that the dogs would be left waiting at the dining room windows, humming anxiously to the brightly lit rooms and colored Christmas tree bulbs while he led me deeper and deeper toward the ravine where the air never warms even on the hottest July days.

He was only the man who fixed the furnace, his name was pinned to the bulletin board below the dinner plates, I would reassure myself. Careful to follow his footsteps, lit by the dull yellow globe of his flashlight, the rifle at his side hanging casually from his ungloved hand, I would want to ask him if his hand got cold gripping the metal. But something about his silence, the way he would dissolve in the dark shadows, would keep me still, half waiting for the hand that would pull me down. Because you see what I had done. I had drawn myself into a trap and now there was hardly anything I could do or forget. "So each man flees himself, or tries to . . ."

7. Here Was Johnny

Steve Heller

In May of 2003 my wife Sheyene and I moved from Manhattan, Kansas, "The Little Apple," to Venice Beach, California. The move was a remarkable uprooting for both of us. Sheyene is considerably younger than I am, but she had lived her entire life in Kansas, growing up in the farm community of Clay Center, which I affectionately refer to as Middle Dirt. Clay Center is the county seat of Clay County, one of the most conservative counties in one of the most conservative states in the nation. Once a hotbed of grass roots populism, in recent decades Kansas has become increasingly known for its flat earth politics, a place where intelligent design is promoted as science, a woman's right to have an abortion is regarded as both blasphemy and legalized murder, and farmers on the verge of economic ruin routinely vote for politicians whose policies speed up the process. Why and how this all happened is answered brilliantly in Thomas Frank's recent book *What's the Matter with Kansas?* What I'm concerned with here is how it feels, as a secular humanist respectful of the views of others, to live in such a state—and how it feels to have left.

Sheyene and everyone on her mother Karla's side of the family, the Henderson/Stunkels, were yellow dog Democrats, contrarians who would rather vote for a yellow dog than a Republican. This made them part of a small but vocal Middle Dirt minority. With the exception of her grandma Mabel, a good Christian who outlived three husbands, the left side of Sheyene's family smoked, drank, joked, cursed, and generally carried on in ways that would make a pastor blush. The right side of Sheyene's family, the Hoyles, her stepdad John's side, was composed of conservative business people. Respectable people, the moral center of Clay County, even if most of them actually lived elsewhere. They all went to church—perhaps not everyone *every* Sunday—and did far fewer of the other things the left side did. Especially Grandma Hoyle, a widow by the time I met her, and one of the most polite, elegant people I've ever known.

When I came into the picture, an older man with four children, going through a divorce after a quarter century of solid-seeming marriage, I expected trouble from both sides of the family. Especially the right.

I didn't get it. What I got from both sides, to my astonishment, was acceptance.

We're so happy Sheyene wound up with a professor, the right side said. *Sheyene's always been such a smart one.*

Half of us thought Sheyene would run away with a truck driver, the left side said. *The other half thought she was a lesbian. Have another beer, Steve.*

The two sides were seldom seen together. Holidays, birthdays, and other occasions were celebrated on separate sides of town. Whenever there were concurrent gatherings, Sheyene and I shuttled between sides, sometimes accompanied by Sheyene's adopted little brother Jackson Reeve, before returning to Manhattan, where all four of my children and their mother still lived. Until Sheyene's mother and stepdad divorced, they shuttled between sides as well.

The left and right sides of the family communicated through emissaries: Stepdad John, the black sheep of the right (a plumber at Kansas State who likes motorcycles and beer), and, less frequently, Grandma Mabel (whose lips have never tasted cigarettes, alcohol, or profanity), the white sheep of the left. And, of course, Sheyene, the darling of both sides, the one who was smart and honest and funny (though never gross, not with the right side, anyway) and loved equally by everyone even though she'd fallen in love with an old married atheist with four children instead of a good Christian, a truck driver, or a lesbian.

I'm sure each side of the family had many heated debates about Sheyene and me. But the heat never spilled from one side to the other.

The shuttle diplomacy of Sheyene and Mabel and John allowed both sides to maintain a kind of civility that in the end seemed bizarrely normal. Of course civility has its price: its effect on the development of one's character.

I'd learned about this effect long before I'd ever set foot in Kansas. My own roots are sunk in the red dirt of Oklahoma, the red state that borders Kansas on the south. From the sixth grade on, I lived in a stone house in the wheat lands five miles north of Yukon, "The Czech Capital of Oklahoma," hometown of Garth Brooks, whose name spans a water tower visible from I-40. Today there are more than 22,000 residents, many of whom work in Oklahoma City, twenty miles east. In 1960, however, when my parents and I moved to Yukon, we found a sleepy farm community of about 6,000, not unlike Clay Center today. The tallest building in town was the Yukon's Best Flour grain elevator. In high school, my male classmates went to church, played sports, drank beer, chewed tobacco, and drove muscle cars and pickup trucks.

From the beginning, I was a misfit in Yukon society. Unlike most of my peers, I was an only child. There were no kids my age within a mile of my parents' house. I was skinny and didn't play sports, although I loved baseball and thought I'd grow up to write for *The Sporting News*. I may have been the only student at Yukon High who read *The Sporting News*. Most had never even heard of it, and this fact made me feel a secret, unwarranted superiority. The truth was that I was uncomfortable with the aggressive, macho behavior encouraged among boys by coaches, teachers, and even their parents. I tried hard not to reveal this discomfort, for in Yukon the consequences of being regarded as different were severe. *There's two kinds of guys*, my friends said. *Guys who like sports and guys who like other guys.*

I belonged to no clubs, and had few friends outside school. I'd been baptized Catholic, but never confirmed. My parents were agnostic, at best. *When you're dead, you're dead*, my father used to say. *There ain't no ever-after.* For my mother, our lack of church attendance was a source of guilt. *I fault myself for not taking you to mass when you were young*, she still tells me from time to time. *You should have had a choice.* Whenever I point out that in fact I did have a choice—an informed choice, after attending Catholic, Methodist, Baptist, Lutheran, and other services at the invitation of my peers—Mother shakes her head and says: *It doesn't work that way.*

Nevertheless, like most teenagers, I tried my best to fit in. When I was a senior, working almost forty hours a week at the postal center in Oklahoma City, I bought a new sky blue Pontiac Sprint: a six-cylinder overhead cam, premium fuel version of a GTO. I joined the yearbook staff, got elected to the student council, made the girls and even the jocks laugh with self-deprecating humor. *Steve's cool*, my classmates began to say.

But my cool was both an illusion and a denial. If I had any idea who I really was at the time, I never gave my classmates a chance to see it.

One warm summer night when I was sixteen, before anyone had begun to call me cool, two of my buddies from social studies (I'm not going to reveal their names) picked me up in the older one's Ford pickup. The driver was a farm kid. Like many other guys in Yukon, between the bench seat and the back window he had mounted a rifle rack. When I climbed into the cab beside my buddies, I found two twelve-gauge shotguns resting behind our heads.

"What are these for?" I asked.

"To shoot," the driver replied.

In Yukon, conversations among guys tended to include as many words as necessary, and no more.

"Shoot what?" I had to ask.

In reply, the driver uttered a seven-letter derogatory term for black people.

"Yeah," the other passenger said. "Damn straight."

Then they both laughed.

City-data.com lists the black population of Yukon in 2004 as less than 1 percent. When my buddy uttered the word, there were no black residents of Yukon at all. And we weren't about to go looking for any black people, either. We were just going to drive around, just like we had all the other times, and pretend to look for a place we could buy beer. Only the driver actually drank beer. My buddies were simply farting off.

Acting cool.

And what did *I* say? Nothing. Nothing at all, until nearly four decades later, when I told the story of that night to a group of faculty, staff, and students at Antioch University Los Angeles, where I was interviewing for a job. *Creative writing is not self-expression,* I asserted to my audience, *but the opposite: the expression of otherness, the connection between the self and other, the writer and experience, the writer and the world. The writer's job is to imagine what it feels like to be someone else. Only then can we know the world and our own place in it.*

Then I told them the story of the pickup ride when I was a teenager.

It took me many years to see it this way, but I was like a gay man growing up among people who would hate me, even harm me, if they discovered who I was, what I thought and believed. So I hid my feelings and my thoughts, hid the fact that I was different, as if I had slipped the differences off my skin and hung them in a closet.

At the core of the character that developed out of that night with my buddies are some questions I've regularly asked myself over the years: When should one speak up? And when should one remain silent? Is silence in the face of bigotry sometimes a necessary tool for survival? Or is it just cowardice?

I was eventually offered the job at Antioch, and Sheyene and I made our big move from the Little Apple to Venice Beach, from reddest red to bluest blue. At last, we told ourselves, as blue as our own blue-collar blood (my father was an electrician and maintenance man, my mother a secretary). Venice turned out to be a little *too* blue, or at least too noisy, so the following year we moved again, this time to Marina del Rey. My middle son, Michael, moved with us. Our apartment on Panay Way overlooked C Basin, and from our balcony we could see a slice of the main channel, the cliffs of Playa del Rey, and many boats. The most impressive boat by far was a brilliant white cruiser called the *Serengeti.* The *Serengeti* is so long that it has to be anchored at the end of a dock where it can occupy a space equivalent to the length of two berths, plus the main walkway. It looks like something you could take to Hawai'i without refueling.

We hadn't lived in the marina long before we heard people talking about the *Serengeti*. The talk was seldom about the boat, but rather about its alleged owner. "Yeah, I saw him on the way back in last night; he waved." "Oh yes, it was him, all right." "I never recognize his guests; must be family." Despite all the rumoring and name-dropping, usually without actually naming names, we noticed the residents pretty much allowed the owner his space and his privacy, which perhaps is why he was seen so often. Oh, there was the occasional dinghy occupied by tourist snoopers, motoring round and round the *Serengeti*, taking pictures of its bow and stern. And one evening a drunk sailed by in a small yacht and shouted, loud enough for everyone on C Basin to hear: "Heeeere's *Johnny!*"

Sheyene and I never laid eyes on him ourselves until one evening a few months after our move to the marina. We were taking Dachshund Hammett on his evening walk. The weather was perfect, and across the basin the lights of the *Serengeti* were lit. As we completed a loop around the long apartment building next door, suddenly there he was, standing alone on the upper deck, white hair shining as bright as it used to in his last years on *The Tonight Show*. He was there for a few seconds, then vanished into the main cabin while Dash marked yet another palm tree.

We're still relative newcomers to LA, but Sheyene and I have learned that seeing celebrities is no big deal out here. You can't swing a dead poet without hitting somebody who's been on television. But later that night I got to thinking about how I used to watch *The Tonight Show* when I was a kid, then a teen, then, less often, as a young adult, then, less and less often, as an older adult, until finally I didn't bother any more. Johnny Carson did all manner of silly things on screen; he'd literally pull his pants down for a laugh. But my lasting impression of him was one of calm. That laid-back Midwestern charm that put nervous guests at ease. When I was going through my Yukon cool guy phase, I used to critique his monologues, which I often thought were tame, even lame. Sometimes I was certain I could write funnier lines myself, but that was youthful hubris. Something I understood only gradually was the power that Johnny Carson wielded from his desk on the set at NBC in Burbank. He functioned as a kind of touchstone for American sensibilities, and he used this authority with knowing discretion. The guest comedians were nice, only a little bit naughty. The musical guests were not too loud. I remembered wondering, when I was still a teenager, why the governor of California was on *The Tonight Show* so often. I didn't see why Ronald Reagan was supposed to be interesting, even if he did used to act with monkeys and sell Twenty Mule Team Borax. Then, of course, I began to see. In the ad pages of magazines I saw Johnny wearing the same dorky suits he wore during his monologues. Like Bob Hope and John Wayne, he began to seem the opposite of cool. But I still trusted him somehow, in some of the same ways I continued to trust my parents, even though our values and sensibilities were very different.

It wasn't until I was in my twenties that I put a label on what Johnny Carson represented to me. And when I finally said the word aloud, the sound of it on my lips surprised me: *conservative*.

The surprising part was that so much of this word was still alive inside me. Familiar. Comfortable. An old friend who might be dorky, even a little backward in some ways, but you could still trust him, even when you knew he was wrong. Like my buddies in the pickup, whom I lost touch with decades ago, right after I headed off for college and they stayed on in Yukon, guardians of a way of life that was threatened only by their own ignorance. I sometimes wonder what happened to the two of them, whether their views may have changed over time. Sometimes I wonder if I really knew either one of them at all, if they too were concealing some vulnerable side of themselves, hiding behind the false bravado of aggressive speech.

And so we come to today. Bush. Iraq. Neocons. The tragedy of New Orleans. And our longtime companions: racism, sexism, greed. And is it any wonder? Recently, I have begun to ask myself some new questions: those of us who watched Johnny when we were kids, but grew up to be liberals and other things left of center, when did we fall asleep? When did we lose the ability to empathize, let alone sympathize, with all those other folks who, like us, were dozing off in their beds during the second skit or the third interview? When did we lose the ability to communicate with the people who continued to empathize with Ron and Bob and John and Johnny? When did the civil conversation, the one we used to have with our buddies and our families, whether they were red or blue, bigots or progressives, whether it was face-to-face or by emissary, when did it end?

Or has it really ended?

Bloggers, columnists, commentators, and spinners fill our eyes and ears with polemics 24/7. The ground shifts continuously beneath our feet, and the hateful din is deafening. Almost. There are still the Sheyenes, the Grandma Mabels, and the divorced stepdad Johns to ferry the news between left and right.

When should one speak up?

When is it best to listen?

If I had spoken my thoughts to my buddies in the pickup forty years ago, what kind of man would I be now?

One morning in January 2005 I woke up and discovered the *Serengeti* had sailed away. I thought little of it at the time, because in a week or a month it had always come back. The following Sunday, when I read the news that the King of Late Night had died, I found myself wondering where the *Serengeti* had gone this time, and whether I would ever see it again.

What I do know is this: Johnny was once here. All I see now is a big hole in the water.

8. America, Where's
Your Sense of Humor?
Michael J. Rosen

In the years following the 2004 elections, a remarkable number of remarkably diverse studies appeared, each assessing the reddish or bluish nature of one or another topic. All but one study, the distribution of humorists within the fifty states, which I personally conducted, are the work of statistics experts, political pundits, or well-credentialed analysts in the given field. (I qualify for none of these categories.) Perhaps the 2004 election appealed to, or maybe even prompted, the public's keener interest in the differences between red and blue states, even as criticism of the electoral college has pointed out that Ohio, where I live, and a couple other persuadable states, have become the only places where campaigning seems to be focused in an election in order to effect a presidential outcome.

It may also be true that studies, such as the ones cited here, provide a wealth of material for the impoverished programming that allows our umpteen conventional and unconventional news sources to find someone or something that requires urgent attention, immediate endorsement, bipartisan vilification, or just a solid round of hot-headed public humiliation, twenty-four hours a day.

Rather than bog us down in post-post-election analysis and citations that might qualify me as something I'm not, let me simply offer, without any smugness or gloating, some of the findings I found most interesting.

Professors

A few studies revealed that in the social sciences and humanities there are 7 blue professors for every 1 red professor. In other fields, the ratio varies: the lowest, in economics, shows 3 Democrats for every 1 Republican; the highest, in anthropology, shows 30 Democrats for every 1 Republican.

Fertility

The Boston Globe featured a story showing that in 2004, Bush carried the 19 states with the highest expected lifetime fertility rate for white women (non-Hispanic). Moreover, Bush won the 25 states with the longest-married white women (between 18 and 44 years). In Utah, where the most fecund white women reside, the Mormons gave Bush 70 percent of their votes. In Massachusetts, Vermont, and Rhode Island—3 of the 4 states with the lowest white birthrate—Bush received 40 percent of the votes. And Kerry took the 16 states with the lowest fertility rates.

Limpness

Men's Health assessed per-capita sales of erectile dysfunction drugs in 100 cities (citing NDC Health as the source), factoring in obesity, which, it claims, increases ED by 79 percent (citing figures from the Centers for Disease Control and Prevention). Providing grades from A to F, and giving approximately 50 percent A's or B's, the study gave F's to the nation's 4 "limpest" cities: Kansas City MO, Montgomery AL, Shreveport LA, and Birmingham AL—all in red states. Of the 50 limpest cities—those receiving a C or below—40 are located in red states.

Population Density

Most of America's *land* voted red—Bush's counties are more sparsely populated. Kerry's counties are more densely populated. Omitting the enormous and barely populated Alaska, the red states still have one-fourth the population of the blue states.

Housing Prices

Bush carried the 26 states with the least inflation between 1980 and 2004. The more Democratic the state, the higher the housing prices. The study even suggests that better views—literally, how scenic are the views out the windows—make more liberal viewers.

Divorce

Using 2002 statistics, the 13 states with the highest divorce rates all voted red. The blue states include 9 of the 13 with the lowest divorce rates. (And 2 of the other 4 were Iowa and New Mexico, which Kerry lost by the smallest margins.)

Teen Pregnancy

Fourteen of the 17 states with the highest teen pregnancy rates voted red. Or 17 out of the top 25. Meanwhile, blue states include 8 of the 9 states with the lowest teen pregnancy. (North Dakota was the one red state.)

Traffic Fatalities

Twenty-four of the 25 states with the highest rates of traffic fatalities voted red. Of the 16 states with the lowest rates, 15 voted blue.

Violent Crime

Twenty-two of the 31 states with the most violent crime voted red. Nine of the 17 states with the least violent crimes voted blue.

Mobile Homes

Twenty-one of the 24 states with the largest number of mobile homes voted red. The 13 states with the smallest number of mobile homes voted blue.

Feral Hogs

In *The New Yorker,* Ian Frazier reported a correlation between red states and states with feral hog populations. Twenty-three of the 28 states that voted for Bush have feral hogs. Three other observations: Texas, the most solidly Bush state, possesses the most feral hogs. Democratic hopes for Florida, according to the feral hog predicator, should have been dashed: all sixty-seven counties have feral hogs. And California, which voted blue, does have feral hogs in all but one of its fifty-eight counties. But, Frazier points out, in California, "5,509,826 people voted for George Bush—the most of any state, even more than Texas."

Now we move to the study for which I can claim some responsibility. The question I posed: where does America's sense of humor reside? Using the same 2004 elections as the other studies as my guide, I believe we can safely conclude that the state—or states, rather, of American humor are blue.

For something close to a decade, I've been an unofficial organizer of an unfounded organization we can call the National Humor Writers Union. Op-ed writers, essayists, screenwriters, satirists, monologue writers, and other humor-penning personalities across this country have shared work for possible publication in a humor biennial I edited. So, if America were a patient and we were playing Operation, we could remove the funny bone, biopsy it, and produce the following data.

This biennial, *Mirth of a Nation,* began in the Clinton administration, barreled through George W. Bush's first term, and launched its third volume, *May Contain Nuts,* during the 2004 presidential debates (which sort of temporarily took the attention off of humor).

In map 1, we see a review of the electoral votes in the 2004 presidential race. Instead of red and blue, I've used a medium-gray to represent red/Bush/Republican and some kind of psychedelic pattern for blue/Kerry/Democrat, figuring the map was going to be hard to read at this size in black and white no matter what I tried.

Looking at the locations from where all the submissions were

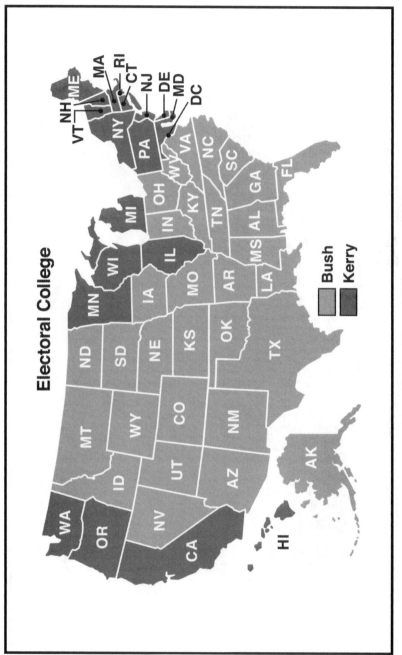

Map 1. The 2004 Electoral College map.

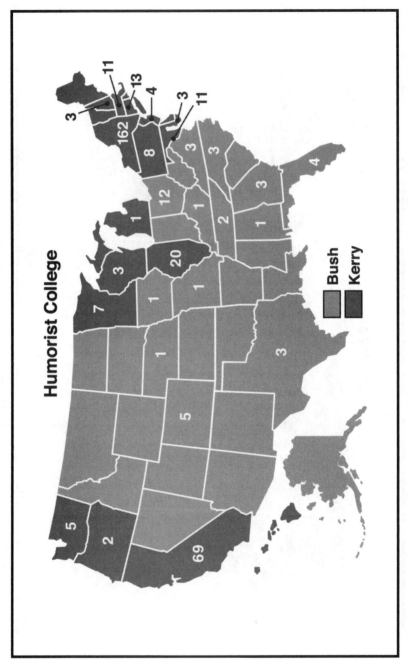

Map 2. The same Electoral College map with the number of identified resident humorists applied to each state.

mailed, map 2 presents a map of where humor writers live in America. Or at least, where humor writers live in America who would like to be published. Or at least where humor writers live in America who would like to be published in a book that I am editing. As you may surmise, this is an acceptable margin of error in keeping with current electoral practices. To be scrupulously accurate about inaccuracy, while I tried to handwrite replies to every submission, I did not always copy the authors' addresses before returning the work. But when the submission contained great work, genuine promise, or sincere flattery (as in "I can't wait to read the next volume, *even if I'm not in it!*"), then the name was logged into my database.

Out of a few thousand submissions, I can put a pushpin in the correct state for roughly as many humorists as there are Electoral College votes in this country: that's 538. I say, "roughly" because, over the years, I, like the presidential candidates, rely on student-volunteers from nearby universities to help register names.

Unfortunately, some humorists were ineligible for our study, namely several Canadian residents (two of whom, in the spirit of NAFTA, are published in these anthologies) and one Englishman. (Curiously, no submissions came from any of America's other allies. *You* try coercing a humorist . . .) Also, as this last election reminded us, people move. So, throwing out returned mail, and people who only exist as Hotmail or AOL addresses (nothing like a university e-mail account for disclosing whereabouts!), the number of locatable humorists drops to 368.

In keeping with the prohibition of employers accompanying employees into the voting booth, this editor did not contact any humorist to inquire about his or her voting record; instead, we'll have to go the way of all statistics and incorrectly presume that each humorist voted along his or her state's party lines. Here's what we find: 324 humor writers reside in blue states, 44 reside in red states.

In case it's hard to remember whether it's the blue or the red states in which 88 percent of our humor writers reside, I have prepared a chart:

RED	BLUE
Virgin Mary	frozen Margaritas (use blue curaçao)
embarrassment	blue funk
box of Hot Tamales	Etta James
Valentine's Day between 1 man and 1 woman	Chanukah
in the red	once in a blue moon
sunburn	blue blood
red meat	soy: the other white meat
hot under the collar	bluestocking
blushing	blue movies
red carpet	periwinkle wall coloring
redskins (potatoes)	bluepoint oysters
red herring	bluefin tuna
red alert	code blue
red tape	blue streak

Number of Humorists Residing in Each Blue State

New York	162
California	69
Illinois	20
Connecticut	13
District of Columbia	11
Pennsylvania	8
Minnesota	7
Washington	5

New Jersey	4
Maryland	3
Wisconsin	3
New Hampshire	3
Oregon	2
Michigan	1
Hawaii	0
Delaware	0
Maine	0
Rhode Island	0
Vermont	0

Red States in Which No Humorists Reside

Montana, Idaho, Nevada, Wyoming, Utah, Arizona, New Mexico, North Dakota, South Dakota, Kansas, Oklahoma, Arkansas, Louisiana, Indiana, West Virginia, South Carolina, Alaska. That's 17 out of 50 total, or 34 percent of the states.

Number of Humorists Residing in a Blue County within a Red State

In order to factor in those decidedly blue counties in decidedly red states (that is, areas that resoundingly supported the Democratic ticket despite the electoral votes all going Republican), a "net" result appears at the end of each state's listing:

Ohio 12 (This swing state is home is 12 humorists. All but 2—Cincinnati residents, both—live in counties that voted blue. In the spirit of full disclosure, I live in a red county here as well.) Net red: 2

Colorado 5 (All reside in either Boulder or Aspen: in counties that voted blue.) Net red: 0

Florida 4 (Only the Tallahassee humorist lives in a county that voted red. He, however, writes crossword puzzles for his livelihood. How blue is that?) Net red: 1

Texas 3 (All 3 live in Austin, in Travis County, 1 of the 16 counties in Texas's 254 that went for Kerry. Moreover, 1 is Molly Ivins, whose book *Bushwacked* suggests that she does not contribute to the humorless state of red in Texas.) Net red: 0

Virginia 3 (The first is in Arlington, which voted blue; the second is a Chicagoan teaching at Virginia Tech who coauthored *My First Presidentiary: A Scrapbook of George W. Bush*; the third is a novelist whose contribution to *More Mirth of a Nation* are letters imploring his senator to end the "McCarthyesque vendetta" to impeach Clinton.) Net red: 0

North Carolina 3 (One resides in Durham, which voted 68 percent blue.) Net red: 2

Georgia 3 (One resides in Clarke county, which clearly supported Kerry.) Net red: 2

Tennessee 2 (One resides in Davidson County—Nashville— which voted blue.) Net red: 1

Kentucky 1 (But this is Bobbie Ann Mason, for crying out loud!): Net red: 0

Missouri 1 (A professor from St. Louis, which voted democratic.) Net red: 0

Nebraska 1 (This is an Omaha resident whose work I never really warmed to; what can I say?) Net red: 1

Iowa 1 (A Johnson county resident—Iowa City—which voted blue.) Net red: 0

Arizona 1 (I can't actually remember who this is, but one of my interns logged in an address, and every address deserves to be counted.) Net red: undetermined

Montana 1 (Someone from Missoula, which has a famous creative writing department and voted blue.) Net red: 0

Utah 1 (An émigré from the DC area on a sabbatical.) Net red: 0

Oklahoma 1 (This is a friend, Rod Lott, who's run a pop culture 'zine for ten years. He writes: "The last Oklahoma humorist I can think of was Will Rogers, and look how that turned out: he died in a plane crash and so, without any sense of irony, our state names our largest airport after him." This is a red voter?) Net red: 0

Louisiana 1 (This is Andre Codrescu of NPR fame, who resides in New Orleans, which voted 77 percent blue.) Net red: 0

Alabama 1 (An English professor whose previous books include *Pensées: The Thoughts of Dan Quayle*, a book that is not exactly devoted to honoring the ex-vice-president's Republican legacy.) Net red: 0

This tallying results in a net red count of 10 humor writers, suggesting that 358 out of 368 humorists reside in the blue areas of the country, or 97.28 percent of the humorists in America.

Once again, to be fair, individual voting records are not being plotted here: only home turfs. Some humorists, such as the very funny and very Republican P. J. O'Rourke in New Hampshire, may not have voted along with the state.

Other Demographic Data

Although no official census was distributed, and submitted manuscripts did not specify their creator's political affiliation, ethnicity, sexual orientation, or age, it is still possible to suggest with the standard level of confidence and cockiness, the following demographic trends. Of the humorists in our "electorate":

- 103 women. (I confidently include "Holly," "Polly," and "Molly," and other female names, but because there are more and more ambiguous as well as ambivalent first names—the fact that even "Michael" can be a woman's name only retroactively underscores my own childhood insecurities—this number may include some men. My apologies, in advance, to authors with the

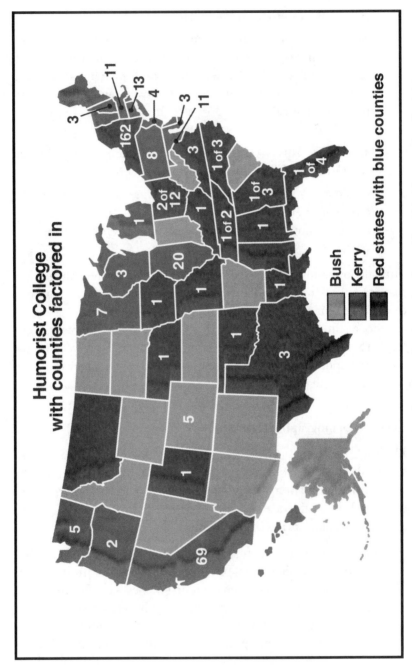

Humorist College
with counties factored in

3

11

13

4

3

11

162

8

3

1 of 3

2 of 12

1

1

1 of 3

1 of

3

1 of

4

3

1

1 of 2

1

1

20

7

1

1

1

1

1

3

5

1

5

2

69

☐ Bush

☐ Kerry

☐ Red states with blue counties

Map 3. The Electoral College map is adjusted to reflect humorists that reside within blue counties of red states.

first name "M.," "J.B.," "JHS," "Kerry," "Kris," and "Rosecrans.") All but 3 live in blue states.

- 20 gays/lesbians. (This does not include metrosexuals or even address the inclinations of Steve Altes, who is a hand model, actor, cover guy for men's hair-color products, as well as a widely published humorist.) All 20 live in blue states.

- 91 Jews (or humorists with Jewish-sounding last names or who do not italicize words like schlep and tchotchkes). All 91 live in blue states/blue counties of red states. (Unfortunately, no other conclusions can be suggested for evangelicals, Protestants, or any other religious background. Had there been any Amish or Sikh last names, I believe I would have picked up on them.)

- 2 Asian Americans. (Easier names to pick out.) Both live in blue states.

- 4 African Americans (the rare humorists who use the "N-word" with impunity). All 4 live in blue states.

- 3 Latinos (or possibly only 2, plus another humorist whose writing will suddenly switch into Spanish and who will not even go back and translate the line for a reader who, for instance, took *French* in high school—or even Spanish, but that could have been a long time ago). All 3 live in blue states.

- 25 humorists in the 18-to-25 age group. This was the hardest to discern from the names or from the writing. But if we're looking for the equivalent of first-time voters, perhaps appearing in a book for the first time would work. There are 48 first-timers. All reside in blue states/blue counties of red states.

As the preparations for the 2008 elections continue, we know this: the states of American Humor are blue. They're fourteen states, to be specific. Throughout history, humor—always the province of minorities and underdogs—has remained pretty darned blue. It's part of being a good loser, part of being hopeful about what lies ahead.

But for me, living blue in a red state, some things remain more important than identifying with one or another tint. I don't know that we need to identify ourselves, more and more, as *either* red or blue, unless, of course, voters cease choosing their allegiances based on one controversial topic (gay marriage, abortions, gun control, raising taxes) and return to basing their votes on understanding what their parties represent.

Now perhaps I lack commitment to the political process. Perhaps I am sheepish about my own incomplete understanding and unsteady resolve on each and every issue. But indignation is a less than neighborly spirit; it goes less far toward earning the confidence or trust of others than compassion or even conversation.

So, at the general store, at a PTO meeting, we have three choices: we can all agree with one another, we can agree to disagree, or we can all be plain disagreeable. Then, back at home, cast in whatever warm pink or cool blue light we imagine our lives, we can get back to the agreeable work of being right all along.

9. Control Issues
Robin Hemley

I missed my connection from Ljubljana to Frankfurt and had to be rerouted, so on my flight to America, I was placed in the last row by the bathroom. A young man, Arabic-looking, sat down beside me. He looked flustered. "I never in this lifetime," he said. "I am through with this planet. You see, they put me here so the other passengers don't have to look at me. They think I am a terrorist, that I want to hurt someone. I don't want to hurt anybody. This happens to me every time. They search me all over and then put me in the back."

Over the next several hours, he told me his story. He was from Somalia but had grown up in Kenya. His dream was to make enough money to move back to Kenya and open a little store. He wanted to taste the sweetness of life, he said. As he said this he looked up toward the plane's ceiling as though he saw right through it. He placed his hands together and then opened them.

I asked him his name.

"Maybe later," he said. "I know what you will think if you know my name. Life is short, and it goes forward, but money goes round and round. The animals, they have legs and they have tongues to taste the sweetness. Even the ants. And they have a soul and if that ant does you no harm you must let it go."

He told me of his life in Chicago. He earned just enough money to share an apartment with several other immigrants, and to send money back to Somalia and Kenya where his family lived. He had a wife in Kenya he rarely saw, and that was why he had made this trip, but now he wished he hadn't boarded the plane back to America. In

Chicago, all he did was walk from his apartment to his job at a gas station on the south side where the customers and his coworkers sometimes taunted him and told him he wasn't wanted in America, and then when his shift was over, he walked back to his apartment. And the next day, he did the same thing over again. Before September 11th, he had been a truck driver, but afterwards they fired him. They didn't want Arabs driving trucks.

He said I asked him unusual questions and wondered if I might be CIA.

"I am ashamed to tell you my name because so many people hate it," he said. I figured maybe it was Osama or Mohammed, odds on the former. I convinced him to write down his name if he didn't want to say it aloud. He wrote down Mohammed and then his last name. After a few minutes, he told me he was worried that he had written his whole name. So I crossed it out, but I told him that I would still remember it.

"I wish you would forget it," he said.

He carried with him light green refugee documents that looked like a passport but informed the reader emphatically, THIS IS NOT A PASSPORT. In any case, his refugee papers would expire in October and he didn't want to renew them. He didn't care anymore. "I'd rather live in Somalia now than America."

At Immigration, we split up. We lined up near the booths and a man with a military bearing faced us. "U.S. citizens," he yelled. "Welcome home to the land of the free." Someone in the crowd cheered and he said, "That's right. I better hear some hoo-yahs when I say that!" He told us he was a veteran of Iraqi Freedom and was about to be sent back and he welcomed the veterans especially.

Mohammed and I spoke once after that on the phone. He wanted money. I could tell. But he couldn't bring himself to ask for it and I couldn't offer because I didn't have the money to send him home to Kenya. He told me we shouldn't speak again and we never did. Most likely, he is back in Kenya again with his family. His wish has come true. I have forgotten his last name.

Traveling from LAX to the Philippines on Philippine Airlines, our bags were overweight and so one of the airline employees offered to help redistribute the weight in our luggage. My wife and I opened all the bags, including our carry-ons, and when we were done we barely met the weight restrictions. After all, we were going there for almost a year, and we needed to bring a lot of stuff. In line at security, something drew the attention of the employee scanning our bags. The man, a friendly looking guy who was balding, asked my wife if he could inspect her bag. He opened it up and found a pair of kitchen scissors inside. Of course, I knew immediately what had happened. We had packed the scissors in our toiletry bag in our largest suitcase and the airline employee had shifted the toiletry bag to my wife's carry-on.

I heard someone mutter behind me mutter, "Jesus, I don't believe this." When I turned around, I saw some guy looking sourly at me.

I didn't recognize him, but I saw the star light go off in Margie's eyes, and I felt her nudge me hard. The man, who once played Dr. Billy Kronk on the television program *Chicago Hope*, finished dialing a cell phone number, then started talking loudly into it. "You wouldn't believe what just happened," he said. "I'm in the security line at LAX and the guard just pulled out a huge pair of scissors from the carry-on of this guy in front of me."

I was startled that he was speaking so directly and loudly about me. "Yeah!" he continued. "It's like a four-inch blade. They shouldn't even let him on board."

I wanted to protest, to say, "Hey, it's my wife's bag! She's the one you shouldn't allow on board!"

Dr. Kronk looked at the friendly guard and gave him the thumbs up. "Good catch!" he said, as though I were a major terrorist. Maybe he was in character and I was on some reality show I didn't know about.

The guard didn't say anything, but waited for me to explain what these honking big scissors were doing in my bag. I didn't go into the full explanation. I didn't protest my innocence. I simply said it was a mistake and I didn't need them.

Then Dr. Kronk turned to me and said as though he were in uniform, "You carrying any more scissors with you?"

My normal reaction would be to say something sarcastic. "Yes, I have a bag of scissors I'm going to pass out to all the passengers." But something stopped me. Maybe good sense. I looked over at the guard who seemed suddenly perky, less friendly, waiting for me to answer the good doctor. I was being set up—I remembered the no joking sign in the security line, how I'd surely get pulled off the plane if I said what I wanted to say. It boggled me how often we have no control over the way others perceive us, how often the viewpoint of others is in conflict with the way we see ourselves.

"No," I said meekly. "I don't have any more."

The character of Billy Kronk had some control issues on *Chicago Hope*, too:

> *Elkes sings in the operating room.*

BILLY KRONK: Shut up.

> *Elkes continues.*

BILLY: I said shut up.

ELKES: Why?

BILLY: Your singing sucks and it's messing up our concentration.

ELKES: You think you can sing better than me?

BILLY: Well that is a question which will remain in the realm of the rhetorical since I don't see a sing-off in our future.

In the 1890s America still saw itself in the shadow of Europe and it didn't want to be in anyone's shadow, except God's, but most of the time, God's shadow and America's shadow were one and the same, and the shadowlands underneath America's wings extended far, but not far enough, for surely America deserved the world and the world deserved America. And America set its sights on the Orient. The Orientals needed uplifting. The Europeans had a three-hundred-year head start and had uplifted the Chinese by their pigtails until their necks hurt and they were walking on tippy-toe to stay on the ground. Opium was the most famous form of European uplift, but there were others. Many forms of uplift unfortunately had bad side effects, resulting in death. In the days before air forces, the Great Powers uplifted by way of navies and navies ran on coal. And coal ran out on the long Pacific journey, and so America needed coaling stations for its ships if it could ever hope to uplift China or to stem the influence of the sole Asiatic power that could uplift back: Japan.

Hawaii, Guam, the Philippines. All soon felt the warm breeze of Liberty generated by the gentle draft of our Eagle wings.

The operations against the sovereign nations of Hawaii and the Philippines did not have names the way they would now. But in retrospect, let's call them Operation Pineapple Surprise and Operation Flamenco Storm.

The power to name something gives you a kind of control over that thing, doesn't it? The Spanish-American War, for instance, lasted only three months. It's aftermath, the Philippine "Insurrection" lasted eight years or more, although President Theodore Roosevelt declared it officially over on July 4, 1902.

Of course, the past is the past and there's no sense crying over spilled blood. But I have long felt a stirring—let's not call it shame. Americans need not feel shame, nor should they because our cause is always Just. So I will not name this stirring. But I feel it when I think about Hawaii and the Philippines, both places I have spent much time in, the latter more than the former. When I think of Hawaii, as I'm sure is the case with most Americans, the first name that comes to mind is Grover Cleveland.

What? Grover Cleveland isn't the first name that pops into your head when you think "Hawaii"? Sorry, I'm being disingenuous. I'm being rhetorical.

I guess most people don't think of Grover Cleveland at all. The first Democrat elected since the Civil War, Cleveland was the Bill Clinton of his day, that is to say, he had some personal problems. He was the acknowledged father of an "illegitimate" child. A bachelor, he was the only president ever to be married in the White House—to a woman half his age! Oh, Monica, eat your heart out.

If you know him at all, you most likely know the fun fact that he was the only president ever elected to two nonconsecutive terms. After his first four years in office, he ran for reelection and won the popular vote but lost the electoral vote. And so he came back for a third try and won both.

As president, he was opposed to the Statue of Liberty.

How could anyone be opposed to the Statue of Liberty? Would that not make him the worst president and not one of the best? But let's ponder what the Statue of Liberty is. It's a monument made of steel and copper, and it is uplifting to behold. Did he worry, I wonder, that we would come to worship the statue, the gesture of liberty, and not liberty itself?

The Hawaiian monarchy had been overthrown in 1893 during the last days of the administration of Cleveland's predecessor, Republican Benjamin Harrison, by a group of American businessmen led by Sanford Dole.

They called themselves the Annexation Club. The reason is self-evident, which is why they decided to keep the club secret. They sent a small delegation to Washington to sound out the Republican president on the matter. He thought the Annexation Club was a wonderful club indeed, and so they went home and plotted and formed a smaller offshoot of the Annexation Club, the Committee of Safety, which anyway has a nicer ring to it than the Annexation Club, though they probably could have come up with an even better committee name if they'd tried:

> The Sons of Liberty Timeshare Committee
>
> The Hawaii Freedom Visitors and Convention Club
>
> The Mission Accomplished Playground of the Rich Committee

In any event, the Committee of Safety took action when Queen Lili'uokalani committed a Revolutionary Act. She wanted a new constitution to replace the old "Bayonet Constitution" that had been forced upon her brother, the old king, by a group of American businessman known as the Hawaiian League. The Bayonet Constitution had limited the monarchy's power and the power of native Hawaiians, which was the only way they could be uplifted by the Committee of Safety. The Safety committee decided it was time to act! First, they went to the U.S. Minister to Hawai'i, John L. Stevens, who assured them that he would not act to protect the queen, that he would recognize the Committee of Safety if they occupied some key buildings, and that, if necessary, he would land U.S. troops from the USS *Boston*, conveniently anchored in Honolulu Harbor, to protect the safety of Americans whose lives were in jeopardy because of the queen and her band of revolutionaries who obviously hated our values and were bent on the destruction of America.

Within a month after the Safety committee had overthrown the queen and established its own republic under President Dole, a delegation had made its way to Washington, where a delighted Republican administration submitted to Congress a bill to annex Hawai'i.

Only a few days after Cleveland was inaugurated for his second, nonconsecutive term, he withdrew the bill, and so started a battle between Cleveland, Congress, and American business interests. In a powerful speech that reaffirmed America's ideals, Cleveland chastised Congress:

> If national honesty is to be disregarded and a desire for territorial extension, or dissatisfaction with a form of government not our own, ought to regulate our conduct, I have entirely misapprehended the mission and character of our Government and the behavior which the conscience of our people demands of their public servants.

He demanded that the monarchy be restored. Grover Cleveland became a minority of one. Congress responded in the way that politicians always respond, with hollow phrases that stand simply as statues of liberty:

> Hawaii must be entitled to demand of the United States an indulgent consideration, if not an active sympathy, when she is endeavoring to accomplish what every other American state has achieved—the release of her people from the odious antirepublican regime which denies to the people the right to govern themselves, and subordinates them to the supposed divine right of a monarch, whose title to such divinity originated in the most slavish conditions of pagan barbarity.

In the face of Congress's opposition, Cleveland gave up, but he had tried at least, and there was nothing disingenuous or purely rhetorical in the attempt. But unwittingly perhaps, Congress overthrew another government with this act, and we have not been the same since, though at least we have the Statue of Liberty, Cleveland's grudging legacy, of Thee We Sing.

A hundred years later, Attorney General John Ashcroft wrote a song and raised his off-key voice, enraptured by the power of his patriotic fervor, and all of us liberals laughed,[1] whistling past the graveyard where the Eagle soared.

It's OK, though, to be in the minority. The role of the minority is to record what the majority would rather forget or ignore.

I'm so accustomed to being in the minority that I can't even remember to be disappointed when my candidate loses. In 1972 at age fourteen I campaigned for George McGovern and was at the height of my audacity when, plastered with McGovern buttons, I walked into Republican campaign headquarters in South Bend, Indiana, and asked for a few Nixon buttons, which they graciously gave me. In 1976 at age eighteen I campaigned in the Ohio primaries for Morris Udall, meeting coal miners at the end of their shifts in the middle of the night to pass out campaign literature. In 1980, as a twenty-two year old graduate student at the University of Iowa, I watched the impossible happen on television with a group of my friends, and I thought the world as I knew it was over with Reagan's election. Twenty-four years later, I was back in Iowa as a professor, watching the impossible happen again. What I've learned to settle for are pyrrhic I-told-you-so victories and a desire to remember and not forget. In 2004 what I told my friends is this: "The only good thing is that four years from now, the Republicans will have no one to blame for the war and all their blunderings but themselves." But even that is the sentiment of a hopeless idealist, I'm afraid.

In the long run, the best service to America's "liberty" would be to do away with the two party system entirely—no less a patriot than George Washington was suspicious of all the harm political parties could do. Maybe an "I told you so" from George Washington would be the wake up call this country needs. Barring this unlikely scenario, maybe what's needed are term limits, not on political candidates, but on the parties themselves—the idea that a political party could exist for a limited amount of time, say twenty-five years, and then all its remaining assets would be given over to the national debt or *even* the Department of Defense. It's an idea that perhaps *could* work if anyone could stand the thought of ceding or losing power. But who wants that? Am I crazy? Probably. I can count on the fingers of one hand the number of presidents in this country who were distrustful of the political Powers That Be: George Washington, who didn't want to be president the first time *or* the second; Grover Cleveland; Dwight Eisenhower, who famously warned of the Military Industrial Complex in his Farewell Address (why did he have to wait until then?); and hmm . . . well, President Warren G. Harding once admitted to a friend that he wasn't fit for the job of president. But he was right. After that, I draw a blank.

And so our system of musical chairs will go on *ad infinitum*, and little will ever really change except for the tempo of the music and who's doing the calling.

I once saw Mark Twain at the Illinois State Fair in the guise of an animatronic life size figure in the Milk Expo. He was dressed in white and had a mustache that looked like the accumulated years of milk mustaches. He told us he had a mighty hankering for milk. He told us how good milk was for us.

He was a lobotomized, soulless Mark Twain, and I thought, how sad that a man as smart as that can be co-opted as a pitchman for milk. This made me think about Ideas in general, and their perversion by others with less than noble aims.

In 1898 Mark Twain, the vice president of the Anti-Imperialist League (now there's a name that doesn't fool around), wrote an excoriating little essay titled, "To the Person Sitting in Darkness." His essential argument was that the purveyors of Civilization, namely America and Europe, ran a kind of trust fund for the rest of the world, "The Blessings-of-Civilization Trust." To "a person sitting in darkness," that is, a native Filipino or Hawaiian, the trust fund seemed peachy because with the trust came these handy and delicious concepts:

LOVE, LAW AND ORDER, JUSTICE, LIBERTY, GENTLENESS, EQUALITY, CHRISTIANITY, HONORABLE DEALING, PROTECTION TO THE WEAK, MERCY, TEMPERANCE, EDUCATION

But only if the light were truly dim. Otherwise, the person sitting in darkness—a Hawaiian, or in this case, a Filipino—-might begin to suspect the truth, that there are two kinds of Blessings of Civilization: one for export and one "for home consumption." "There must be two Americas," Twain supposed the persons sitting in darkness might conjecture: "one that sets the captive free, and one that takes a once-captive's new freedom away from him, and picks a quarrel with him with nothing to found it on; then kills him to get his land." Twain went on to describe some of the acts committed by American forces against the Filipinos in the name of Liberty, including a letter from a boy from Decorah, Iowa, who told his family of the heroics of battle: "We never left one alive. If one was wounded, we would run our bayonets through him."

The New York Times and other True Patriotic Outlets were outraged by Mr. Twain's essay. He had his facts wrong, they clamored. And anyone who believed him had already made up his mind about the Philippine Question. Anyone who believed Mr. Twain did not care for the truth and what's more, was close-minded, *The New York Times* railed.

So there! Mr. Twain. Nyaaa nyaaa nyaa. Support our Troops.

True patriots understood then as they do now that the Blessings-of-Civilization Trust was big enough for everyone to have a piece of the pie, as it were. Sometimes, as in the case of the Philippines in 1901 and Iraq in 2006, you had to pinch their little noses closed so that they would open their mouths and allow the pie to be consumed, or else it became necessary to administer it through another orifice. The reasons for Pie Administration vary of course from case to case.

In the case of the Philippines, we were there to overthrow the Spanish tyrants and replace them with . . . well, us.

And, of course, we were there to Christianize them. While it's true that they had been Catholics for three hundred years, and while it's true that Catholics are a kind of Christian, they are not the best Christians by far.

In the case of Iraq, we were there to hunt for weapons of mass destruction. When we didn't find any of those, there had to be plenty of other good reasons. And there were.

Saddam had something to do with 9/11, didn't he? I'm sure he appreciated 9/11 at least. I think I heard somewhere that he programmed his cell phone with an image of the towers imploding. That's a good reason.

And the best after-the-fact reason is: may we have the envelope please? Liberty for the Iraqi people. As a nation, we are very service-oriented and this was a service we wanted to provide Iraqis because we never support cruel dictators. We only want to overthrow them, unless of course we want to support them with billions in aid.

Liberty for the Iraqi people was the bestest reason ever.

Dr. Kronk, Dr. Kronk. You're wanted in the er *to tell someone to shut up, to remove the scissors from our backs, to stop all that goddamn singing.*

"Life is short," a fearful stranger named Mohammed once told me, "and it goes forward, but money goes round and round."

I better hear some hoo-yahs when I say that!

Note

1. The definition of the word "liberal" is, of course, in dispute. Depending on one's political affiliation, "liberal" means either "anti-fascist idealist operating not only out of greed and self-interest" or "weak-kneed, bran-farting son of a bitch." For the sake of clarification, I'm using the word in its former and original sense of the word.

10. A Campaign That Failed

Deb Olin Unferth

I talked them into it.

I said we could change the course of history.

I asked them if they knew how many Democrats there were one hour from where our feet at this moment rested.

I said I had figured out the election would be decided by ten electoral votes.

Guess how many electoral votes Missouri has, I said.

Then I had this whole thing about how a hundred thousand votes would decide the election, something about some other election that had been decided by a hundred thousand votes. "Remember Florida," I said knowingly. And guess what was in Kansas City, one hour from our resting feet, just over the state line. Guess.

A hundred thousand newly registered Democratic voters.

But how could we know they were Democratic voters if they were newly registered and therefore had never voted?

They were previously hidden Democrats. The forgotten ones, nearly left behind but now rounded-up, roped in. As numerous as train whistles, as crickets. As close and as far as the sun, the heart of the sky.

The thing seemed vaguely flawed even to me. I mean, how dim did I think those hundred thousand people were? They needed to be reminded to vote? But listen, they were forgetful Democrats (aren't we all?). They needed a note pinned to their sweater, or a little party favor, a sticker or a magnet: Vote November 2.

I imagined this: I'd stride from house to house with my clipboard. "Interesting point of view," I'd say. I'd click my pen, pause. "Have you considered . . ." I imagined myself speaking with grace and ability, rubbing their own views from their minds. "Hell, what else am I doing this afternoon?" they'd say and untie their aprons or put down their wrenches and so on. "Gimme a list, I'm coming along."

Then the Democratic National Committee announced they were pulling out of Missouri. They were stopping the ads, not coming for visits anymore. They had given up on Missouri. Missouri is lost, they said, all the Democrats said. Lost as a lone kernel in a Kansas cornfield. They closed up their office and left. My phone wouldn't stop ringing. "What is going on?" said the volunteers. "What about the plan?"

"Don't listen to them," I said. "Who knows Missouri, us or them?" (I had never actually been to Missouri, that is, off a highway and outside a gas station.) "Who's got a hundred thousand newly registered Democrats just over the state line?"

On Saturday October 30 I caravanned out with thirteen or fourteen volunteers. We showed up for the training session in the biggest theater in Kansas City along with five hundred other people and we were so excited. A man got up and talked. "We've got five hundred people here!" he said and we all shouted back, "Yeah!" This went on for about an hour, then suddenly he was gone and someone else got up and said, "OK, all precinct leaders, come get your packet. We're ready to go!"

Everyone in my group looked at me. "Are you a precinct leader?" one of them asked.

"I don't think so," I said.

"Are you sure?"

I thought about it. "What's a precinct?"

Everyone admitted they didn't know but that I better damn well go up and ask. I didn't want to go up and ask. It was a mess up there, people crowding around, everybody shouting and waving their hands.

"Maybe we should just wait and our precinct leader will come," I said.

They looked at me.

"We came all the way here for you to sit there like a rock?"

I went up.

"How many?" asked the woman who seemed to be in charge.

I frowned. Just what we were talking about here?

"How many precincts do you want?"

"How many are there?" I asked doubtfully.

She handed me a stack of large manila envelopes and a pile of door hangers stamped with a picture of a local Democratic candidate I'd never heard of.

"What's this?" I held up the envelopes.

"Precincts," she said. Even I knew no precinct could fit it an envelope but I went back to my group with the manila envelopes and door hangers. I was a little afraid. They were gathered around a table and immediately started in with that infernal Democratic whine: "What exactly are we going to be *doing?*" We opened the envelopes and found lists of names and addresses. "What *exactly* are we going to be doing!" they screeched clutching the lists.

Someone at the microphone was saying, "If you have any questions, ask for a volunteer!"

"That's what we need," they said. "We need a volunteer."

"But we are volunteers."

"We need another volunteer, a *better* volunteer," they accused. "One of the ones they've got up there."

"All right, all right, all right," I said, walking back up.

Our special volunteer arrived and we said, "Where are these places?"

He shrugged. "I just flew in from Massachusetts last night."

Suddenly I had an epiphany. I thought: I'm the leader. "You," I said, pointing to one of them. "Go find out how to get to these places."

She scurried off.

"And you," I pointed to another. "Write a script for us to use."

It took another hour to get ourselves organized with highway maps drawn on backs of napkins and scripts written on flyers and all of us divided into six groups, with two or three volunteers each, maps, envelopes, cell phones, snacks, door hangers, and so on, and then we spent another twenty minutes in the parking lot arguing about what marks we should put on the lists, what codes we should use, et cetera, and then we drove off in our caravan but we got a little lost and turned around and one of the cars got left behind at an exit, which set off cell phones ringing up and down the highway but we did at last arrive.

We fanned out into the town of Independence.

The first address on my group's list read something like: 762781 Grove, Building H, #26. We pulled into a complex of housing units, really dismal stuff—flat, razored land, gas station signs, a couple of skinny trees, a few feet of grass, acres of parking lot. Building H had a three-foot-high letter H posted on its side. Outside number 26 a little girl sat on the top step. She was blocking the front door. "Hello," I said brightly, "is your mommy home?" She didn't answer. She started humming, buzzing sort of. Loudly. I tried to talk to her again but she ignored me, closed her eyes, kept humming.

"Lean over her and ring the doorbell," one of the volunteers said.

"I can't reach," I said. "Hello!" I yelled through the screen. Inside we could see hands in a sink lifting and soaping dishes. "Hello! We've come to remind you about the upcoming—" but I had to stop because now the little girl on the step was nearly screaming.

No one came to the door.

It may have been this moment, at the very first house, or it may have been another moment—it may have been an accumulation of moments that slowly ended the moments of me still believing this was going to be fun. I had thought that once I got through the messy parts, the planning parts, the boring parts, and despite the difficult prelude, that in the end the experience would be a good one. But now, as I peered through the screen into the cool apartment beyond, I understood that no part of this was going to be fun, and it wasn't.

At the next stop, in building F, a young man opened the door. We proudly stomped out our speech. He blinked, rubbed his eyes. "I'm sorry," he said. "Are you selling something?" We wavered, then proudly stomped out our speech, again. Which required that he answer questions. Which he did not. "Are you a charity?" he asked. We looked at each other. "If you have some literature," he said wearily, "proper brochures explaining where the money goes, I can give you five bucks."

At the next address, a giant-sized poster was plastered to the door. It read: Vote George W. Bush.

"Now what?" said a volunteer.

"Their name is on the list."

"Maybe they're undecided?"

I knocked. A man opened the door. I offered our door hanger. "What do those words say?" he asked. He pointed to the poster. "Can you read? They say: Get out."

I don't have our script anymore. I've been looking for it. I recall it ran something like:

1. Hi, my name is _____. Are you _____? Good morning! I'm here with MoveOn and America Coming Together and we're going around today reminding people that the elections are this Tuesday and we're hoping you're going to go down and vote.

2. Do you know where your polling place is? (We knew where their polling place was and would write it down for them on little cards if necessary.)

3. Do you have a ride to your polling place this Tuesday? (We had a number you could call if you needed a ride.)

4. (And most importantly:) Are you planning to vote for Democratic candidate John Kerry on Tuesday, November 2?

A lot of people said no to this question. An enormous number of people said no, despite being on the list. Despite being in Independence, hometown of Harry S. Truman, Democratic stronghold.

People refused to open their doors. People weren't home. People were home but didn't answer to the name on the list. People were Republicans. People stared at us, said a few words I couldn't hear, and shut their doors. The neighborhoods were unattractive, desolate, isolated—clusters of buildings huddled against each other on empty mottled plains. Houses tucked in cul-de-sacs, semi-identical houses made out of siding and painted beige or gray. The people were white and I had heard there were lots of African Americans around Kansas City. I had brought special African American posters for that purpose. A lot of them. I had distributed them to the volunteers. We were all armed with big, beautiful, expensive posters. Paid for by a woman in France. Designed by artists in Ann Arbor. Mailed in from Detroit. That read in bold slant lettering:

If you are African American,
The Republican Party doesn't want you to vote.

I knocked on exactly one door all weekend that was opened by an African American. When she opened the door, she looked like an angel to me. She was young and slim and wore a smart suit. I held out my poster. I held out a handful of posters, she could have the whole pile, she could plaster her house with them, give them to her African American friends. She looked at my poster. She was really angry.

She said, "I'm a Republican."

She said, "You better not come back here."

The second day was worse than the first, I think, although it's all a dark wet blur now. We got an early start, drove the string of cement that wove through the landscape and receded away into thickets of parking lots. One address was at a senior citizens home. We walked down a long hallway lined with wheelchairs and gurneys.

"Let's leave these people alone," said my co-volunteer.

"No way," I said. "They're probably all Democrats. Somebody should just pile them into a bus and take them down on Tuesday." We asked a nurse, who pointed to a room and we went in. The woman on our list lay stretched out on a bed. She was small and still. "Ms. Parks?" I called softly.

"Leave her alone," said my co-volunteer.

"We should remind her to vote," I said, uncertain. "Ms. Parks?" Her eyes were closed and her mouth was open. She didn't move. "We'll just put this here," I said. I stuck a door hanger on her iv tube.

We knocked on one door and a woman came out, listened to our speech. "How long has this one, the one we have now, been in office?" she said.

"Four years," said my co-volunteer.

We came to a house with John Kerry signs on the lawn. *John Kerry!* We rang the doorbell with pride. "Just wanted to remind you that this Tuesday . . ." I began.

The woman did not open the screen door. She spoke through the screen. "Do you think we don't remember when the election is? You think we're complete idiots? You come around banging on our doors like Paul Revere? Like hit men? Like the law? You come once more— any of you—and I'm voting for Bush."

We ran back to the car.

Some said, "Well, now, I haven't decided." By the second day, these people made me feel like a fool. "What issues are important to you?" I'd say hopelessly and I ended up in bizarre exchanges that made no sense to me.

"No, I wouldn't *make love* to a flag, if that's what you mean."

At one point, I was standing on a porch full of undecided, unregistered citizens. We were talking about the war or politicians or welfare or God. One of them said, "They're a load of crooks, every one of them," and we all nodded. I could hear my co-volunteer a couple doors down, the murmur of her voice, earnest and coaxing.

"And liars," I said. "Those people can*not* tell the truth."

Kansas: God signs on the highway. The ten commandments on a slab in the park. The creationism bill.

Creationism. Imagine.

One of the volunteers called me on my cell and said, "The last six houses we've been to are Republican. What is going on? You better find out."

"All right, all right, all right," I said.

I called headquarters. "We've got Republicans on our list. A lot of them."

"What code do they have?" said the woman.

"Code?"

"Look all the way on the right, do you see some letters and numbers?"

Yes. Far from the names and addresses, all the way on the right was an unlabeled column of letters and numbers. "7R," I read.

"Oh, that's Republican."

Something behind my eyes exploded. "What's the code for Democrat?" I asked.

"1SK."

I hung up and called the volunteers car by car. "Do not," I said, "do NOT go to the homes of Republicans and remind them to vote. If it says 7R, cross them off the list."

"What if it says 4S1?" they said.

We did not take any lunch breaks. We talked about it beforehand, the lovely meal we'd have in the middle of the day, a glass of wine, a light salad, a cheese board. We didn't see any restaurants out there and went home hungry. The second and third days we brought yogurt and bananas in the car. We stopped at a gas station and bought potato chips and Hohos. Garbage got all over the car and somebody spilled a soda. The volunteer in charge of the lists got overwhelmed. I glanced in the back seat and saw a hurricane of papers, crumpled on the floor, flying around in the air. Some of the papers were scrunched between the seats.

I turned back around and faced the road.

On the third day, a man opened his door and said, "What do you want?" He sounded bewildered. I didn't know what to say. I felt a deep inferiority, a deep sense of defeat and loneliness. I felt clownish, loud, presumptuous. I was humiliated. And I knew: these people were not going to vote for the Democratic candidate or maybe vote at all and I would never know why.

I felt the heavy weight of things I did not understand.

The afternoon of the third day it started to rain. By this time we weren't fanning out into neighborhoods, going in twos on foot. Instead several of us huddled in one car and I'd drive a few feet to the next address and then we'd bicker about whose turn it was to run up and ring the doorbell. It rained harder. It got dark and we still had people on our list. We couldn't see the addresses on the houses or the papers—the light inside my car didn't work. I went up to a door with a Bush sign on it, tore it down and ran back to the car while the sky thundered above. One by one the other cars called and dropped off their unfinished lists with us and went home. My volunteers tried to be stoic but I could see they were almost in tears. We were damp and hungry and carsick and cold. "Just a few more," I told them. "This election may be won by a few votes. Think of that," I said. "Imagine those votes coming out of Independence, Missouri, Democratic stronghold." I opened the car door and a packet of door hangers slipped out and fell in the mud.

By election day, everyone had quit except me and one other volunteer. We had stacks of papers, all the lists, all the houses we had visited. We each took half and went home to call the ones with phone numbers. People hung up on me. "Quit calling or I'll phone the police," they said. Or no one was home or they weren't answering. I left messages. I kept dialing and dialing, the sheets spread over the floor. I was still calling when the results starting coming in. "Did you vote?" I said.
"There's still time, by God. If you run. Run!" I yelled. "RUN!"

Part 3
South

11. Playing Debussy in the Heart of Dixie

David Case

I have simply worshipped pianists—two at a time, sometimes,
Harry tells me. I don't know what it is about them. Perhaps it is that
they are foreigners. They all are, ain't they? Even those that are born
in England become foreigners after a time, don't they?
—Oscar Wilde, *The Picture of Dorian Gray*

Ten or twelve years ago, Mark Childress published a novel (*Crazy in Alabama*) that enjoyed some notoriety and was made into a film by Antonio Banderas. I recall picking up the book when it first appeared, thinking it looked interesting. Then I reread the title: *Crazy in Alabama*? Isn't that a bit like *Chilly in Fairbanks, Cranky in DC, Foul-Mouthed in New Jersey*, or *Boring in San Diego*? Alabama *was* crazy in the mid-'60s (the setting for Childress's book), but it is perhaps even crazier now. Please allow me to explain.

I have lived in California for most of the last twenty-three years. This is where the reader expects a "but," and I have a heavy one waiting: *but I lived in Alabama until I was twenty-one*—that is, until I had a choice in the matter. At seventeen, I was a skinny androgynous white male liberal Democrat, already an alien. Now it is far worse: at forty-three, I am an openly gay white male liberal Democrat with a PhD from a school in California. Worst, I have "lost" most of "my" Southern accent. Since "my" Southern accent is mostly a Hollywood-based concoction, I use it mainly to frighten my students when they are behaving badly or to fuck with the minds of native Californians. I must say, however, that *I* am still frightened to hear strong Southern accents: Alabama haunts me, night and day.

Yet I typically visit the South only for a few days once or twice a year. It can't be as bad for me as for those instinctively Coastal people who actually live there: I am thinking now of my brother Mark, in Birmingham, my sister Susan, in Gainesville, Florida (where, as my brother-in-law Gary says, they are "doubled-Bushed"), and my friend James, in Montgomery. Montgomery, you see, is redder than red. In Montgomery, there is still a separate golf course for Jewish people . . .

Was I a blue-stater from the very start? It will sound improbable, but the evidence shows that I was. I credit this to my mother, who, in informing me that her family was partly Native American, made white chauvinism disgusting to me, and to my older brothers and sisters, who were far more liberal than average: they actually read interesting books and left them lying around the house for me to pick up. I learned quickly from their conversation and their behavior that they considered racism to be, if not a moral outrage (crimes against humanity are hard for young people to understand, especially when they are standing too close), then at least highly uncool.

One friend told me, about ten years ago, that he actually enjoyed living in Alabama because, he said, "It's so easy to be the coolest here." When very young, I quickly sensed the basic uncoolness of Alabama: the slogans the governors kept proposing and putting on highway billboards (ALABAMA THE BEAUTIFUL! or the ambiguous ALABAMA HAS IT ALL!) were transparent compensation. Beautiful? In a few places, the mountains of North Alabama are lovely, especially in fall, but they are threatening as well: former strongholds of the KKK—and now strongholds of Eric Rudolph disciples—where travelers can innocently stop and never be heard from again. *Has It All?* In my childhood, Alabama had little even when compared to Florida, Tennessee, and Georgia. (Mississippi is a subject I must leave to more courageous writers.) Alabama has no impressive symphony, opera company, acting troupe, or museum—and the problem is not a lack of talent or wealth; it is a simple absence of public interest, even among the wealthy.

The state also lacks "natural wonders." Let's undertake some comparisons. Instead of Niagara Falls, Alabama has Nokolula Falls (and there's a reason you've never heard of it); the highest mountain measures about 2,700 feet above sea level, barely outdoing the Hollywood Hills. The rivers are broad but perpetually muddy and full of chemicals dumped without regulatory obstacles. Instead of the Grand Canyon, Alabama has the peanut-and-pecan-dominated coastal plain. Instead of New Orleans for Mardi Gras, Alabama has Mobile; only Mobile could make Mardi Gras dull. There is no metropolis like New York, or even lowly Atlanta. I grew up in Birmingham, a fairly large town, but one known mainly for racist police brutality, blast furnaces, and bad religion.

Landmarks? Birmingham has an enormous statue of the ugliest Roman god (Vulcan) overlooking the city and flashing a naked butt at Homewood, a conservative middle-middle-class suburb. It also has a Civil Rights Museum that most white residents would probably like to see blown apart. The chief attraction in Mobile? A retired battleship. In Enterprise? The statue of an insect fond of ruining cotton boles. *I'm not making this up.* As for politics, you probably know most of the sordid story already—but did you know that, about seven years ago, when a Republican lieutenant governor was loath to relinquish the podium of the State House of Representatives to its new Democratic speaker, he held the stand for several days without pause, at several points pissing into a jar hidden behind the stand?

Was E. B. White thinking of Alabama when he wrote the admirable line, "I have often gone miles out of my way to avoid places of historical interest"?

When I was young, Birmingham did have an airport. I saw the few jets landing and taking off as ambassadors of hope, at least for those astonishing people getting on board to go elsewhere. They were escaping: what unheard of good fortune! This airport now has a sense of humor: it sells postcards reading WELCOME TO BIRMINGHAM, ALABAMA! PLEASE SET YOUR WATCHES BACK TEN YEARS. (Only ten? I'd say *fifty*.) Birmingham also had a public library—where Proust was kept behind the desk rather than on the shelves. When I was sixteen, I stared down a librarian who looked at me askance when I asked for it

(I mean the old two-volume Moncrieff translation). He finally gave it to me, frowning all the while, but without a word. God knows where they kept Henry Miller or Kurt Vonnegut.

Birmingham had Samford, not Stanford, and it was at *Samford* University that I underwent three years of preparatory training in piano before college. (I'd previously been taught by a rather somnolent woman who let me read through whatever I liked without asking me to refine it.) Although Samford was nominally a Baptist school, there were no Baptists (maybe one?) on the music faculty, and I was exhilarated to have actual blue state types, spiritual exiles, now teaching me. Their company was a wonder to me: allusions to people and places that I (made pessimistic by my surroundings) believed I'd never see; the free play of ideas; mockery of religious fundamentalism. I recall one of them mentioning Wittgenstein.

So I was luckier than I realized at the time to have parents who encouraged me to play concert music and who actually had a piano for me to practice on. At first my playing was insensitive and sometimes just loud, but that began to change when I hit fourteen or so. I read Harold Schonberg's *The Great Pianists* and realized that, as my students now would put it, I was *drowning in a cesspool of slack*. I began to practice several hours a day, using the standard exercise books but never losing sight of Mozart and Chopin.

Would I have survived Alabama without having people make allowances for me as a musician, that is, as a foreigner of sorts? To know how to play the music, after all, they might have thought, I had had to learn the meaning and approximate pronunciation of phrases like *allegro ma non troppo, main gauche dessus, con fuoco* (my favorite), and *nach und nach wieder auflebend*—and we all know what that can do to a person. For interpretive inspiration, too, I was expected to listen to recordings by people with names like Arthur Rubinstein, Radu Lupu, Antonio Barbosa, Ivan Morevic, Robert Casadesus, Martha Argerich, and (most exotic of all) Guiomar Novaes.

I had to study the lives of the composers. This project did not go exactly as planned. First I read a biography of Chopin, then a biography of George Sand; then I went further astray with a book on Lord Byron. On the recommendation of a mysterious visitor (I don't remember the name, the face, or the number: he simply appeared one day and was gone before the next), I read *The Picture of Dorian Gray*. After that, the cause was lost. I was a foreigner willy-nilly and could remain an honorary Southerner only by affecting and exaggerating the manners of Southerners in the Great Southern Literary Tradition, something I wasn't exactly prepared for.

As for this Great Literary Tradition, a glaive that defensive Southerners swing at those who, like Mencken, conceive of the region as "The Sahara of the Bozart" [*sic*], aren't most of the great Southern novels and short stories about how miserable it is to live in the South? Among the great writers born in the South (assuming that Twain is uncategorizable), only Zora Neale Hurston gives off any sense of joie de vivre; as my therapist says, she should have been a serotonin donor. Most sobering of all to me was the realization that none of these Great Writers *came from Alabama*: Richard Wright, Eudora Welty, and William Faulkner were from Mississippi (Don't ask me . . .), Tennessee Williams from Tennessee(?) or Missouri(?), O'Connor from Georgia, Katherine Anne Porter from Texas, and Zora Hurston from Florida. Alabamans were less articulate even in expressing their misery.

As for the grammar and high schools I attended, the less said the better. Although I escaped much teasing from other students and earned a little credit because I could play many songs by the Beatles, Elton John, Warren Zevon, Joe Cocker, and others on the piano (by ear), I laid myself open to abuse in the most hellish years (fifth grade, sixth grade, and junior high) by objecting to the anti-black and anti-progressive slurs my classmates uttered as naturally as crows caw. In retaliation for my unheard-of views, I was informed that I myself had "a nose like a n——'s." When I replied "So what?" my classmates shook their heads in mingled disgust and pity: I was a lunatic, or perhaps mildly retarded. Above all, a *foreigner*.

And what were our carefully selected history textbooks telling us? Brace yourselves: they maintained that slaves had been treated gently and fairly under the *ancien régime*, that Reconstruction was a bad idea from the start, that the KKK existed solely to protect the honor of Southern Womanhood (no pun intended), and that the accomplishments of African Americans were limited pretty much to the clever things George Washington Carver had done with peanuts. Most of us got the impression that Jim Crow was a kind of pie with black-berries. In high school, I must admit, the books grew more realistic. We learned of the connivings of the "great" corporations and hold-ing companies, of Teddy Roosevelt the heroic trust-buster; Marxism was discussed in an almost evenhanded tone. Senior year, we had a psychology textbook (had no one on the school board actually read it, I wondered?) that described "the authoritarian personality" as the root of all national and family evils (I immediately thought of my father and George Wallace) and that openly denounced racism and homophobia(!). One photograph clearly depicted two shirtless males embracing.

I read all of this senior textbook during a couple of idle hours in my freshman year. Needless to say, the progressive sections of the textbook were not actually assigned when senior year came along. The teachers must have counted on students never to read pages that were not assigned. I owe a great deal to their negligence.

In my contempt for my budding authoritarian schoolmates, how-ever, I deepened my isolation by announcing (rather like O'Connor's Hulga, yet without so much spite, I think) that I was a communist and an atheist, and that *I supported gun control*. When it was my turn to lead class prayer in the early morning, I was allowed to read Li Shang-Lin's poem "The Patterned Lute" rather than to recite a standard inarticulate Protestant mumble. I had no idea what the poem was about, but then no critic ever has had an idea, either. The act was pretentious. *Foreign.* Could a student get away with it now, I wonder?

When informed by the school principal (and, apparently, school censor) that I could not finish my valedictorian address with a quote from Martin Luther King, under pain of having my diploma with-held, I replaced it with a quote from Oscar Wilde (kept behind the desk in the school library but whose plays I knew by heart from read-ing at home). The quote from Wilde passed without comment.

Wow, I thought: *this Alabama high school rejects the words of a Bap-tist minister but accepts those of an infamously gay playwright.* Looking back, I see that this could only have happened in Alabama, and only in the late 1970s.

Why didn't I go ahead and read the quote from King? I wanted my diploma: I had to get the hell out of there. (I still have nightmares in which I imagine that I cannot receive my Ph.D. because it has been discovered that I didn't take all required high school classes—and suddenly I am there again, ugly lockers and all.) Frankly, I also feared for my life: the parents of my classmates were even more ferociously racist than were their children.

College

Something strange happened next. I went to the University of Alabama for three years and had a wonderful time. Yes, at this college, where George Wallace had tried to block an African American student from enrolling only seventeen years before (and where the Greek system was *still* very strictly segregated), I found many progressive and high-minded friends. Eventually these friends included both Mark (my brother) and James Tucker (later, the lawyer who took Governor Fob James and Alabama Supreme Court Justice Roy Moore to court and whose motto in school was GET INTENSE!), along with Tom Cantey, Fred Williams, Grant Pair, Karl Fattig, James Floyd, Bruce Steele, Mark Vines, Anne Klinefelter, and believe it or not many others. By way of several mutual friends, I got to know a small enlightened crowd at Auburn, a school on the other side of the state, a group including an amazingly talented brother-sister team, poet Margaret Renkl and artist Billy Renkl.

I should note that these cross-state friendships are rare. Most students at Alabama and Auburn are football junkies who hate fans of the opposing team, perhaps even more than they hate gay people or Arabs. Fanship seems to be genetically or geographically determined, not a matter of choice: my family was split almost in half, maybe because the distinct regions of the state intersect in Birmingham. (South and east Alabama go for Auburn, but the north and west adulate the Crimson Tide.) People don't abandon their early fan loyalties even if they enroll at the school they detest. My brother, for example, remained a fan of Auburn throughout his year and a half at Alabama.

The Auburn-Alabama football game is the true culmination of

the year for Alabamans: the intensity of the occasion, the effect of a maelstrom, is impossible to describe. Now in many ways, the football games are undeniably fun, especially for drunken nineteen-year-olds: the shockingly cool breezes of October bring out energy and camaraderie in Southerners that you might not have expected to lurk inside them.

Other side-effects, though, are despicable. People become petty, boastful, and childish when football is discussed, and discussion of it accounts for about 50 percent of spare time—even more during football season itself. When I was a freshman, Alabama fans were at the peak of their arrogance, for Paul Bryant was still coaching then; the team went 12–0 and won the national championship at the Sugar Bowl. I gave up on attending the games midway through that year, when I saw the home crowd booing the players, as they jogged off the field, because *they had won by only thirty-eight points.* There was something deeply Roman and bloodthirsty about that coat-and-tie crowd.

These mobsters never taunted me (though they once taunted and threatened my friend Bruce at another home football game, provoking the assembly's beefier members to stand and, with yells and primate noises, face down the jeering homophobes), but I did feel about a half bottle of bourbon poured onto my back at the Baylor game earlier that season. The September evening was still hot, though, so the spill, intentional or no, proved only to be refreshing.

Another night, as I was walking home alone down University Boulevard, a car full of SAEs sporting many football emblems pulled up alongside me so that one of its occupants could yell out, "Cocksucker!" I simply quickened my pace, staring ahead, knowing that doing anything else would have invited a severe beating. These days, I would probably yell something even nastier in return—and get killed. Why hadn't books like *Insult and the Making of the Gay Self* been published yet? Ah, but where would I have found them in Alabama?

So the football obsession dovetails with "the policing of gender" and with the terrorizing of foreigners—all of whom learn very early the importance of knowing one's place, or, better, knowing that one will never *have* a place at all.

Educational consequences: football coverage eclipses reporting on political and world affairs in all of Alabama's "major" newspapers. This year, they will devote much more editorial space to the performance of the football coaches at the two major schools than to the dismantling of Social Security or to the appointment of extremist judges, ambassadors, and attorneys-general.

Do you think I'm joking? While I was in Birmingham for my father's funeral, two years ago, enormous headlines (presidential assassination-level) were screaming out reports of a sex scandal involving the Alabama football coach; radios and televisions delivered updates almost hourly. Meanwhile, George Bush was destroying Iraq and eviscerating whatever was left of American democracy, and nobody gave a flying fuck, to use a phrase I picked up in the South, where I also learned the importance of uttering the word "shit" as though it contained three syllables.

Getting back to college—I don't object to drinking. I believe I've turned down a drink only once or twice in my life. There is, however, as you see above, something ugly about the *way* many people drink in the South, and about the way that they speak and drive during and after. It is not what anyone would call *comme il faut*. Johnson said that drunkards made beasts of themselves to escape the pain of being men; in Alabama, people make beasts of themselves to feed their racism and xenophobia, at worst, and at best to escape being Alabamans.

The weather may explain some of this. For four months (mid-May to mid-September), simply being outside amounts to heat prostration, either day or night. After you have been outside fifteen minutes or so, your skin will be covered by a loathsome compound of dried sweat, dirt, and slapped-dead mosquitoes: drink is the easiest relief. For another two and a half months of the year (mid-December to early March), truly vicious cold can hit the state, usually in the form of howling winds from the Midwest; again, whisky to the rescue! In autumn, the kindest season, football provides another excuse for constant inebriation. Baudelaire would have approved, but he would also have been puzzled.

A father's advice to one of my friends at school: "Son, never drink before 2:00. Unless there's a football game." Quite often, the drinking weekend lasted from Wednesday afternoon to early Monday morning. I went to my morning classes hung-over, wondering why my head hurt and my hands trembled.

How then did I gain so much from attending the University of Alabama (not to be confused with UAB: make a note of it), this racist, sexist, and homophobic football and drinking school? Credit must go to the Men's Honors Assembly, or, as it was usually known, "Mallet." In other epochs, this honors dorm has been dominated by, uh, less than tolerant and open-minded young men (and a few women, despite the title), but in 1979 it was crowded with drunken, drugged out, generous-minded folk who listened to a lot of David Bowie and Neil Young. One night my freshman year, people marched into the "drawing room" (a well-designed but by then hopelessly ratty *salon*) for a dorm meeting while Tom Cantey blasted the Tom Robinson Band's "Glad to be Gay" from the windows of his dorm room, only a few yards from the meeting site, on his massive stereo speakers: even the straight folk were singing loudly on the chorus. Tuscaloosa, Alabama. What was going on?

Three and a half years later, in the *plus que chaud* summer of 1983, a male exchange student entirely lacking the shyness stereotypically associated with his culture insisted on dancing with me at a Country-Western bar on the outskirts of Tuscaloosa. Although I feared violence and bottle-tossing, I was drunk enough to go for it. (It was the night before the poor man had to return to his more crowded and even more conservative homeland, and I was a little in love with him, you see.) When we had danced for about fifteen minutes, I saw the C&W crowd staring at us, "loose-lipped and slack-jawed," as my friend Michael would say, but seeming too stunned to carry out a lynching, or even a beating.

Did this all *really* happen in Alabama, you ask? (My creative writing teachers at UCLA asked this question so often that I began to doubt the reality of my own past.) I admit that the Mallet of that time and place, with the university under its peculiar influence, was a diplomatic enclave—that is, *foreign soil*. One sorority member was overheard, speaking of the place: "All they ever do is read Chaucer and sit around singing strange songs." Hm. She left out a lot, including people's having sex under the grand piano in the drawing room, but she did sense the foreign flavor, confirming for us its existence (and reinforcing our desire to preserve it?).

I loved this foreign place so much that the prospect of leaving for graduate school brought on panic attacks, and during my first three years at UCLA I was often homesick—a stunning thing in someone who should have welcomed the change of atmosphere and accepted the exile with relief—but please keep in mind that I was homesick for this anti-Alabama, Mallet, and a few blocks on the Southside of Birmingham (where one found a gay bar called Mabel's Beauty Shop and Chainsaw Repair), and not for the state as most people know it.

I blame R.E.M.: their music was so good that they made the South seem glamorous for much of the 1980s. I had absurd daydreams of crawling into kudzu patches and drinking there forever—with my friends who had already scattered around the world. I had temporarily forgotten the weather, the marauding Republicans, the governor, the mosquitoes, the "aesthetic ribaldries and theological buffooneries" (Mencken). The release of R.E.M.'s *Fables of the Reconstruction* in the late spring of 1985, with its dreamlike "Green Grow the Rushes," "Driver 8," and "Life and How to Live It," brought on complete emotional meltdown. I hope you're *satisfied*, Messieurs Stipe and Buck.

After the first two years, however, my visits to Alabama began making me nostalgic for California. I landed at the airport (after changing planes in Dallas on the way!) and looked around: Where did all those white people come from? Were they dangerous? Was I acting straight enough to survive their company? Would they confiscate my drugs? I carefully hid my Julien Green novels and memoirs, replacing them with Graham's.

Godawful Religion and Prospects for Change

As you can see, the two halves of this subheading are not exactly compatible. Alabama is not the place for change or reconciliation. Remember that *Congress* has never even apologized—and I realize that the word "apologize" sounds very lame in the context of a phenomenon of this sort—for slavery: if the U.S. Congress won't do it, don't expect the state legislature of Alabama to take action. If tolerance and nobility of mind advances in the South, it will do so in urban Tennessee, Georgia, and North Carolina, not in Alabama, Mississippi, Texas (though Austin may revolt . . .), or South Carolina. These four states *pride themselves* on their stubbornness and their contempt for civilized ways—unless you mean, by "civilized," the backwater starch of Charleston.

The last week's news has given me doubts about North Carolina, too, I must say. I've read reports of a Baptist church where the pastor expelled nine members for *being Democrats*, and interviews with judges and sheriffs who continue enforcing an anticohabitation law. We must not forget that North Carolina repeatedly reelected Jesse Helms to the Senate, or that North Carolinians hospitalized my friend Paul in 1985 to cure him of homosexuality—forcing me to collaborate with a few fine citizens of Chapel Hill on a (successful) escape plan. The staff at the hospital assumed that, since Paul was gay, he must also have AIDS; they posted several large red warning signs at his door.

Alabama, like most of North Carolina, is *coincé*, stuck. As an entity, it instinctively despises dialogue, compromise, progress; indeed, most Alabamans probably deny the very existence of social progress. As far as I can tell, being "progressive" among Alabama whites means reaching out to Catholics, learning to dislike African Americans a bit less, and reserving most of their current hatred for feminists, Hispanic immigrants, and gays. Homophobia will be a hundred years in disappearing, *if* it disappears.

During the 2004 Presidential campaign, a woman in Demopolis, Alabama, was fired for having a John Kerry bumper sticker on her car. I have seen Demopolis. You don't want to see it.

To understand Alabama, you must first grasp its *poverty*. It is not simply material poverty, but a poverty of the spirit and the imagination. Its cities have many new subdivided suburbs and exurbs, but these are equaled in number by rural shacks (yes, in some places, human beings still inhabit *slave shacks*), inner-city houses with tumbling brick pillars, and trailers, trailers, trailers, some of them called "luxury" coaches, others rusting and squalid. People surrounded by such mind-numbing ugliness may not develop the power to think at all—or may focus on one powerful thought: get me out of here! If Alabamans do get a little learning (a dangerous thing, remember), it will most likely be channeled into racist resentment or into bad religion. About eight years ago, in fact, a man was arrested in South Alabama for shooting his best friend. The motive? Anger over having lost a Bible-quoting contest.

About fourteen years ago, *The Birmingham News* obtained a copy of a map of the state being distributed by the Alabama Baptist Convention: the counties were color-coded according to the percentages of the inhabitants assumed to be "saved" or "damned." Even many Alabamans were stunned by this level of hubris and condescension. A further outrage ensued when interested parties determined how the percentages were arrived at: apparently, the project managers were assuming that humanists and atheists would be joined in hell by their hard-drinking Episcopalian, Lutheran, and Catholic friends. Perhaps they had trouble categorizing the Methodists and Presbyterians. Jews? They never had a chance; after all, Baptists had been told by Jerry Falwell in 1980 that "God does not hear the prayers of a Jew"—a declaration that forced even Ronald Reagan to distance himself slightly from the Lynchburg gang.

Am I starting to sound like a less witty Molly Ivins? Could it be that there is only one way to write about the South while remaining sane? No. For another way, look again at W. J. Cash's *The Mind of the South*. Though partly based on racist assumptions and trapped in an early-twentieth-century worldview, many of its observations strike me still as pertinent, especially the discussion of "The Savage Ideal" and the resulting regional contempt for education, a fortiori science. Considering the malfunctioning "Southern Mind" today, many are apt to blame the squalor on bad religion—and there is no worse religion than that of the Deep South, except, perhaps, in Saudi Arabia or Utah. Blaming the mindlessness of the South on this bad religion, however, may amount to confusing effect with cause.

Many blame Baptists. Jerry Falwell is, after all, a Baptist. The Baptist church did arise in Northern Europe among Puritans who thought that the Lutherans and, more incomprehensibly, the Calvinists, were still *too Catholic*. Extremism would seem to be built into the Baptist way. There are millions of Baptists, however, all over the United States, and they are often progressive, gentle, and reasonable people. Why are (white) *Southern* Baptists so hateful? And where did Pentacostalists (more fanatical still) come from?

When you catch a reasonable Southerner in an expansive mood, ask her to describe Pentacostalist *hair*.

I am not a religious historian, but I know that Southern Baptists have devolved since my childhood. We once ridiculed them for their focus on Jesus: how naive we were! Compare *that* with the new focus on the carefully selected (i.e., the meanest) words of Saint Paul, their selective embrace of Levitical law, and their embarrassing enthusiasm for all that relates to *Apocalypse*. They are now "Christians" who think little of the teachings of Christ, unless by "Christ" one means the hallucinatory king of heaven in *Revelation*, the one who, at something called "The Rapture," will hover off the surface of the earth like a cosmic vacuum cleaner, sucking the true believers up into heaven and leaving the rest of us to rejoice. Or lament, as they would have it.

In Alabama, especially in the 1980s, many cars sported the semifamous bumper sticker IN CASE OF RAPTURE, THIS CAR WILL BE WITHOUT A DRIVER. Things of that sort perpetually recall Nietzsche's true, most deeply felt objection to the worldview of Saint Paul and his henchmen: "I *feel* these bad manners whenever I read the New Testament." If a person becomes so disgusted at these unseemly displays of sanctimony and relentless proselytizing that he or she retaliates, say, with the DARWIN lungfish emblem, she is likely to have her car vandalized and beaten beyond recognition (as happened to an instructor at the University of Florida nine years ago) or to be tailgated by a man with a tight mouth and murder in his eyes, speeding downhill (as happened to me, also in Florida and also nine years ago). Astonishingly, it appears that there is nothing so dangerous as offending people who are under strict orders to turn the other cheek.

Still, I refuse to attribute Southern cultural psychoses entirely to bad religion. I think, instead, that Southerners have made bad religion worse and have persecuted good religion—which I would define as a focus on the teachings of Christ, the Buddha, Lao Tse, or someone of similar spiritual stature—almost out of existence. As I have said, few Baptists elsewhere in the nation are as nasty as Southern Baptists; the nationwide United Church of Christ bears little or no resemblance to the "Church of Christ" and "Church of God" (or "Chuhchagod," as most people say) that terrorize the countryside in the old Confederacy. (When these "Pentacostalists" walk into *United* Churches of Christ by mistake, some faint dead away upon seeing same-sex couples holding hands.) Presbyterians, Episcopalians, and Methodists, I believe, have also established special congregations or subdenominations, chiefly to satisfy antimodernists in the Deep South.

The splinter Episcopalians, predictably, have their conventions in Dallas, where the worst of the South merges seamlessly with the worst of the West.

Puzzlingly, many "religious" Southerners will not even read the Bible. When I had a fundamentalist (unbeknownst to me) Southern lover, I slowly discovered that he had tormented himself all his life because of his and his family's belief in the "literal truth" of the bible (and all that was supposedly implied by that belief). I took him very carefully through the first few chapters of Genesis, showing him the absurdity and crudeness of the cosmology and theology behind it all, and he was amazed. When he used my observations in an argument with his sister, she yelled out "HE MADE YOU READ IT, DIDN'T HE?" The religious right, it appears, has gone full circle and has now adopted the positions of the late-medieval papacy. As for poor Jesus, he can hardly be the subject of much Southern Baptist study these days: among these people, the word "peace" has become taboo, and the only context in which "love" is acceptable comes in the recently coined term "tough love."

Saint Francis? Vincent de Paul? Thérèse de Lisieux? Bah! Saints are for sissies. Martyrs, though, especially surly Christian teens who refuse to learn science, are *huge*.

I say that the meanness, the essence, predates the bad religion. Resentment is a precondition for meanness, and white Southerners are the exemplary people of resentment. *Still* discouraged by defeat in the Civil War, *still* unwilling to recognize the horrible crimes of their slave-holding ancestors (the story of Noah and his sons and Paul's letter to Philemon are even today used to justify slavery in some white Southern churches), ashamed of their relative poverty and obscurity among U.S. citizens as a whole, hobbled by their refusal to master the sciences, and maddened by the most intolerable weather in the country, white Southerners *must* insist on their "moral superiority," the supposed "foolishness of Christ" (from Saint Paul: who else would be dumb enough to call Jesus a fool?) that they must prefer to "the wisdom of this world," their much overrated "fine manners," and the memory of Robert E. Lee's battlefield prowess (which gets confused with the football-field prowess of Paul Bryant) to compensate for the wreck they have made of themselves. ("Alabama, you've got the rest of the Union to help you along: What's going wrong?" Neil Young asks in his inimitable anguished voice, guitars roaring.) The fact that meanness and bad religion drive away many of the state's most promising young people is, to many Alabamans, so much the better: they have no desire to have others remind them of their intellectual inadequacies or true ethical failings.

Best of all, if education can be eviscerated, if the "brain-drain" continues, if homophobic, sexist, and xenophobic public discourse can drown dissenting voices, and if the true character of Jesus can be forgotten by Christians, Southerners will be electing representatives like Tom Delay and senators like Trent Lott for generations to come. Such representatives will find themselves able only to shout at Henry Waxman or Xavier Becerra—if they can communicate at all.

12. The Kreskin Effect
Jim Peterson

It was Friday night. No school tomorrow. I was a kid, and I loved *The Tonight Show*. Permission requested and granted. Watching Carson with my father is how I got to know his sense of humor, an affinity for slapstick and other forms of silliness. My own sense of humor fell in line. I laughed until I cried. And I learned. It was on Carson that I first saw Martin Luther King, Muhammad Ali, Lenny Bruce. Strange heroes for a white kid in the Bible Belt, son of a conservative business man. Maybe my favorite guest on Carson was the Amazing Kreskin. My father and I were both literally glued to the screen any time Kreskin came on, and he was a frequent guest. I like that I could have both King and Kreskin as heroes. Kids don't draw so many boundaries, so many lines in the sand. I loved King for his idealism and courage; Kreskin for his feats suggesting an important mystery, and for his perceived ability to control others with nothing but the power of his mind.

Black and white in those days. A flickering light. A youthful Carson in a conservative suit and tie playing the consummate straight man to his guests: Tony Randall, Elaine Strick, Mickey Mantle, Liza Minnelli, Don Rickles. And suddenly Martin Luther King. If my father had not loved Carson so much, he probably wouldn't have kept watching. But he did watch, with a certain grave concentration. Carson treated King with the greatest respect, gave King this popular forum to put forward his important ideas. King was confident, relaxed, charming, righteous, brilliant. How difficult it was for my father to process the power of this black man and the truth of his words. Especially since

King's power stemmed from being morally right, and from passive resistance as opposed to violence. In our country we know what to do if someone threatens us: we get out our big gun and blow 'em away. There is clarity. But when someone stands passively in our way with their truth, we may not know what to do; we feel doubt, confusion, and impotent anger.

Any sense I have of my political engagement with the world, with my connection to praxis in other words, goes back to my relationship with my father. My mother was a presence also, but she was much more in the background, a voice reassuring or coaxing. My father was dominant. Patriarchal dominance was the case in most households of my generation, as it has been in most households going back to the dawn of the Iron Age. Perhaps we are on the cusp of breaking through both the matriarchal and patriarchal structures of culture into a more balanced understanding of power and responsibility, but this more healthy hierarchy hasn't emerged yet; and we continue to suffer under a hierarchical imbalance that places the father (god) into dominance. Before the Iron Age, and for thousands of years, the mother (goddess) was dominant, but that's another story. I wonder if it's possible for us to harmonize these two essential energies in ways that produce a more open and yet stable society where everyone has a realistic chance to learn and grow and prosper. But harmony is not our strong suit so far; now dominance, that's something we can really sink our teeth into.

There is no point, of course, in faulting my father for who he was. Like each of us, he was the product of many factors inherited and environmental. My father's father was even more dominant in his household than my father would ever be. He had a violent temper and favored corporal punishment to get his point across. Thus, his three sons and his daughter were often afraid of him. My father was the middle son and was the most resistant and rebellious. My father liked to tell a story about wanting to play football for the high school team in the little Georgia town of Waynesville. But his father was against it, wanted my father to get home after school, to have a job, and not waste his time with a stupid game. But my father sneaked away to practice and to play in the games. When his father discovered the deceit, he came after my father with a poker one night as he was sitting down to dinner, and my father had to seek refuge with the family of one of his friends. If I ever complained of my father's discipline, he could bring out this story to demonstrate just how moderate his own techniques were by comparison. "Son, you don't have any idea what real discipline is." If that was true, then I didn't want to know. My father eventually paid a price for his rebellious, independent thinking: his father disinherited him, leaving everything to the other three siblings. His reasoning was that James, my father, could take care of himself and thus didn't need the money, while the others were not as strong and needed more help. Beneath the compliment lay the still unresolved battle for control. It was a painful rejection that left a permanent scar on my father's psyche.

Unfortunately and ironically, my father, like so many rebellious sons, took on some of the worst as well as some of the best traits of his father. He thought of himself as a fighter and took pleasure in physical confrontation with anyone who tried to intimidate him. He was fierce, strong, agile, not someone you wanted to cross. He was always eager to prove himself. When he was young and courting my mother, if another man so much as spoke to her or looked at her the wrong way, my father tended to kick ass first and ask questions later. In his middle and later years, he was always working out, jogging, playing sports, working on his boxing skills. Like his father, my father had an excellent business mind, starting out in the insurance field and expanding into a substantial real estate company. For thirty years, he was the primary developer in the South Carolina town I grew up in, building housing subdivisions, apartment houses, condominiums, shopping centers, and even a par-three golf course—and all of this without completing a high school education, which had been interrupted by the Depression. Like his father, my father believed in the old adage, "Spare the rod, spoil the child." I was a well-behaved and courteous child who stayed out of trouble, yet I remember two painful belt whippings my father administered when I was growing up. When he was disappointed, he had the fiercest set of eyes of anyone I've ever known. Having to confront that look was even more difficult than facing the belt. I had to learn to match that fierceness with my own eyes. He had control, but I refused to let him win, to let him dominate me. My style was different from his, but I carried on one of the family traditions and became a rebellious son. I had determined that my father was a deeply flawed man, and thus any position he took on any issue deserved close scrutiny. I discovered that he lived a conservative lifestyle on the surface while indulging in a profligate lifestyle in secrecy. Fascinating and disgusting, though not unusual I suppose. Still, it was a difficult landscape to negotiate for an idealistic son.

When I think about my father's politics, I can begin to understand much about my own brand of liberal praxis. For a rebellious son to do battle with such a strong father, he must contain many of the strengths of that father. I have the stubbornness of both my grandfather and my father. My stubbornness is almost legendary in my immediate family. They tell me that as a little boy, I preferred switchings and spankings to giving in, especially if I thought I was right, which I usually did, another trait, more unfortunate, that I carry on. I like to think that I have some of my father's and grandfather's intelligence, though I channel it into much different kinds of action. I like to think I have their courage. I needed all of that and more to remain standing in my father's presence. I rejected his business as a teenager, and then went off to college to study literature. Though he continued to support me financially, I know that decision hurt him. Literature of all things. What the hell was I going to do with that in the real world? This dance, this prolonged argument between myself and my father, was training, preparation for holding unpopular, liberal views in the midst of a conservative community. For I have always lived in deeply conservative parts of the country: Georgia, South Carolina, Montana, Virginia, and the "country" of my home. From the beginning, my father taught me to stand up for myself. Bullies didn't fare well with me. But I don't think it ever dawned on him that I would turn that strength back on him.

For the longest time, my father was basically a god to me, beyond criticism and beyond reproach. I worshiped him. Values often grow out of the epiphanies of childhood. One of my earliest and most cherished memories of my father goes back to the days when I was "small."

For a long time it seems, my father's hands were always just above and touching the top of my head, were at eye and face level, or were at neck and chest level. He had strong and graceful hands. Sometimes, on a lazy weekend afternoon watching a football game, or in the evening, I would sit in his lap or lie beside him on the couch or in his bed, and he would almost absently stroke my face and neck. When I was little I sought this kind of attention from him often. There really was nothing better than that touch in which I felt his unconditional love and the gentleness at his core. As I became older, he expressed less and less of his physical affection towards me. Maybe he wanted to toughen me up and that sort of affection between father and son betrays weakness. Or maybe he began to become keenly aware of his betrayal of the family pact, and he felt guilty when he was with me. But I still believe that my own attitude of gentleness, my own sense of the frailty of children and of people in general, comes from those blissful times in the company of his gentle touch.

When my father began to have his own success in business in the 1950s, he took up sports again. For years he played volleyball on a local YMCA team that earned a high national ranking. He loved boxing and promoted boxing programs for boys in the city of Augusta. I have an old photograph of him refereeing a match between two kids. I like seeing these pictures that show a man who was volunteering his time in the service of the community. But his increasing success as a businessman eventually changed all of that. There can be no more stilted, formal, rigid conservative landscape than the country club as it is manifested in Bible Belt America. I would rank it above the church as a place where conservative politics is nurtured and crystallized. A kind of cynical, self-serving politics. From an early age I was put into the country club atmosphere, in which I felt about as alien as it is possible to feel. As a child, of course, my alienation had nothing to do with politics, but a kind of shyness in the presence of so much self-importance. I think my father loved all sports, but as an adult golf became his great passion. It was and still is a game that attracts successful people into the country clubs. Though he never had a classically beautiful swing, his strength and feel made him a good player, about a five handicapper for most of his adult life. Yes, my father strode the green pastures of Augusta Country Club solidifying his standing as a successful man, befriending politicians, doctors, lawyers. My father grew up in a small town and dropped out of high school a year before graduating. His success was due to his intelligence and hard work. When he began to hang out with men who were more educated, more sophisticated, he discovered that he wanted to be respected by them, wanted to be like them, and wanted to have the privileges that alpha males everywhere have always tended to expect.

My father was charismatic, charming, attractive to women, confident, masculine, fearless in his interactions with other men. A man who supported Nixon but was ironically Kennedyesque in his youthful appearance. He was, in short, pretty much everything I thought I wanted to be. And yet I fought him. I think I began my first feeble resistance when I was around twelve, in the year 1960. In the year Kennedy and Nixon battled for the presidency, I discovered that my father was having affairs, lots of them. This all makes sense. I was entering puberty, had been feeling an attraction to girls for a long time, though I was very shy around them. And I had exactly no comprehension of the complicated life my father was living. All I knew was that his affairs were hurting my mother, and they were damaging the family. Secretly, of course, I wanted to have the power to do what he did, to have what he had. But that wasn't an idea that I allowed any space. For years I was powerless to do anything about this situation. But then, when I was sixteen, I found a way. I became a born-again Christian. The one thing my conservative but sexually wayward father didn't want to confront every evening when he came home was a righteous, Christian son.

Or an angry wife, for that matter. And so, increasingly he came home only long enough to eat dinner, and then he was back out the door on "business." And my father and I grew farther and farther apart, though I'm not sure this split would have been apparent to others. When we were together, we often fought over issues, the presence of which I had only begun to become aware. I admit it: I was wrapped up in a dream world; I was slow; I was a bit spacey. I listened to Joan Baez and Bob Dylan and the Beatles. I read books like *Catcher in the Rye*. I wrote poetry and strange short stories. It was the 1960s, and the world was exploding with revolutionary ideas. And I fell in love with Jesus. I can find fault with falling in love with Jesus, but I confess that it was a good thing for me at the time. I became involved with an evangelical, youth-oriented, nondenominational organization. I was accepted. I was a part of a loving, compassionate group of people. There was, after all, a purpose in life. There was a real Heavenly Father who trumped any earthly father. Suddenly I was armed with the authority of the mostly highly regarded Book, and with an irrefutable irrationality called "faith." I could stand toe to toe with my unreligious father on any moral question of the day. I had power. I suddenly had more friends. My main claim to fame before this was that I was a starter on the varsity football team. In high school, that's usually enough to get you invited to parties. But now I became respected for my understanding of religious fundamentals; I was wise; I was asked to give talks on religious topics such as forgiveness and salvation. I wrote a play entitled *Why Be?* that was performed at our high school assembly. For the first time I had a philosophical and spiritual basis from which I could take a significant step intellectually as well as personally. I wasn't just stubborn now; I was formidable.

And, increasingly liberal in my politics. Though I'd never set foot in a black church, I was a Martin Luther King kind of Christian, or at least wanted to be. Consider these battle lines. I was a born-again liberal doing battle with my conservative libertine father. Truly libertine. It has been only in later years I've discovered that my amazing father was living an undercover life of orgies that would make Bill Clinton grin with glee. And he had drawn my lovely, reserved mother into it against her better judgment. She loved him and wanted to please him. But eventually the heartless hollowness of it drove her out. And drove a barrier between them that they were never able to knock down. He continued with his affairs. She did battle with her rivals whenever she could find them. There was a tension and a coldness in that big house that sent us each to our own disparate corners. I made up baseball games with marbles and pencils and football games with checkers, and I disappeared into these lonely escapes for hours. As a child I was often left in the care of a black maid. I was practically raised to the age of six by a compassionate woman named Beatrice. After she died, a series of black women took care of me. One of them, Mary, played Beatrice to my parents, but when she had me alone became a harsh disciplinarian who belittled me and struck me when I angered her, which didn't take much. Where were my mother and father, and why had they left me alone with this disturbed woman? I have to say that there were times growing up when I felt abandoned. Mary told me if I ever told my parents that she hit me, she would kill me. I was just plain scared, and I never told them. It was a sweet day when I learned that Mary had quit. But the tension in that house remained palpable, and it wasn't going to go away. My parents were so busy tying and untying the sick knot of their love life that I hardly existed. It affected my sisters also, but they were seven and ten years older than I, and they had gotten out. I was alone in this pressure cooker, and the older I became, the closer I was to boiling over. The only way I could channel this energy nondestructively was to resist, to reject my father's way of life as I understood it. In many ways, the battles within a family are analogous to the broader political battles within a culture. Our presidents are carrying on the line of our founding fathers. The president is our surrogate father. We have such idealistic hopes and expectations for our Father, our President. A man cannot live up to this image. We watch him every minute of every day. We find his faults and we turn against him, and we bring forth another father to lead and comfort us until our paranoid probes discover his failings and we reject him and start the pattern over again, alternating between liberal and conservative like the confused children that we are.

There are many reasons that I became a Christian. I had then and I still have a genuine spiritual longing. The church provides a community and a sense of belonging. The teachings provide a great sense of relief and release from guilt. They also give the believer a feeling of purpose: to spread the word and save as many souls as possible; to develop one's relationship with the most powerful being in the universe. And that relationship is supposed to be personal, which makes it all the more meaningful. For many people, especially in current times, being a Christian links them to the most powerful political movement of our day, the faith-based conservative right. As I look closely at the political climate of our time and of recent decades, I cannot understand why there is a connection between the teachings of Jesus and political conservatism. They strike me as antithetical. For example, for a Christian reasonably to be a hawk on defense, Jesus himself would have to come down from Heaven and erase about half of what he said. The fact is, people on the religious right today appear to have very little knowledge of the actual words and teachings of Jesus. He was truly a left-wing radical, an extremist whose words rang true in the mouths of the flower children of the 1960s. The Jesus hippies with their belief that love is the guiding principle of the universe were closer to the truth of Jesus than the so-called Christians of the religious right will ever be. And the people in our culture that I idolized, even as a Christian, were far on the left, the scarily mistaken left as far as my father was concerned.

My father and I both liked late night snacks, and we would often find one another at the kitchen table in the middle of the night slurping up a bowl of cereal or ice cream. There he'd be, his reading glasses perched precariously on the tip of his nose, his boxer shorts gaping open. And there I'd be, sitting across from him in our kitchen nook, in my jockey shorts and T-shirt.

"King was right tonight, on Carson, wasn't he?" I'd say.

My father would take another bite, set his spoon down, and think. "Yes and no," he'd say.

"He's either right or wrong."

"If every nigra was hard-working and smart like him, then he would be right. But they aren't. Now son, you've got to understand I'm not a racist. I know what I say from experience, not from prejudice. I hire nigra men all the time, and not one of them will come to work on time, if he shows up at all. And then he gets mad if you don't pay him. If you give a nigra a chance to make good, to prove himself, he just acts like it ain't nothing. He throws it away. Here I am trying to give 'em a good job, and the turn over is more than I can keep up with."

"What do you pay 'em?"

"I'd pay 'em better if I could count on 'em."

"Maybe if you paid 'em better, they'd have a reason to be more dependable."

"Son, it's your kind of thinking that's bringing this country down."

"No, Daddy, it's your kind of thinking that's holding this country back."

My father would start trembling with anger. And I swear his eyes could cut. I learned how to make mine cut back, invisible swords in the air between us.

"Son, you talk like you know something, like you'd ever done something in the world. You don't understand the way things are in the real world. It's nice to be an idealist, Son, but that won't do you much good when it comes to making a living and taking care of a family. Things are more complicated than you think."

"What's right is right. Ain't it? And what's wrong is wrong. You've got to admit King is right. Under our constitution, everybody's supposed to have the same opportunities. Regardless of color. Is that right or wrong?"

My father slid out of his side of the nook. He ran his hand through his pillow-mashed hair. He raised his right fist between us and shook it. "He may be right, Son, but he wants too much, too fast." And he walked out of the kitchen, slamming a hall door that we didn't usually close.

I stayed in the nook for a minute, trying to quiet my shaking body. I knew we'd been talking about King, and racism, but I also knew it was more than that: we'd been talking about ourselves, our respective values, our sense of right and wrong and justice. What my father said was right at the heart of it.

Too much, too fast.

One point I want to make here is that a person's political evolution is not a simple matter. My critical attitude towards our current president, for example, springs out of many complex issues and experiences that can't be simply analyzed in terms of liberal and conservative, Republican and Democrat, red and blue. The conceptual division of red and blue states is a perfect demonstration of the ways we delude ourselves by drawing imaginary lines in the sand. I have lived in some of the reddest states that there are, and yet I find that I am not alone in my blueness. Even in my home states of Georgia and South Carolina, you can find strong elements of liberal thinking and politics. In South Carolina, for example, I think of the longtime Democratic senator Fritz Hollings and the many people who supported him across the generations. In Georgia, I remember the progressive governor Carl Sanders of the 1960s. And of course there is Jimmy Carter, a born-again Christian liberal. Now that's my kind of Christian, and I quite frankly don't understand why there aren't more of them. I do not understand why the hawkish, rights-denying right has taken possession of Christianity in the mind of the public. If we stop to think, we realize that many Christians are Democrats and liberals. But the popular perception mitigates against that reality. There can be no doubt that Carter made some bad decisions as president that opened the door to his defeat when he came up for reelection. But Carter, in the years after his presidency, has done a lot of meaningful work in the world that has little if anything to do with partisan politics. Carter is a man who attempts to live the principles he claims to hold. His practice of Christianity is closer to that religion's true heart than most of what we see coming from the right. For me, he is one of the true heroes of our national life.

Red and blue. How strange it is to see our country divided into these little blocks of color, these artificial and truly misleading divisions. I would like to suggest that a balanced blending of these two colors, red and blue, is what we need. The blending of red and blue yields magenta. Is it not interesting that many color therapists believe magenta to be of the highest order, oriented toward spirituality and meditation? It is considered an instrument of change, of the purging of old attitudes and obsessions. Magenta stands for making a break with the hardened and destructive past. We need to find leaders in this country who can mix these two primary colors of red and blue into magenta, instead of always drawing the sharp lines of division between them. I want to call for a magenta nation, a people who recognize that finding common ground and cooperation are the important values for our future. Those who understand that listening and tactful responding are superior in the long run to inflammatory rhetoric. Superior because they bring us to the center in our national consciousness where resolution and solution can be found. In the governor's race going on in my state right now, the Republican is running the most vicious sort of ads calling the Democrat every name in the book, twisting everything in the Democrat's record to make him appear evil. The Democrat is having to run ads detailing newspaper articles that defend him, demonstrating that the Republican's ads are false. It seems never to end. It's becoming who we are.

After all I've said, I hope it won't surprise you if I say that my father was primarily a good man. I think I knew this all along, but it became much clearer to me as I grew to an adult and understood the pressures of being a human being in this culture. He made a lot of mistakes that hurt me and him and the whole family, but all of that is part of the learning. I forgave him a long time ago, and I hope that before he died he forgave me for my sometimes angry opposition. The fact is, he was always generous with me. He supported my education through the masters degree. He argued hard and well to convince me that I should take over his business, but he also knew that if I didn't follow my own path I would resent him forever. I don't think my father ever denied me anything I truly wanted or needed. Indeed, I had it too easy. I was spoiled. In the days approaching his death, he worried aloud about that, wondered if I were ready to face the world without his help. I know he loved me, but I think I always puzzled him. I wasn't the kind of son he was supposed to have. He respected the toughness I displayed on the football field, but he always suspected that I wasn't tough enough as a man to cope with the hard reality of making it on my own. My liberal and spiritual values were too soft and idealistic to be practical.

The one exception to my claim that my heroes were radical liberals is the Amazing Kreskin. Perhaps Kreskin is neither liberal nor conservative, neither Republican nor Democrat, as he claims. Nonpartisan. In any case, the most important aspect of his influence on me has little to do with politics directly.

It has to do with liberating one's thinking and analytical processes. In order to do that, one must see, confront, and transcend one's conditioned thinking, one's habits of thought. By "confront" I don't mean "battle." I mean "stand up to and accept." Doing battle with them will only strengthen them. Instead, one must recognize that they are created at least in part from the outside, that they are not one's own awakened and original analytical mind. It is my belief (yes, I am forever the idealist) that when you really see these habits of thought for what they are, you can move beyond them.

There is something vaguely comical about my father's small town libertinism. Something vaguely enviable about it, if only it had been more joyous. The anxiety and existential angst it eventually caused him may well have had something to do with his health problems. Kidney stones that led to major surgery. And the leukemia that he battled for nearly four years. The stress of a guilt-ridden secret life may have contributed to these problems that eventually killed him. There can be no question that his sexual addiction damaged all of us who lived at the center of the storm that was his life. But it seems to me that finding one's way in the storm is what the whole thing is about, at the personal level, and at the national level. What John Keats called negative capability, the ability to remain alert, calm, receptive in the midst of uncertainty, is not just an aptitude necessary for artists; we all need it, now more than ever.

When you realize that a hero who is vitally important to liberal causes and issues such as Jackie Robinson was a political conservative, a Republican who supported Nixon, you may begin to understand just how complex a person's personal political evolution can be. In breaking baseball's color barrier, Robinson was hated by conservatives; and yet he was one of them. There is something hard-wired about our political views, though that wiring may have been laid down during childhood. As I look back on my relationship with my father, I realize that in the beginning many of my liberal political stances were designed to annoy and frustrate him. As time passed and I moved out of the shadow of my father's influence, my views had to stand up to my maturing rational powers. Most of my positions survived the intense scrutiny I gave them and have thus become the true and worthy positions of a free-thinking adult. And I think this process demonstrates to each of us that our beliefs may be the result of unresolved emotional battle lines in our lives, not unlike grudges, and that we have to let go of them, clear the air, in order to be able to see that our beliefs are true to our deeper selves. I haven't been a Christian for many years and I belong to no religion. But that doesn't mean that I don't have a connection to spiritual life. I believe that each of us has a deeper self, an awakened center capable of possessing Keats's negative capability, a self that can be in the midst of uncertainty without becoming unhinged.

As a man who is living blue in the red states, I have become exhausted by the constant and bitter warring between these factions. As a writer, I am looking for the metaphors that will enable us to envision a new nation of functional, compassionate, far-seeing, and far-reaching decision making. I am looking for a rising up of the Magenta Nation. Another metaphor that works for me is the functional family. If it is a traditional family, male and female energies harmonize through love that goes beyond sex. The circle of that harmony draws the children into unconditional nurturing. Parents teach their children how to locate credible information, how to listen to both sides of any argument, how to weigh the evidence and make an informed decision; in short, how to think for themselves by staying in touch with their own deeper selves, by developing necessary negative capability. In such a family there would be no demonizing people of other races and religions and political stances. I realize this is a typical hippie dream, an ideal that will be difficult to achieve on a wide-spread basis. But I for one would rather go down struggling to be the best we can be than to survive by nurturing the worst in ourselves. In such a family, each individual is not operating out of the superficial values of self-promotion and self-service. Rather, they are moving deeper into themselves where higher values are waiting to be engaged. We all have this deeper place inside of us. What if our leaders, Democrats and Republicans and Independents, could lay aside their concerns about re-election and lucrative post-tenure business involvements, and could move into their deeper value systems and begin to think and vote from that level of themselves? It's not that they would all suddenly agree with each other, but that they would all be operating from a common ground, from a deeper center of values.

My father's deeper values were triggered by memories of his mother. She was Jewish and much beloved by her children in contrast to their fear of their father. My father's father was Baptist. On Saturday my father went to the synagogue, and on Sunday he went to church. This was not a happy conjoining of two very disparate belief systems. Rather, it was a competition. On her deathbed, my father's mother brought her children into the room one by one, calling them over to her bedside where they could hear her last feeble words. She made each of them promise never to become Christian. Thus my father never became either Jew or Christian. When I became a born-again Christian, I unconsciously carried into the new generation this polarizing family tradition. In some ways, I became my father's father, and the battle was renewed. Though my father died in 1977, though we had made a fair amount of peace between us by that time, even now I carry in my psyche the scars of this division. As I have understood more about how I have come to be who I am, I have wanted more and more to dissolve these boundaries that have brought great anxiety and inner turmoil. Thus I continue to be spiritually inclined without belonging to or supporting any particular religion. I think through each of my political positions, trying to make sure they can stand up to any arguments, regardless of whether my conclusion would be considered conservative or liberal by others. I ask myself what is the deeper value, not what will people think of me when I make my views known. If I am to be any kind of free-thinking adult, a human being, I cannot continue to allow my father to have a judging presence; I cannot allow him to produce in me either conformity or rebellion. I must purge myself of my father.

In those old days when I was lying in front of the TV with my father, I did not understand the psychology behind Kreskin's demonstrations. As a child, I was simply amazed and delighted. But as a young man in college, I saw Kreskin twice in person. Huge crowds had come to see him. It was exciting, mystifying, entertaining. In many ways, Kreskin is (or was in those days) a traditional magician or illusionist. But I am not concerned with that aspect of his performances, fascinating as it may be. I am interested in that aspect of his show when he invites people to volunteer to come on stage to be part of his act. The label Kreskin most often uses to refer to himself is "mentalist," and that term certainly applies to this part of his work. As people walk down the aisles toward the stage, one is reminded of the huge tent revivals of evangelists. Quite frankly, the question at the center of these seemingly very different operations is essentially the same: do you believe? If you believe, come forward. As people arrive at the edge of the stage, Kreskin's assistants make them wait. As the people in the audience see the line forming, they ask themselves if maybe it wouldn't be exciting to be on stage, and they join the line too. As the lines grow even longer, those remaining in the audience finally decide that they have waited too long; they no longer have a chance of making it to the stage. When there are no longer any people coming down, then Kreskin's assistants stand aside and allow the people to scramble up on the stage. When the crowd on stage reaches a size that Kreskin feels is the optimum, he has his assistants once again close off the stage entrances. Many people are sent back to their seats. It is important that those remaining on the stage see that others have been sent back. This is the leverage that Kreskin uses. If you do what I say, you get to stay. And people are motivated not only to walk down to that stage, but to stay on it for as long as they can. On stage, Kreskin works his gathering of people like a horse trainer works a horse. If you have ever seen a master trainer work with a green horse in a round pen, you know what I mean. Using only voice commands and body language, such a person can get virtually any horse to do anything he wants within minutes. If you were witnessing this, you would think the horse and man were communing by mental telepathy. Tackless training is what it is. No physical contact. The horse cannot take its eyes off the trainer whose knowledge of horse psychology, whose skill at focusing the horse's attention, are finely tuned.

Over a period of time, Kreskin trains the people on stage to focus on him in a similar manner and to do what he suggests. Those whose concentration wavers, those who falter in their response to his commands, which at one point are much like a game of Simon Says, are asked to leave the stage. Those who remain are now all the more determined to focus and to obey so that they can stay on the stage. Of course Kreskin is suggesting to them all sorts of simple but sometimes silly actions to demonstrate the power of his hypnosis. Their arm becomes so stiff it can support Kreskin's weight. They become so cold that their teeth chatter and they ask for coats. They become so hot they break out into a prolific sweat. And with each round Kreskin sends more of them away. Finally he narrows them down to a small group of highly suggestible people. In some cases, he can get these people to do odd and embarrassing things or to perform feats of strength or balance that they would not be able to do in ordinary circumstances. Finally, there is only one remaining person, someone so responsive that he is virtually a puppet. A mental puppet, for Kreskin can manipulate this person's actions without touching him or speaking to him.

Living blue in a red state, or living red in a blue state for that matter, may well be a continuing process of resisting the powerful attractions of conformity and acceptance. Through fear of rejection, through just plain fear, through the promise of loving acceptance, many of us are manipulated by the suggestions of influential people and organizations, just as we were led to conformity by our parents when we were children.

Many of us are drawn out of the unified state of magenta into the more defined conditioning of red or blue by the power of suggestion, by our desire to please either a powerful individual or the crowd, or through our desire to be accepted as part of a status granting group. One day, as I was watching Kreskin on stage, I suddenly realized that I was being hypnotized. How many forces in our culture operate the way Kreskin was working his stage crowd? How many forms of leverage were being used to turn us and move us where someone wanted us to go? Perhaps for the first time in my life I felt the various forms of pressure to conform at work in my body. I literally *felt* them. I felt again the presence of my father, of church, of friends, of the university, of all forms of authority in society. On that day I began my quest for freedom. I also felt a center in myself that was deeper than any place I had ever reached before, a place out of the reach of the superficial pressures of conformity-producing authority. The question became, how often and how long can I remain in that deep center of myself, a process akin to acquiring Keats's negative capability?

My father's beliefs were the result of his desire to be called up to that stage and remain there. He wanted to be part of the gang that was running the show, and so he adopted many of their attitudes and views. He played golf with them, played cards with them, partied with them, had sexual adventures with the women that hung around them. He knew that if he didn't play along he would be asked to leave. He had worked too hard and too long to be a member of the club to risk it. He was smart, tough, ambitious, but he struggled when it came to finding a source of deeper values. Neither Jew nor Christian nor atheist, he was adrift spiritually and morally. He just wanted to stay up there on the stage as long as he could. He never figured out how to live his life in a way that gave him satisfaction and peace. Maybe the most meaningful part of his life was the sexual pleasure he had with his many girlfriends. After I left home, my mother and father finally separated. On a visit home, I went to see my father in his apartment. He was at the lowest point emotionally that I had ever seen him. A much younger woman that he had been in love with for a while had left him for another man. He knew it was the right thing for her to do, considering their age difference. But he couldn't let go. He was waiting on his bed with the telephone beside him. He thought she would call at any moment. He cried and cried. I tried to comfort him, but on that night he was too far gone. He warned me not to live my life the way he had. About a year later, a girlfriend of his was watching TV with him at the apartment. She excused herself to go upstairs to the bathroom. When she didn't come back after a reasonable time, my father found the bathroom door locked. She wouldn't respond to him. Then he heard her body hit the floor. He tried everything he could, but he couldn't break the door down. By the time paramedics got to her, an inch-thick ocean of blood covered the tile floor. Miraculously, she survived. My father described the whole night to me in detail. He said that when he first made love to her, he discovered that her body was covered with scars, knife wounds administered by her ex-husband. My father was way beyond his depth. He had studied the art of sexual love; he knew how to give her body exquisite pleasure. But he didn't know how to relate to her at a deeper level where maybe he could have helped her. He said it took him forever to get her bloodstains out.

Near the end of his life, he had become involved with yet another beautiful younger woman. He built an extravagant house for her, and they were going to live together. My mother and father were finally going to be divorced. But then my father found out that he had a difficult form of leukemia. My wife and I were living in Colorado, but we pulled up stakes and moved back to South Carolina to be close to home. When his girlfriend discovered that my father had leukemia, she left him, never even visited him in the hospital. My father came home to my mother, who took him back in and stayed by him until the day he died at the age of fifty-nine.

When I went off to college, I started a Christian club in one of the local high schools. I remember one night I was preaching the fundamentalist principle that one had to accept Jesus as one's personal savior in order to enter the Kingdom of Heaven. I said that Jesus was the only way. After the meeting a young man walked up and challenged me. He hadn't realized I was so narrow and rigid in my religious practice and teaching. He told me I was wrong, that there are many ways to God, and he never came back to any of my meetings. Now, after all these years, I salute that young man who was wiser than I was though he was younger and less experienced. I wish I could remember his name, that I could know who he is today, that I could walk up to him and somehow tell him how much I respect him for his courage, his honesty, his ability to think for himself. Soon after that, I began to question my beliefs that had become my boundaries, my battle lines with the world. I began to make a more thorough study of other philosophies and religions. I became more involved in environmentalism and civil rights. I began to earn my blueness in a world that had become increasingly red.

October 2005

13. Faith

John Lane

Tell me about your despair, and I will tell you mine.
Meanwhile, the world goes on.
—Mary Oliver, "Wild Geese"

Last week at my Aunt Libby's funeral I sat halfway back in the Baptist church in the suburbs of Greenville, South Carolina. The pews were hard and dark. It was a tag-team service that went on way too long. I brooded while the two preachers talked off and on for an hour about how my aunt was waiting for us in heaven, up there somewhere just above the sanctuary's sheet rock ceiling. Both men took their Bibles seriously, reading from them, quoting them, holding them aloft like shields or antenna whenever the spirit moved. They were bony men with thin wrists and practical black suits and hair trained back from their foreheads. They wore dark lace-up shoes creased by making the rounds of the sick and dying. I looked up at them as they prayed the opening prayer and thought I'd landed in the presence of Flannery O'Connor's *Wise Blood* preacher Hazel Motes, or the tall wiry coal town preacher with the neck like a turkey in John Sayles's movie *Matewan.*

"No one here voted for John Kerry in the last election," my wife, Betsy, said as the prayer ended and we scanned the choir and the pews in front of us. "No one but us."

I chuckled and thought for a moment about what it really meant that two far-left liberals were marooned for an afternoon deep in what we perceived as the soundless void of South Carolina's religious conservatism. Politics and religion were coming together in a strange way for me there at the funeral, as they seem to be in the whole country. To balance our karma we'd already decided we'd pass on Aunt Libby's graveside service and get back to Spartanburg for a vegetarian picnic put on by a youthful group of anarchists, Southern hip-hop revolutionaries, and local artists. Our political, intellectual, and social values definitely placed us on another planet than those surrounding us at my aunt's funeral. As the service began I took some comfort in our status as blue state secularists among waves of red state believers. Or so it looked.

But the class and social order surrounding me in the Baptist church was my origin, my home ground. I grew up among these people in the red hills of South Carolina. Though I voted for him, I was no John Kerry blue blood. I still talked like most of those around me in the church, enjoyed many of the same foods in spite of an occasional meatless meal, honed a sharp sense of humor based on making fun of the rich and powerful. As the organ prelude played I tried to leave the easy clichés behind—red/blue, liberal/conservative, believer/infidel. I tried to think instead about the common sadness of my aunt's recent death, the grief still present from my mother's death the year before, and a colleague's death a few months before that. Weddings and funerals are really the only occasions I go to church now, and in a little over a year three unexpected deaths had created an uncomfortably long string to reflect on as the first Baptist hymn began to wash over us.

My mother's funeral service had been held at the graveside, so I'd actually avoided a sanctuary. My mother grew up poor, conservative, and Southern, so she had invited the preachers in when her final decline began, even though it was clear to them she felt she was right with her God and didn't need them. When my mother died we kept her service low-key, honoring her wishes. My relatives were not happy when we passed on the church service, the long, black limos (what my Aunt Libby called "a family car") from the mortuary. My uncle's Free Will Baptist preacher, selected from the rabble of holy men clustered around my dying churchless mother, had honored our wishes and kept the service as close to nondenominational as he could. He'd even joked that "Mary Ellen," my mother, often reflected on how she'd been sprinkled once and Baptized twice and none of them took. Her sense of humor held until the end, holding off even the power of family and organized religion to make her into one of their believers.

My English department colleague had died the July before my mother, after slamming his Mercedes into a water oak at the South Carolina gated beach resort where he lived during the summer. Like me, John had grown up in Spartanburg and returned to teach college at his alma mater. At fifty he was our Mr. Chips, beloved by the students and faculty, a gifted teacher of Shakespeare and tireless committee worker. We were from different sides of the tracks though. My childhood church was in an outlying mill village with a prominent member who was South Carolina's Grand Dragon of the KKK. John, on the other hand, was a communicant of the Episcopal church downtown, and six or seven generations of his family were buried in the cemetery outside the church's front door. As a lay-reader John intoned the scripture beautifully to Spartanburg's gathered elite. He always seemed at home and committed in his conventional upper-class faith and the weekly rituals needed to maintain it.

The scene at John's funeral was quite different from my mother's and light years from that of Aunt Libby. In the pew in front of us a former lover gripped John's copy of James Joyce's *Ulysses* to her chest and rocked back and forth in grief so deep we thought she was going to implode. After the ancient rituals from the *Book of Common Prayer*, John's daughter read a passage from Shakespeare that he had told several people he wanted spoken at his funeral. Standing around in front of the church after the service, one of my English colleagues had pointed out that the young woman had edited out two or three lines. Had she done it on purpose or dropped them out of grief? A spirited discussion worthy of a graduate seminar ensued about the meaning of the passage with no consensus, causing several of us to miss the internment. We all agreed John would have approved and given us a high grade for "class participation" in the funeral.

Obviously if all these memories were roaring through my mind, I was not really listening to what Aunt Libby's Baptist preachers preached as I had to the Shakespeare at John's funeral, though I did catch how in alternating fashion they talked of her biblically based faith in Christ and their assurance that Aunt Libby sat, even now, as the Bible promised, somewhere above us and smiled down, free of the cancer and suffering that had taken her away at sixty-three.

I was unrepentantly, though deeply, moved when the choir broke into "The Old Rugged Cross," but when the preacher to the left of the podium stood up once again and suggested Aunt Libby had taken her seat in the heavenly choir, trading her weekly seat in the real choir behind the pulpit for one above, I lost interest. Then the preacher on the right stood up and put the nail in my theological coffin when he added some rote scrap of scripture, and assured us all that if we wanted to see Libby again we needed to get right with Christ. "Knowing Jesus," the preacher said, "is God's requirement to enter the gates of His Heaven."

"Gates? It sounds like heaven is some sort of country club," Betsy said, as we stood for another prayer.

Fifty years ago when I was born, everyone in my mother's South Carolina family would have been a Democrat. Now I'm the only Democrat and they're all Republicans. What happened? What changed in those five decades? When I parted ways with my mother's family this was one of the issues that had driven my departure. Those same political and social differences with Mama's relatives kept me away from them during the last year of Libby's life. They put faith in things I didn't understand or trust—the Bible, what they called "family values." Conscious of it or not, a generation or two before this one they had also placed their faith in a fragile economic life based on wealthy people exploiting poor people. In my eyes this faith had eaten my family alive for three generations before most of us crawled out of mill work and marginal farming into the lower stories of the crumbling middle-class.

The year of my Mama's death was the year of George Bush's reelection, and Betsy and I felt under siege everywhere we went in Spartanburg and Greenville, I-85 corridor communities where a 30/70 split between Democrats and Republicans makes a liberal political life begin to feel marginal. John had died in July of '04 and my mother fell in August and died at the end of September. In early November we stood in line for two hours at our local precinct to cast our vote for John Kerry and the values we perceived he might support in his private most liberal moments—we were "green" (environment over business), anti-war, pro-choice believers in evolution and equal rights for people of all sexual persuasions.

The line of registered voters snaked through the church parking lot all day and the large turnout, even in South Carolina, made us hopeful that our side would win, even in the South. Next day's results showed us the split in our precinct had been even higher than the up-state average, and I slinked back home from work that evening, sick with grief—at John's death, at Mama's death, and the loss of openness and love, at the complete collapse of the dream of removing George Bush from office and replacing him with a liberal.

I had been close to all nine of my Mama's brothers and sisters in childhood, but the year before, in the months leading up to mother's death, we had clashed over Kerry's campaign, over religion, over social issues. It had been silly, the sort of thing grief and suffering should put aside but often doesn't. When it became obvious my mother was dying—bedridden in a nursing home, fighting for breath, on dialysis—my aunts and uncles all set about to make sure Mama's soul was saved. Soon after she fell and we realized it was serious, a steady troupe of Baptist preachers of multiple flavors began to hover outside the ICU.

As my mother lay dying last October I fought my own ill-advised war against her family's fundamentalism. Any time issues arose I voiced a contrary opinion. My mother would not have wanted it that way. Her faith was not easily explained either, though she seemed more comfortable with these preachers than I was.

One morning I arrived at the family waiting area to find a Free Will preacher from my uncle's church reading the local paper. The governor of Rhode Island had just been caught in a homosexual tryst with one his aides. The preacher's face was beet red. He held the paper out at arms length and a deep steady rumble worked its way out— "Aaaaabomination! Abomination!" he said over and over, bouncing like a teakettle.

When Mama moved to the nursing home the preachers continued to visit almost every day. As death finally approached, Mama still didn't seem to mind. She liked the company. My Aunt Libby was concerned that her Southern Baptist preacher, one of the men who preached Libby's funeral a little more than a year later, had not had a chance to pry into Mama's faith.

I was standing in the hall the day before my mother died and Aunt Libby was particularly concerned that her brother's Free Will preacher had been in again. Libby came out and began talking to her brother, sighed and said, "Well, I guess there's room in heaven for both Free Will Baptists and Southern Baptists." She paused for a moment of reflection and said, "There might even be some Jews up there."

I was furious and stood, crossed the narrow hall of the nursing home, and said, "Libby, I'm a Buddhist. Will there be any room in your heaven for me?" She began to witness to me on the spot, cycling through her questions, "Do you believe in Jesus Christ, God's only son?"

"No."

"Do you believe He is the Way, the Truth, and the Light?"

"No," I said again.

Betsy pulled me back to sit beside her. My aunt, crying, disappeared into my Mama's room. I sat there brooding in the awkward silence in the hall as my other uncles and aunts tried to ignore what had just happened.

After a while Betsy touched my arm, said, "You can't let your religious differences with your aunt keep you out of your dying mother's room," so I went inside to join Libby and my sister beside the bed. After a few minutes Libby touched my arm softly. "Johnny, you aren't really a Buddha are you?"

"No, Aunt Libby, I'm not a Buddha," I said, holding her hand, and it seemed to settle things for the moment.

In the following year I drove the thirty miles from Spartanburg to Greenville once with my sister to see my mother's youngest surviving sister soon after she entered the hospital. Lung cancer had been diagnosed. Libby was a nonsmoker and it was a surprise to all, the way the cancer attacked and took her in a few months' time after Mama was gone.

As we drove over I decided to put aside our differences. It proved to be a pleasant enough visit. Libby had lost a great deal of weight and she complained of not being able to swallow. She struggled to eat a helping of mashed potatoes while we stood in the room. On the way back to Spartanburg my sister was more talkative than usual. You could tell Libby was on her mind. She said she had been thinking a lot about heaven now that Mama was dead and Libby was dying. Sandy and Libby were close to the same age, and I'm sure that had a great deal to do with it. My sister didn't usually talk about spiritual things. Like me, she'd never really been a churchgoer. "Do you ever worry about whether you are going to heaven?" my sister asked.

"I don't believe in heaven," I said. "I worry instead about how much suffering there will be in the end. That's what I think about. I don't want to go like Libby and Mama, though I know there is a chance I will."

It's obvious I have little of what my mother's family and many of my friends in the South would call religious faith. Unlike my dead colleague John, I have found no way to balance orthodox religion and the life of the mind and body. There is no church membership that pulls me out of the house every Sunday morning, no Bible study, no rote memory of hymns from a happy Protestant childhood of Sunday school and prayer meetings. Though I grew up Methodist, little of the ritual and community rhetoric of Wesley's church motivates me. When I wake up Sunday morning I never feel I should be somewhere else rather than where I am, sitting on our screened porch or in front of the fire in our living room, worshiping at what my wife in jest calls "The church of the Sunday *New York Times.*"

My loss of traditional faith did not happen slowly. I first lost interest in the church when I went off to college. There I discovered that I liked the things my mother's Free Will Baptist brothers and sisters called sin—sex out of wedlock, beer and whiskey, the theory of evolution, and the sharp intellectual landscape of '60s liberalism still hanging above the horizon when I was twenty in 1974. Old-time religion, as defined by Southern Protestants, fell off like a glacier calving. In the thirty years since my college years there's been a slow, steady erosion of anything still connected to organized churches. Though I no longer practice sex as a sin and my drinking is confined to a Friday afternoon beer with friends, the rules of organized faith hold only unconscious sway with me as a value or moral system. Church is still a drag, as it was on my adolescent soul.

Not being a businessman, I did not need the church for networks of customers. Being a faculty member at a small college, I have been surrounded for decades by a community of like-minded souls. Having married in my late forties into Betsy's ready-made family of us and two grown boys with values already formed, there was no reason for church membership to assure what Christians call "family values."

Now approaching fifty I have ascended into a comfortable college educated skepticism in spite of the age of faith creeping around me like kudzu in the Bush South. I'd have to say my faith, if someone needed to be convinced for some reason that I have one, is in a force that is bigger than the human but has no human attributes. This force includes the human drama in its universal process, but this force is no more concerned with our small story than with the parade of fire ants through the vacant field at the corner of our lot. My faith's in a force close to evolution. It's not a joke like George Lucas's force in *Star Wars*, but I'd be the first to admit that faith, as I know it, has more in common with Yoda's *Star Wars* force than it does with anything in the *Left Behind* series.

I wasn't lying when I told my Aunt Libby I'm a Buddhist, so I'd have to add that my faith is in the Buddhist principles as well. For a Zen Buddhist practice is belief. Though not a very good one, I have been a Zen Buddhist for thirty years and I've come closer to religious practice as a Buddhist (paying attention, cultivating each moment) than as any other person of faith. I sat cross-legged and compulsively for several years, read *Zen Bones, Zen Mind* three or four times, and even explored the Buddhist scriptures. Twenty years ago I took part in several meditation retreats. But like my mother's baptisms, it just didn't "take." I drifted away, back-slid to Sunday morning papers instead of meditation cushions and mantras.

What would those tag-team preachers think, finishing off Aunt Libby's service so the interment could proceed? I realize, as I watch the Baptist preachers proceed, that it's not that I don't have a faith, it's that I have a mongrel faith, part Methodism, part Buddhist, part Charles Darwin. They would not be impressed. They'd say I don't know Christ, or seem to have much interest in meeting him. I certainly do not praise the Lord if that Lord exclusively blesses those who vote for George Bush. I'm more likely to put a bumper sticker on my truck that says, "My boss is a bodhisattva" than "My boss is a Jewish carpenter."

When the service was over we made our way slowly to the back of the sanctuary and quickly exited to the parking lot, avoiding the tears and the family members loading into three long black limos for the drive to the nearby cemetery. The pallbearers had loaded Aunt Libby's silver casket into the hearse and shut the door on her life, a life I'd witnessed in part. When I was a child she'd loved me and I'd loved her back. As adults we each loved as much as our own conscious and unconscious prejudices would allow. We'd been unlucky in the year since Mama's death and never really spoke again about our separate faiths and how they sustained us, and now the opportunity had passed. Libby and the preachers would say there was nowhere left but heaven.

We crept past Aunt Libby's limos full of my relatives, my Southern kin, nursing their communal grief in the dark space behind the tinted windows. As we drove past my aunt's idling funeral procession I felt an unexpected pang of guilt. I looked out the sunroof at that cloudless blue sky and thought of Flannery O'Connor again and the fallen South she'd so accurately imagined in the 1950s and 1960s through vivid characters like Hazel Motes and the Misfit in "A Good Man is Hard to Find." I thought of the Misfit's famous statement after he's shot the grandmother dead—"She would of been a good woman if it had been somebody there to shoot her every minute of her life."

I felt like I'd been shot dead three times in one year. Of course, all these deaths made me think of my own mortality. It also made me realize how similar we all are—fragile, human, puny—and how little the political and social issues really matter at the very end. No matter how painful, these three deaths made me better, made me hang onto every detail of life rushing past. I wondered if there was any chance

Libby and the preachers had been right? Was I simply a backsliding Christian like my aunt had always assumed? Is faith as wide and deep as the sea itself? Is there a heaven, and if so, could there be room in that heaven for all faiths, even the Jews? Could that paradise actually be big enough to hold Flannery O'Connor, Billy Graham, the Baptists, the vegans, the gay governors, the Earth First supporters, the anti-war activists, and bless his heart, even George Bush?

It was a half-hour back to Spartanburg, and as we sped down the interstate Betsy listened to me reflect back on the afternoon. She pointed out that Libby had only been a member of the church where the funeral had been held for a year. Libby was completing her search for a new "church home" during the month her beloved sister had died. It had been a tough time for everybody. Maybe the church Libby had joined was more liberal than the one she had left, and so that moment in the hallway when Libby admitted Jews to the kingdom, a moment I had perceived as prejudiced and mean, may have been a moment of vast spiritual growth for her. "Libby was a searcher like you and your mother," Betsy said. "She'd come a long way, as you have, from the faith of her childhood."

Driving home, I felt a deep comfort I haven't confirmed in years. To those we left back at the church I am the lost sheep in the biblical parable, and they are still my family, my flock. The metaphors of childhood Bible training in the Methodist Church still creep back from the shadows during those moments of crisis and joy. There was nothing in my neglected Zen training, my New Age philosophy, my "Green" consciousness that was quite as comforting as that lost sheep resurfacing. It settled something within me and allowed me to let go, though the answers are still elusive.

14. How to Ruin a Perfectly Good Swamp in South Carolina

Gilbert Allen

1. The Interview (February 1977)

The air is bright and windless. In the shade, the temperature hovers in the mid-fifties. But here, in the campus parking lot, in the sunlight behind the magnolia trees, I can imagine it's summer. To me, this is truly amazing.

Before today, I'd been south of the Mason-Dixon line only once—on a brief trip to Washington DC. When I left upstate New York yesterday, it was snowing. When I return tomorrow, it will still be snowing.

I've just turned twenty-six, and I successfully defended my doctoral dissertation (on the poets of World War I) two months ago. I'm headed for a meeting with a half-dozen of the college's brightest English majors. (One of them will eventually become a celebrated novelist; another a prominent eighteenth-century scholar and college administrator.) All are lively and respectful, interested in my thoughts on Wilfred Owen and Edward Thomas, and even curious about my own poems. They call me Doctor, as if I had the power to heal the sick.

I've just had conversations with the English department faculty. Everyone seems to like me, and everyone seems to like each other. To me, this is beyond amazing. This is miraculous. I have come from a university where people routinely turn around in a corridor and walk away, leaving those present to wonder whose face was responsible for the scowling change in direction.

This, I think, *is a better place to be.*

Late that afternoon, I return to the office of the department chair. He looks and sounds like Faulkner's Colonel Sartoris auditioning to play Shakespeare's Henry V. But beneath his theatrical bearing is authentic hospitality. He, a full professor, will personally chauffeur me to the airport at 6:00 a.m. the following morning! Without either of us knowing it, we will drive, in darkness, past the empty house that will become my home.

But first, before this day is over, he must take me to the Administration Building, to meet the Man in Charge. As we walk, he opens fire doors for me, as if we were out on a date. "You might hear some questions that sound—strange," he says, stopping before the final door. "Just answer them honestly, and be yourself." He sounds as if he already knows what that self is. He is destined to become a dean, and (despite our more-than-occasional differences about university governance) a lifelong friend. He points to the office of the Man in Charge and says, "I'll wait outside."

The Man in Charge looks as if he'd been born in this dark, wood-paneled room. Indeed, he has been at the college for over three decades. He asks me what I think of the local weather (splendid, I say), and nods when I mention my wife's passion for gardening. After a few casual questions about my literary interests, he asks me where I go to church, and whether I have a personal relationship with Jesus Christ.

Even in 1977, these last two questions seem more than strange. If I hadn't been forewarned, God knows how I would have responded. What I say is this. "I don't attend church regularly. But I consider myself a Christian. I can't imagine my personal or my professional life outside of the Christian tradition."

The Man in Charge seems to be reading something—it could be my letter of application, my references, or my curriculum vita. Or it could be his church newsletter. He nods, without looking up. "I see," he says.

I already know that the Man in Charge has only recently abandoned his practice of walking around campus, telling men not much younger than myself to tuck their shirttails inside their trousers. What is he thinking? Perhaps that in a benighted decade—a decade in which even the president of the United States admits that he has committed adultery in his own heart—some bland, blond Yankee might be the best thing lurking at the bottom of the barrel.

Months later, after I've moved to South Carolina, the Man in Charge will host a luncheon for first-year professors, from all departments. He will tell a long, rambling story—about a former member of the faculty who mowed his lawn on Sundays. About the telephone of the Man in Charge, which never stopped its indignant ringing on the Sabbath. "Now, I'm not telling you when to mow your lawn," he will smile. It will be the first time I encounter such a smile. A smile worn by Southerners who stop to help a person—occasionally, a black person—change a flat tire. A smile worn by Southerners who direct an unwanted person— usually, a black person—to a doorless alley behind a building when he asks where the rest room is. For years, I will think I'm seeing two different smiles, and my own two eyes just can't tell the difference. And then, I will discover what makes the South the South: those two smiles live on the same faces, often on the same day.

No, the Man in Charge doesn't forbid anything. But his message is clear: wherever you go, people are watching you, and they see where you work. They know what is in your heart. And if they don't like what they see there, you'll upset them—and they'll upset the Man in Charge. There are things in South Carolina more important than your grass.

2. Nothing Could Be Finer (July 1977)

It's still dark, early morning. In our new-to-us house, all windows are open, to no avail. I can't tell if yesterday's heat is still radiating from our minimally insulated attic, or if even warmer weather is on the way. Our air conditioning is broken, neither my wife nor I will receive a first paycheck for two months, and we've decided we need to spend our savings on more important things than refrigerated air—things like cat food and our monthly mortgage.

Directly across the street from our bedroom window lies a sunken swamp: forest, with dense undergrowth, honeysuckle and blackberries and cattails, and some huge trees—mostly poplars and sweetgums, although I don't yet know their names. They muffle most of the ordinary traffic noise from the highway, so what remains is indistinguishable from running water, or from a light breeze through the lofty leaves.

The overpass bridge, however, is banked the wrong way—slanting down, to the widest point of the arc. The engineer, we joke, must have been Jesus's brother. A month ago, my wife and I woke up to an enormous crash. I thought something had run into the house. (When I was eleven years old, living on Long Island, a car full of drunken teenagers actually *did* drive their car into my family's dining room, claiming that they thought it was the entrance to Southern State Parkway. They collapsed part of the foundation, rupturing the oil tank in the basement, but our family was watching *Ben Casey* in the living room at the time. No one outside the car was hurt, and no one inside the car was killed.)

Fifteen years later, I checked the perimeter of my own house, I saw no damage, and I went back to sleep. When my wife and I drove to the supermarket that morning, we beheld a flatbed truck perched on the guardrail of the overpass, its load of logs spilled to the highway below. A man in a baseball cap—the driver of the truck, most likely—was standing with a state trooper, leaning first one way, then the other, making gestures with his hands, as if he were unsuccessfully trying to keep his balance. The cop kept nodding, up and down, smiling his Southern smile.

Cacophonies just before dawn have become commonplace. Overloaded out-of-state truckers, unfamiliar with the road, can't make the turn and get hung up on the guardrail. A formidable guardrail. Only one truck has actually plummeted to the pavement below the overpass.

My wife is a sound sleeper, but even she sometimes stirs at the squeal of desperate air brakes, followed by an eighteen-wheeler scraping to a nine-wheeled stop against the rail. "Don't worry," I whisper. "It's just a truck falling."

3. School Days (August 1977)

My wife is an elementary-school teacher, with four years' experience, a master's degree, and lifetime certification in the state of New York.

Before she is eligible to teach in South Carolina, however, she must successfully complete the National Teacher's Exam.

I drive her to the downtown high school where the exam will be administered. When I return to pick her up, six hours later, she's drenched with sweat and fury. It seems that only the school's library is air-conditioned, and the library was large enough to hold only surnames L–Z. So A–K were sent to the sweltering cafeteria. I almost tell her she should have stayed a Szigeti when we married three years ago.

"No wonder this state scores dead last in everything," she says on the way home. Her brain feels like steamed cauliflower. She didn't even think while she answered most of the questions, and she's convinced she failed the exam—although no one at the test site seemed to know what a failing score (or a passing score) would be.

Weeks later, when she receives the results by mail, she's amazed: ninety-ninth percentiles, across the board. "My God," she says. "If cauliflower's as good as it gets, this place is in trouble." (In the meantime, cauliflower has become a family joke.) She interviews for several positions, and takes the one at the elementary school just a mile from the college. We'll be sharing a car, a Ford Fiesta, and we'll be able to drive to our separate jobs, together, in ten minutes.

Around here, public school starts in late August. A week before the beginning of classes, we visit her new room, together. When we open the door, she nearly cries. Of course, there is no air conditioning. We knew that. But the paint is mildewed and peeling, the rickety small desks look like the leftovers from a slumlord's yard sale, and the window sashes have cracks that let in as much light as the glass does. She opens her own desk. Only two things are in it: a piece of chalk and a paddle.

The chalk is white and normal. The paddle is not. I pick it up and study it carefully. Its heft surprises me. Actually, it is made from *two* paddles, taken from those kids' toys with the red rubber ball attached by an elastic cord. Her predecessor cut off the cords, glued the two identical pieces of wood together, and neatly drilled six holes into the flat surface—to decrease wind resistance without diminishing structural integrity. The center seam is still holding fast. Her predecessor clearly took a lot of care to make it, and to leave it behind.

In the coming months, my wife will never use the paddle for its intended purpose—although she will wave it around, on occasion, for purely rhetorical effect. Instead, she will come home each afternoon, peel off her damp clothes, stride naked into the shower stall, and scream—loud and long.

She thinks we've landed in hell. "It used to be better," her one African American colleague smiles. "Before integration." Her principal insists that if she takes her students on a field trip, or if she uses the bathroom during the school day, she will be personally responsible for The Consequences. "It's your class." He bares his Southern teeth. "Don't expect me to protect you."

4. Rezoning Hearing (1)

The overpass near our house is being redesigned, and the wetlands across the street will provide the space necessary for the new configuration. The county will be condemning most of the land, designated "residential" in 1974 when county zoning began.

The project itself is a done deal. We and our neighbors know that. And, despite our mailing addresses, we live *near* this tiny city, not *in* it. Officially, we're in "an unincorporated section of the county." But we're all here, at a city council meeting, to witness a landowner's application for rezoning. He wants his land designated for "Commercial" use, and he will agree to be annexed into the tiny city (and to pay the tiny city's tiny taxes)—*if* the city agrees to the zoning change.

The city's fathers study the highway department's maps, and they discover that only a small portion of the land would remain after the highway reconstruction. The main effect of the rezoning would be to raise the owner's compensation for the condemned land by at least a factor of ten.

The city fathers deliberate, long and hard. Money is at stake. Finally, they deny the request, saying the windfall to the city would be small, and the cost to the county would be large. City residents, they add, still pay county taxes.

The landowner is angry. Before the highway department officially condemns the land, he clears it himself, harvesting all the big trees. It aches our hearts to see them go, but we realize they would have been bulldozed anyway, to make room for the new overpass system necessary for the safety of residents and travelers alike. But the almost-five-acre patch directly across from our house will *not* be condemned, and, for this small blessing, we breathe in relief.

Then, the owner starts cutting these trees, too—beginning from the soon-to-be-highway and working steadily back, toward our house. My wife is distraught. She hand-letters a sign on a sheet of the oaktag she's bought, with her own money, to construct posters for her classroom. She Magic-Markers SAVE ME in block letters, and she ropes the sign around the biggest tree—a poplar that must be four feet in diameter and sixty feet high.

For two days, the loggers cut around it. Then, on the third day, when we come home from our teaching, the tree is gone. The loggers have left only a half-dozen saplings behind, too small to have any commercial value. The rest of the land is a broad, sunken red-clay ruin, with an open ditch leading to the river.

Soon, with the owner's blessing, the highway department dumps the blast-shattered concrete from the old bridge into the basin. Word spreads throughout the county, and beyond. A new landfill! If the highway department does it, then it must be okay! Refrigerators, stoves, dishwashers, dining-room furniture, old rafters, and brush too wet to burn raise the site from a steep, marshy pit to a gradual depression. While the new four-lane is being built, there's too much red clay around the roadbed. So the surplus gets steam-shoveled into the pit, and bulldozed over. Still, household appliances stick up from the mud, here and there, like post-apocalyptic weeds. We complain to The Authorities. Eventually, somebody plucks them out.

We plant trees in our front yard, to hide ourselves as best we can.

5. Rezoning Hearing (2)

Fifteen years later, the landowner (the same landowner) applies for rezoning, again—this time for an "industrial" designation on the almost-five-acres remaining from the highway project. The county planning commission turns down his request. He is undaunted. The county council turns down his request. He is undaunted still. He announces his intention to apply for annexation to the still-tiny city, contingent upon the rezoning of the property. The city's own planning commission turns down his request. He still applies to the city council, and there is public hearing on the issue. The landowner announces that he already has a buyer—a local machine shop seeking a new, larger facility.

During recent years, our neighborhood has become surprisingly diverse. Right behind us, in the old house built by the couple who once owned this whole side of the mountain, live a retired Navy nurse and her Buddhist husband. (They met while she was stationed in Florida. A native of South Carolina, she ran away after high school, but quietly returned to her home town after she'd put in her twenty years elsewhere. Her parents still live in the house she grew up in, about five miles away.) Across the street is a local contractor who bought his land from the man petitioning for the rezoning. (The landowner had promised at the time that the adjacent land was, and would always remain, residentially zoned.) Down the street, we have a retired Jewish pediatrician and his wife, both from New Orleans, who came here to escape hurricanes and oil refineries. And north of our own woods, in the neighborhood's largest and most elaborate house, live the director of the school district's science center and his wife—a painter who teaches at a nearby high school.

A few days before the public meeting, we all gather in our living room to get organized. Only five people can formally object to the proposed rezoning request, and each can speak for a maximum of five minutes. Our contractor-neighbor will speak of promises made and promises broken; our Buddhist will speak about the hazards that an industrial site would pose for area children who play and who wait for their school buses nearby; our pediatrician will speak of restricted access for ambulances and fire engines on narrow, truck-clogged streets; I will talk about the visual prominence of the property, and explain how an active industrial site would diminish the quality of life for residents and passersby alike; my wife, a frequent admonitory presence at public meetings for the past two decades, will outline the land's recent environmental history, first as a wetland, then as a dumping site that was bulldozed flat and covered with a thin layer of soil—to remind the city council, and the prospective buyer, of the springs and quicksand under the deceptively firm-looking turf. While a bulldozer was moving red clay there during the highway project, it got stuck so deep that it had to be towed to safety. Then, from the audience, Georgia, the painter, will spontaneously explain why she and her husband moved to the area, and why the machine shop would turn it into a place where they might no longer want to live.

One hundred and fifty-four local residents come to the meeting, to oppose the rezoning. We're all on time—except for our resident Buddhist, who blunders into the meeting ten minutes late, and ends up speaking third instead of second. The rest of us perform on cue. At the end of her planned outburst, Georgia, the painter, impulsively adds: "This land would be perfect for a park!"

The landowner, his real estate agent, and the prospective buyer speak in favor of the proposed zoning change. The buyer explains, rather uneasily, that he is an honest man, that he wants to be a good neighbor, and that his business will be an asset to the community. He swivels his head to smile, in our direction. He will construct a high-quality all-metal structure, fence his property, and plant shrubbery to screen loading docks, which will face our neighborhood. I suspect he *is* an honest man, and that he intends to keep his word. Yet I want to stand up and shout, *You can't screen it! Drive on the road! Or check a topographical map—the neighborhood looks down on it! The trees would have to be a hundred feet high!*

But I've already had my say. The city council votes to annex and to rezone the land. That decision, however, won't be final until the second reading, in two weeks' time. The property owner and his real estate agent look happy. The prospective buyer, however, stands apart from them, and he looks a bit worried. His wife is in tears.

There is no second reading. The would-be buyer asks an independent firm to take a core sample on the northwestern corner of the property, where he plans to locate his main building. As the sample rises, the truck starts sinking into the turf. My wife and I watch, in dark amusement, from our living-room window. This could be an outtake from a bad science-fiction movie: *The Revenge of the Merdes.*

The driver barely manages to get his vehicle back onto the service road. When the buyer withdraws his offer, the owner withdraws his rezoning request—he doesn't want to pay city taxes on land that he won't be selling anytime soon. A sign appears on the door of city hall: *Zoning Meeting Canceled.* The realtor—not smiling—tells my wife that she cost him his commission. All of the nearly-in-the-city-residents applaud, in the city hall parking lot.

But our happiness is brief. Within a few weeks, stobs and pink plastic tape carve up the property. The owner has hired a surveyor to mark out eighteen plots, with shared driveways, for double-wide trailers. We check with the county planning commission: current regulations don't distinguish between double-wide trailers and houses. No zoning change or city annexation would be necessary. The owner is perfectly within his legal rights.

I call the landowner, and I ask him to consider donating the property to the county for use as a public park. (Law prohibits the county recreation district from using tax revenues to acquire land.) I mention the considerable IRS advantages of such a donation. He tells me that he's still willing to sell the land for the same price he'd have gotten from the man with the machine shop. I can hear his smile through the telephone wires.

My wife decides it's time for another neighborhood meeting.

6. The Document (August 1996)

POINSETT PARK PROJECT

Background

The Pine Forest Drive community lies at the foot of Paris Mountain, just south of the city of ——. Since the highway redesign in the 1980s, many residents have been concerned about a 4.559 acre tract along both the totally residential Pine Forest Drive and the frontage road. The land is very prominent; its appearance greatly affects the character of the highway, Paris Mountain, and the surrounding neighborhood. Two tributaries from the northwest Paris Mountain watershed pass through it. This water then travels under highways 25/276 before winding through parts of the Green Valley Golf Course and joining the Reedy River.

In November 1995, 154 area residents opposed the rezoning of this property from residential (R-12) to industrial. The land remains residentially zoned, adjacent to the city of ———. The Pine Forest Drive community presently has no recreational areas. Since the zoning hearings in 1995, many residents have come to the conclusion that a park would be an ideal use of the land.

Goals

In August 1996, The Poinsett Park Project was formed by concerned residents and friends of the Pine Forest Drive community. Our goal is to raise $110,000 (plus incidental expenses) to acquire the 4.559 acre tract. The Friends of the Reedy River, a local 501(c)(3) nonprofit organization, has agreed to set up a special Poinsett Park Project fund to accept donations for this purchase. The Friends of the Reedy River has also agreed to be our agent in purchasing the property. During our option period to buy the property, we will have a limited amount of time to raise this money through donations from private individuals, businesses, and other interested parties. Once the property has been acquired, it will be presented as a land gift to the County Recreation District, which enthusiastically supports developing it as a Greenspace/Neighborhood Park. Any monies raised in excess of acquisition costs will be used to establish a restricted fund with the County Recreation District for the development of this park.

7. How to Spend Two Years of Your Life

Donate $1,000.00 of your own money. Then donate $1,000.00 more.

Send thousands of letters to foundations and to prospective donors. Persuade hundreds of them to contribute anywhere from $1 to $30,000 to the project.

Write weekly newspaper articles for your local papers. Persuade your husband to duplicate their typefaces on his computer, to provide them with camera-ready copy that's too easy a space-filler to pass up—even if their editors think you're crazy.

Walk door to door, visiting every local business. Spend a sweltering hour at a driving range, explaining the project to the owner. Watch him give you his Southern smile while he says, "Everybody at Hardee's reads about you and your project and laughs. I sit with them at breakfast every day. But I tell them I can't laugh, even if I want to—because that woman's a member of my church."

Get the Local TV News Heartthrob to walk the property with you. Bask in her thousand-watt smile. Make sure her cameraman films those cute little fish in the stream. (People feel better about parting with money when they see fish. That's why so many doctors and dentists have aquariums in their waiting rooms.)

Meet frequently with the director of the county recreation district. He's as frustrated as you are by the prohibition against using tax revenues to acquire land for new parks. To help buy the land, he decides to allocate money from skate rentals and swimming-pool admissions—before he retires, beyond the reach of official reprimands and reprisals.

Visit the bank where you've done business for twenty years. Sit down with the president (a father of twins, a member of your church) and explain your project in painstaking detail. Provide donor lists, letters of support from United States Senators, and a young architect's dazzling (donated) rendition. Then listen to him say that he doesn't see how a public park would help the city of —. After all, people don't need parks. Subdivisions have recreational areas.

Put collection jars in local businesses and restaurants—especially those that serve a high percentage of persons who don't live in subdivisions with recreational areas. Return periodically to collect $1,439.08 in loose change that you and your husband will count, roll, and deposit in a local bank, while the president watches through the glass walls of his office.

After the project has reached its goal, give that same president one more chance to donate. Find the check in the next day's mail, and add his bank to the donor list publicly displayed in the post office.

Pay the landowner $110,000.00, while he smiles at the cashier's check and tells you how much he enjoys performing a service to the community.

Receive a plaque from the city of —, proclaiming you a model citizen. Smile your best Southern smile, while you're thinking that you wished you lived near a model city.

Wait five more years before the county recreation district can find enough money to construct a picnic shelter, a children's playground, a walking trail, and a small parking lot. (In the interim, however, they do mow the grass, though never on Sundays.)

8. Dedication Day: September 20, 2003

At dawn, the hot air is already rising. Half-inflated, an enormous balloon, bearing the logo of a real-estate company, prepares for its initial ascent. A nylon mesh play cage, with its floor already pumped up and bulging, is surrounded by neighborhood children, each eager for the first bounce. Near the entrance to the permanent playground, more kids wait for the yellow ribbon to be cut. Portable gas grills line the new concrete like robotic sidekicks from *Star Wars*, programmed to provide service for the Empire: in this case, free hot dogs.

An open-sided tent overarches five rows of metal folding chairs and a podium. Most of the chairs remain empty while children play and adults talk with their mouths full, beyond earshot. Politicians speak words that no one remembers. There is polite applause. My wife receives special thanks for her community service. There is more applause, somewhat louder.

Morning turns into afternoon. The balloon is long gone, but the kids are still playing. The local politicians gather in the high-impact plastic tree house, at the very top of the slide, ready to send down the First Official Child. November, after all, is not so far away. They catch the eye of the photographer from a local paper—a young man who grew up nearby, in a parkless community. He snaps the shutter. When the photo appears the following Wednesday, the politicians are nowhere to be seen. In the cropped version, only the child remains—in gleeful descent, toward my wife. PARK OPENS.

9. Even a Ruined Swamp Has a Moral

Acre for acre, the park is the most-used outdoor recreational facility in the county. Parents can exercise on the walking trail and still keep sight of their young children in the playground. The open field offers opportunities for kites, Frisbees, Wiffleballs, and batty games whose rules only kids could make up, or understand. My wife and I routinely hear the playful, high-pitched squeals from our yard, across the street, as we go about our gardening. The scrub trees left from the first clearing—the ones with no commercial value—have grown big enough to cast usable shade for benches and picnic tables.

In the evening, we often walk in the park ourselves. Because we don't have children, we have come to think of the park as our child—something that wouldn't have existed without our presence, and that will continue in the world after we've left. We might even scatter our own ashes here.

As the sun lowers, we often remark upon how the neighborhood has adopted this space—upon the level of civility that has become the norm here. Whites, blacks, and now Hispanics all visit the park, in roughly equal numbers. To the best of our knowledge, there have been no fights, no crimes, no deliberate rudeness. The park has become a showcase—a model for public development, funded by private support.

We sometimes wonder what the park would have been like in a different world—a world in which a politician who promised to raise taxes could get elected, a world in which local governments perceived and met their citizens' needs, a world in which city councils did more than bestow plaques upon persons who successfully circumvented their apathy. Such a world would have given us two years of our lives, to do other worthwhile things—and would still have promoted responsible land use, for the public good.

And yet, we wouldn't be the same persons. We wouldn't have the same sense of adversity overcome, of neighborhood solidarity, of enduring accomplishment. In all likelihood, we would feel the same way about that hypothetical, struggle-free park as we feel about the asphalt on the street in front of our house—necessary, yes, but not anything we have an attachment to, despite its proximity and despite the fact that our tax dollars helped pay for it.

No, we did things The Red State Way. We watched the remnants of a perfectly good swamp ruined, in the name of Free Enterprise. When what was ruined was about to become even worse, we and our neighbors decided to protect ourselves. We had no local park, and we made one, while our government watched—and, at the end, smiled for the camera.

Hand in hand, we finish today's final lap. As we look over our lengthening shadows, stretching toward our own home, across the street, we never doubt that it was worth it. But we'd never ask anyone else to walk that trail. And we could never walk it again.

15. Rescue the Drowning, Tie Your Shoe-Strings

Sidney Burris

I.

In the spring of 2005, I attended a banquet for a few dozen of our brightest students who'd come to Arkansas on a Sturgis Fellowship, one of our university's most sought-after scholarships. We only award seven to ten of them each year, and so in any semester, we've got about forty articulate, charming, ambitious, intelligent, accomplished, and utterly driven students who call themselves Sturgins and, as far as I can tell, come from all sorts of backgrounds, but mainly and recently from five states: Arkansas, Texas, Oklahoma, Louisiana, and Missouri. Red states, every one of them. Because I chair the committee that selects the winners and direct the honors program that oversees the administration of their fellowships, I attended the banquet. Because our chancellor and our provost are very proud of what these students have accomplished, and are very hopeful about what they will accomplish, they were at the banquet too. When I was an undergraduate, I couldn't have told you the names of my chancellor and provost, but when you've posted the test scores these young people have posted, when you've written as well as they've written, and when you've interviewed with their particular brand of candor and wit, you get to hang out with chancellors and provosts at a very early age.

I turned eighteen in 1971 and voted in my first presidential election in 1972. I supported George McGovern, and so was baptized into electoral politics by a history-making landslide—Nixon claimed over 60 percent of the popular vote. Because I came of age during this period in our nation's history, I assumed that the greater part of politics was protest. I protested the Vietnam War, I protested the destruction of the environment, I even protested my university's financial investments in South Africa when I probably couldn't have told you exactly where South Africa lay except that it was likely in the southern part of Africa. I did use the word "divestiture," though, and I liked using it because it stymied my parents and seemed vaguely philosophical to me, but I haven't used the word since then and can't at this point foresee an occasion when its use would have the punch it once had. That saddens me.

I protested these things partly because I thought the government's behavior both at home and abroad deserved a public show of disrespect from its citizenry, but I also protested these things largely because I couldn't conceive of not protesting them. And I couldn't conceive of not protesting them because all of the people I admired, or wanted to meet, or wanted to be like, were protesting them. No doubt about it, political activity for me was partly ideological, partly social. I'm uncertain about the exact proportion of each—it's probably an unflattering ratio.

In the nine Presidential elections I've voted in, Democrats have won three times. I was living in Vienna during the run-up to Jimmy Carter's first bid for the presidency, and on a trip to Budapest I was held at gunpoint for four hours at the border crossing back into Austria. I had to sit in one of those rooms that littered the American Cold-War imagination in those days—a featureless, dirty green bunker with one window. Standing beside that window, of course, was a guard, a small man whose eyes were pinched together over a precipitous nose. He was chain-smoking and talking into his walkie-talkie to another guard with equally small eyes who was standing at the gate chain-smoking and letting all the other cars pass without incident. It was a scene from early John LeCarré. I caused an incident, apparently, because I was an "American"—I could understand that much—and because I was wearing "bloo sheens," which I figured to be blue jeans. At any rate, I responded to this incident by firing up an ugly nationalism—suddenly, I was hearing tin whistles and seeing tricorn hats and white shirts with balloon sleeves. I was angry. When I returned to America, I voted for Gerald Ford because Carter had stupidly confessed in *Playboy* to having desire in his heart, and I figured he wasn't the man to part the Iron Curtain. By the time Carter ran for reelection, and was defeated by Reagan, I was working on advanced degrees in several arcane subjects, and figured I'd need all the help I could get in this life, and that a muscular military presence in the world wasn't going to give me that help, and so voted Democratic—another losing ticket. Since then I've voted Democratic continuously, and won twice with Bill Clinton. Two out of nine. Twenty-two percent. Those are my numbers.

The older you get, the less likely you are to know instinctively what's on your students' minds. Music, food, clothes, language, technology, even the fundamental assumptions of living—all the coins of the undergraduate realm have long fallen from your pocket and you sometimes feel as if you're at another border crossing as you work your way through a conversation toward some common ground of understanding. I often don't know where my students stand politically because they don't protest anything that I'm aware of, and so I can never be sure what they think about the headline issues of the day.

Because this age gap yearly yawns wider between my students and me, I realize that the older I get, the more they have to tell me about what the world looks like from where they're standing. Once I let them in on this discovery, I began to get regular updates, particularly on the technology and the music that I've missed. One student thought our class should have a Web log and that I should administer it—she sent me the information, I followed the links, and so began my blogging life. Another one thought I should listen to Radiohead, which I did. I don't think I heard their music, or got it, as naturally as I get, for example, Led Zeppelin. That's bothersome to me because it means I can't tune my internal radio to the Radiohead frequency. Millions do; I don't. Which means accordingly that I can't come to a reasoned opinion about the band. So it goes. Yet another student informed me of a site that translates any text you give it into Snoop-speak, and for a while I had a link to our English department's Web site done up in that exotic and childlike language.

After the banquet was over, I was drinking coffee with several of my students when one of them told me about another Web site that I ought to visit. It was called the Facebook (thefacebook.com), and I was told as well that I ought to join because there were some interesting—my student's adjective—discussions going on, even about one of the classes that I and several of the faculty team-teach. So I went to the Web site and joined before I even knew I'd joined—it's that simple. Odd things started happening within the hour. I got a request saying that so-and-so wanted to add me to their "Friends List." Confirm or Deny? I got another request from someone I'd never heard of who wanted my Xbox Live name so we could play Halo 2—I confessed that I didn't even have Xbox Live yet, that I actually liked Halo 1 better than 2, and saying this felt distinctly like a confession. I was gaining access to a community whose expectations I couldn't equal, and I was feeling deficient. I currently have eighteen friends, which compared to my students' numbers is abysmally small, but I also learn from my home page that through these friends, I am "connected to 1,821 people," which means that each of my friends averages over one hundred friends. Many have hundreds more, so their "connected-to" numbers are surely five digits. Maybe there are six-digit networks out there. I don't know.

Of course, the Facebook is a kind of e-dating service, except when it's not, which is a lot of the time. Because its immediate field is confined to the campus, a lot of the students already know each other, take classes together, go to the same parties, belong to the same clubs. So it's partly a chat room among friends. Each member has a "Wall" where others can leave messages—there's a lot of flirting, some boasting, some gossip, but nothing serious. Occasionally, it sounds like the copy you'd find inside the cover of a school yearbook—"Hey man! Laughing at random crap in econ was the only way I made it through that class," exclaims one. But it's the Profile section that got me. When I hit the edit button to create my profile, I had a range of choices: Basic, Contact Info, Personal, Professional, Summer Plans, Mobile, Courses, Picture. Under Personal, I found a drop-down menu entitled "Political Views" that gave me the following choices: Very Liberal, Liberal, Moderate, Conservative, Very Conservative, Apathetic, Libertarian, Other. I decided not to create a profile. I felt as though I were at the Austro-Hungarian border again, and I flinched.

Michael Oakeshott, one of the twentieth century's leading political theorists, once defined politics as "the activity of attending to the general arrangements of a set of people whom chance or choice have brought together." He continued by pointing out that in this very broad sense, "families, clubs, and learned societies have their 'politics.'" And so too does the Facebook. Because I've been having so much trouble figuring out exactly what it's like to be a Democrat in a Republican state—with my success rate of 22 percent in presidential elections, it's like figuring out what it's like to be alive—I decided to ask my students about their own political preferences as listed in the Facebook. I devised a questionnaire and sent it to them. Here are the five questions I asked them:

1. Why list a political preference?

2. What does it mean to you in your day-to-day life to hold the political designation that you profess?

3. If you jumped the fence, and embraced the political orientation opposed to yours, how would your life change?

4. Could you reasonably conceive of a long-term relationship with someone residing in the political camp traditionally said to be opposed to yours?

5. What are the crucial issues, the wedge issues, as they're called, that allow you to claim your political designation?

Joan Didion reminded us years ago that "we tell ourselves stories in order to live. . . . We interpret what we see, select the most workable of the multiple choices." Likewise, we choose our political parties, and they become part of the stories we tell ourselves. I want to summarize the answers I received to each of these questions, and make a few generalizations as I go, hoping to throw into relief the story of my own political life in a red state by excavating those of my students. It might seem, on the face of it, a backward way of doing things, but I was surprised enough by their responses that my own interpretations of what

I see, my own story, seem to me now less certain than it once was. After all, my students are the ones, as Edward Hoagland has written, "who need to face the future with more than curiosity," and maybe that intoxicating mixture of curiosity, anxiety, and drive that stokes their own vision of the coming days would give me a Zen-like whack in the head. And maybe a Zen-like whack in the head would spill some clarity over my own little stretch of ground. There are *always* choices, I reminded myself, current-changing choices, to be made, and it's still the workability of them that ought to concern me. Why this choice and not that one? And what is the nature of the story that drives the choices?

II.

1. WHY LIST A POLITICAL PREFERENCE?

I suppose the reason that Oakeshott's work appeals to me is that he sometimes worries about the relationship between politics and human knowledge, and that's not a worry that gets much press. Newspapers, and the politicians clamoring to get into them, have traditionally wielded their political opinions as if they were baseball bats, and as our technological capabilities have expanded, the bats have become even heftier. I read Oakeshott because he isn't interested in the kinds of knowledge we might use to prepare ourselves to talk politics or to do politics; he wants to know what kinds of things "we unavoidably call upon whenever we are engaged in a political activity." He wants to understand our political instincts.

The difference here is between political knowledge as a formal preparation and political knowledge as a more immediate, personal response. "I chose to define my political views (in the broadest sense)," one student wrote, "because I want, actively, to be identified with a particular mindset." Or, wrote another, "I think it is important for people to know where I stand." And then, with foreboding, still another one warned that "some people chose to list their preferences so people will be warned not to bring up certain issues while talking to them." My students, in Oakeshott's terms, are attending to the general arrangements of a set of a people whom chance or choice have brought together. Of course the Facebook relies on both choice and chance. You choose to join, but then the network hooks you up by chance with those friends of friends that spiral outward like a nebula. The vision to me, in fact, is distinctly astronomical: one star among a crowd of them, flashing its signal, its, to any or all of the others who've got their dishes pointed in the right direction. The politics here, the general arrangements that are being attended to, are distinctly social, and even more distinctly personal.

Most of us play out our daily lives in the local arena—home, office, grocery store—and so it's in the local arena that we field-test our ethics. Yet as I've gotten older, I've cultivated a smoldering anger over the larger ideas that are played out in places many thousands of miles away, far beyond the grocery store: Iraq, Afghanistan, the Balkans, Rwanda. I have seethed, at times, over our country's foreign policy, while paying far less attention to a student of mine, for example, whose boyfriend was mugged, bound, duct-taped, and placed in a dog-cage by his ex-girlfriend. The current girlfriend was naturally undone by these events and on the verge of tears as she told me why she would be absent the next day. There were hospital visits, court stuff, that kind of thing, and I expressed concern, of course, but quickly got back to my seething over Iraq.

Conclusion: I'm becoming suspicious of the entire enterprise of forming political opinions. I'm beginning to believe that a political opinion amounts to a social decision, first of all, a way of joining one club, while declaring non-membership in the others, and it's this latter declaration that seems at times more important.

2. WHAT DOES IT MEAN TO YOU IN YOUR DAY-TO-DAY LIFE TO HOLD THE POLITICAL DESIGNATION THAT YOU PROFESS?

Taking the political pulse of my students has put me in mind of my own student days. I graduated from Duke University in May 1975. A few weeks earlier, South Vietnamese president Duong Van Minh had surrendered unconditionally to the North Vietnamese colonel Bui Tin, and as the few remaining Americans hightailed it out of Saigon, the last two U.S. servicemen to die there were killed when their helicopter crashed. Other things were coming to an end too; the snake's tail, lodged so securely in its mouth, was rolling into view. I noticed that some of the freshmen that year began carrying briefcases to class, cutting their hair, wearing different looks on their faces—they kept schedules, entered stuff in date books, didn't cut across the grass, walked with purpose. The fellow who lived beside me in the dormitory, the son of a retired Navy admiral, had a big boxy computer he used to catalogue his extensive classical music collection. His records filled four long shelves, and I used to go in and ask for something obscure so I could see the fat green numbers and letters pulse across his screen.

"Yes, here it is!" he'd exclaim. "Number 475B, Bach, 'Three Partitas for Viola.' How long will you be needing it?"

His sense of order and regimen was partly inherited from his father, but it was partly a political choice, the outer signs of an inner conservatism still struggling to find its public costume. A few years earlier, military sons like him would've revolted against their fathers and poked flowers into gun barrels. But no one in those days knew what conservative students looked like: what they wore, how they wore their hair, what music they listened to, what they ate, and so I see now in this young man—I didn't see it then—a real sense of frontiersmanship. It wouldn't be too long before *Family Ties* would air on NBC, with Michael J. Fox playing Alex P. Keaton and reprising for all the Reagan world to see the exotic character who'd lived beside me for a year. By the time the show finished its long run in 1989, conservatism in America had become an entrenched institution, although conservatives were surprisingly adept at portraying themselves as an endangered species. Everything they said and wrote had a kind of Alamo urgency to it, and the strategy worked for them then and is still working for them now.

Aside from the standard uniforms of the various contemporary tribes—Goth black, body piercing, and so forth—I can't typically tell by looking at them whether my students are conservative or liberal. Nowadays, political affiliation in the traditional sense seems more an inner phenomenon, an internal rhetoric, and less a matter of attending to the general arrangements of a group of people. "In my day-to-day life," one student writes, "being liberal means that I don't just 'tolerate' diversity, but value it." Or this: "It is not because I am conservative," another student declares, "that I try to live morally; rather, it is because I value morality that I am conservative." My liberal student values diversity; my conservative student values morality, and yet my liberal student wouldn't claim to support immorality nor would my conservative student come out in favor of racism. Both opinions would seem, on the face of it, to be constructed by looking inward and then outward; both, it would seem, are involved in the labyrinthine process of determining individual value, and then finding the community that shares that inner conviction. Yet I wonder if they aren't finding their community of friends first, and then internalizing the group's way of doing things; I wonder if they aren't adopting their politics after they've found their friends.

Conclusion: Maybe our social behavior reflects at some level our political and moral ideals, but social behavior within a community is nearly always negotiable, while political and moral ideals typically aren't. I'll share and enjoy many things—food, drink, hospitality, committee work—with my friend who supports the war in Iraq, but I won't share his political or moral ideals concerning our foreign policy. I won't share it because I don't have to share it; I can negotiate the demands of my daily life without my opinion on the Iraq war ever once appearing. So what kind of opinion is it that lives most of its life in a dark closet until a politician snaps the light on at election time? "Individual happiness," Nietzsche wrote, "springs from one's unknown laws, and prescriptions from without can only hinder it." What are the laws of happiness? What are the policies that will make us happy? Nietzsche's right; we haven't discovered them. We know when we are happy, but less often do we know how to make ourselves happy. And so we keep looking, generation after generation, placing our hope in ideals and moralities, looking outside of ourselves when we feel lonely to see who agrees with us, to discover those who share our known laws and might therefore share the unknown ones too. Political opinions are our hedge against loneliness—attracting those people we'd like to claim as friends, warding off those who can't do a thing to ease our loneliness.

3. IF YOU JUMPED THE FENCE AND EMBRACED THE POLITICAL ORIENTATION OPPOSED TO YOURS, HOW WOULD YOUR LIFE CHANGE?

My divorce was finalized during the Bush II administration, while the marriage it dissolved was conceived under Nixon's. I've never lost a friend over a political opinion, but I lost many friends, and gained a few as well, when my wife and I finally called it quits. And my father committed suicide the year Reagan was elected. I would be happy to blame the Republicans for these perilous events in my life; yet I know that political administrations, and the ways in which they attend to the general arrangements of a set of people, have little impact on the very things that cause us the most pain: sadness, depression, death, rupture, loss. It feels ungrateful, however, to say that the changing colors of our political guard make little difference to me, and yet during my voting life in the presidential elections, the nine-fold palette is fairly monotonous: red, blue, red, red, red, blue, blue, red, red. And they bear no traceable correlation with the changing colors of my personal life.

Yet, because maintaining an interest in politics requires that I believe in the reality of the party and its daily effect on my daily life, I invest myself from time to time in "having an opinion." For me, it's difficult, withering work. Once, I dutifully looked up the voting records of my senators—I have forgotten now what the issues were and how they voted, but I felt at the time that I'd become a knowledgeable part of the citizenry. Still, the imposing abstraction behind this notion of "the citizenry"—who constitutes it? where is it? when am I a part of it? when not?—soon wore me out, and I felt as though I were working for an entity I'd never seen. So I stopped looking up voting records.

My Democratic students don't want to be Republicans and my Republican students don't want to be Democrats, not because the events of their lives would radically change if they switched allegiances but because their self-conceptions clearly would. I am talking about a sense of inwardness here, and I am suggesting that political parties can manipulate it without ever substantially changing the immediate world in which we live and breathe and work and love. Polls suggest that most Americans feel radically disconnected from the government that petitions them to vote, but they don't feel that way about their jobs, their children, their vacations, their retirement. To them, and to me, the American national government is a massive and inwardly potent abstraction. I can lie by the pool and read Montaigne, thinking of myself as a Democrat, and have a fine day on my hands. Then I can think of myself as a Republican, lying there with Montaigne, and the day is shot to hell. Nothing has changed and everything has changed. It is not in the interest of politicians to encourage this insight.

Conclusion: We are made to feel that our vote counts, and of course it does, as long as it gets counted. But if one hundred million people vote in a modern presidential election, then I'm one hundred millionth of that total, and I'm not accustomed to thinking of myself in that particular fraction. When I do think of myself in these fractions—as a member, say, of BlueCross BlueShield, which serves ninety-two million people—I also think of insignificance, belittlement, and anonymity of the most debilitating kind. I will always vote, but not because I believe that my vote will feed a hungry person; nor do I believe that my vote will have much impact on the events that occur in Congress. I will vote because I believe that while it will do little to change the affairs of state, of the American national abstraction, my vote directly impacts how I think about myself as I'm lying by the pool. "Not being able to rule events," Montaigne wrote, "I rule myself and adapt myself to them if they do not adapt themselves to me." That is what it is *really* like to vote in America. I vote as a way of ruling myself, and so do my students. Our political opinions are dear to our hearts because it is our hearts, and not the national interest, that we are tending to when we utter those opinions.

4. COULD YOU REASONABLY CONCEIVE OF A LONG-TERM RE-
LATIONSHIP WITH SOMEONE RESIDING IN THE POLITICAL
CAMP TRADITIONALLY SAID TO BE OPPOSED TO YOURS?

As I finished breakfast this morning, I was watching the eminent Hungarian-born historian, John Lukacs, on C-SPAN2. He was talking to one of those American audiences that congregate in bookstores for a reading. The clothes are pastel, the handbags canvas, the paunches slightly noticeable, and the faces reflective of a sober-minded devotion to self-improvement. Lukacs, as they say, knows his stuff, and he has about him the kind of intellectual *noblesse oblige* that I've always vaguely associated with being a European thinker: he's come to these shores to help me with his vast stores of knowledge, not to embarrass me or confuse me. And from the looks of the bunch assembled here, a ragtag army of oatmeal complacency, we need his help.

His latest book had something to do with the global triumph of liberalism, although the word itself, paradoxically, he pointed out, had been successfully vilified and hounded into hiding. He never read from his book, nor did he appear to have a copy of it—another trait, this very old fashioned aversion to self-promotion, that I also fantasize as somehow being European. Instead, he rather modestly spoke off the cuff about the book's central concerns, and then opened the floor to questions.

The microphone was located in the central aisle between rows of folding metal chairs. The first question came from a man with those large, square-framed glasses scientists used to wear in the black-and-white NASA films I saw as a boy whenever we launched a space capsule. In fact, the man looked like one of those scientists: he wore his hair in a crew cut and had on a white short-sleeve shirt with a dark tie. For a moment, I wondered if this were a Halloween costume. There was a good deal of clanging and scraping as he moved chairs to get to the microphone, and at one point his umbrella got so tangled up with an elderly woman's canvas bag that both of them almost went to the floor, and I realized this guy was the real deal. This was no costume.

He was nervous, and so he started asking his question before he got to the microphone.

All I heard was: "... and yet of all the 'isms' you've spoken of today, you haven't said anything about the polar opposites, idealism and realism. Would you care to comment on those?"

What had I missed? Had he chastised Lukacs for using so many "isms?" Was he a scientist, as I'd fancied, and was he impatient with all of this unempirical speculation about political history? If the man were assaulting Lukacs, you couldn't tell by looking at Lukacs. Or by the tone of his response.

"Quite right. Excellent point," Lukacs said. Now in his eighties, and no stranger to controversy, Lukacs was well practiced at public equanimity. Besides, I said to myself, he's European, even if he *has* spent over half a century in this country.

"But actually, you see, I take the opposite of 'idealism' not to be 'realism' at all, but instead, 'materialism.'"

I finished my cereal and made a mental note to incorporate the phrase, "you see," into my own conversational repertoire. I put the cereal bowl into the dishwasher, added a small cake of detergent with a pearl-like thing in its center, latched the door, turned it on, and sat down to thumb through my students' responses to the fourth question. At some point, I began to identify the whirring, slurping noise of the dishwasher with the notion of realism and the responses I'd gotten from my students with idealism. Most of my students thought they'd have no problem in a long-term relationship with someone of the opposing political camp. I realized that my questions required my students to construct a series of ideas, coherent stances that were largely speculative and at times idealistic, and being the intelligent young people they are, they did so admirably. Yet most of them weren't about to let these ideas get in the way of the social realities that stared them in the face every day. If they got serious about someone whose political opinions they didn't happen to share, they reasoned, so be it. If they could pluck a couple of well-scrubbed ideas out of the churning forces of their social lives, that was all to the good, but for most of them their days were lived well beyond the polemics of consistency that we associate with a system of coherent ideas and which of course political campaigns claim to represent.

Oakeshott has argued that just as a cookbook presupposes the very act of cooking and only exists to describe one way of doing what has been done for millennia and will continue to be done for millennia, whether we have cookbooks or not, so a political ideology is not a beginning, or a prescription, for political activity, but rather amounts to "knowledge . . . of a concrete manner of attending to the arrangements of a society." A kind of knowledge, I might add, that is already in place, but is seen to be dormant, in need of mobilization. The rallying cry of an ideology, in fact, demands an act of memory; it intends to activate forgotten patterns of behavior, ways of negotiating and valuing the real world that for one reason or another have been laid aside or temporarily submerged by other ideologies. As such, an ideology has a lot in common with Lukacs's use of the term "idealism," just as my students' unwillingness to let these ideologies govern their daily reality reveals the power of "materialism," the swirling round of ad hoc decisions they make to negotiate their world without reference to principle or ideology or any other set of nationally mobilized abstractions.

Conclusion: The lead editorial in the *New York Times* today is speaking out against American prison abuses at Abu Ghraib, Guantanamo Bay, and Bagram. In the U.S.-run prison camp at Bagram, Afghanistan, the editorial claims that the "common peroneal strike" was used regularly. I had never heard of it, but I learned that this particular torture amounts to "a blow to the side of the leg just above the knee that can cause severe damage. It is clearly out of bounds for a civilized army, but it was used at Bagram routinely." I read the editorial online, checked the weather page for Fayetteville, Arkansas—did several of those anesthetic things—and then realized, after the anesthesia wore off, that I had no capacity to stop the common peroneal strike. I felt diminished. You know the feeling. My students know the feeling. It is very common nowadays, and nothing we do or say, no vote we cast, no party we elect, will ever do anything to lessen the terrible gravity of that feeling.

As soon as we abandon political ideology in the name of political realism, we confront the fact that our theater of operations is constricted to an exceedingly small space, and that perhaps basking in the protective shade of an ideology was more comfortable because while there we flattered ourselves that holding an idea was nearly the same as enacting an idea. Now, realists that we are, we know that holding and enacting ideas have little in common, and we must live with that. And so, with diminishment.

5. WHAT ARE THE CRUCIAL ISSUES, THE "WEDGE ISSUES," AS THEY'RE CALLED, THAT ALLOW YOU TO IDENTIFY YOURSELF AS A LIBERAL OR MODERATE OR CONSERVATIVE?

Equal rights, gay marriage, separation of church and state, social benefits, women's rights, the Middle East, censorship—that's part of the litany of issues that divide the camps. They echo perfectly the national chatter around election time and, increasingly, the times between. It's sometimes difficult to tell when these issues are being seriously addressed by our politicians and when they are being used to mobilize a vote—so it's sometimes difficult to know when we should pay attention and try to help, and when we should resurrect the old honesty that leads to the old diminishment I just mentioned.

My students struggle with this political currency too, bartering it whenever they can, but always remaining aware of how political allegiances, with their ghostly abstractions, are always changing shape. Here's an anecdote I received from one of them that makes the point:

> During the elections, I wore a political sticker on my book bag, but I took it off before entering my classes. Officially, and still honestly, I didn't think my classrooms needed any more politics, with or without an election; more, though, I didn't want my instructors to have reason to associate me one way or another. I was really conscious of that sticker outside of class, too. I had a hard time balancing what I knew I believed, what I wanted others to know of what I believed (and whether that knowledge was necessary to them truly knowing me), and what I hoped, by wearing that sticker, I might change.

You could chalk this up to an undergraduate angst about grades and dating, but I don't think that's entirely accurate. I think we're talking about the social manipulation of information. All sorts of information. The abstractions of a political sticker can't possibly reflect the whirring allegiances that rise and fall throughout the course of a day. Agendas of every sort—grades, dating, abortion, war, starvation—nip at us continually and force us into reactions we hadn't expected and can't conceivably corral inside the comfortable confines of a slogan.

And yet so much of politics is sloganeering; so much of it amounts to an unwieldy abstraction that we can only carry around for so long. "To me," another student wrote, "people are a little too complex to place in two or three camps of political persuasion."

We're made to feel that a political affiliation entails a vision of life, with all of its ups and down, and that we should naturally belong to a camp of political persuasion, and yet such an affiliation, after we've taken it on the road, amounts to a sluggish instrument at best. Political opinions often arise out of those inner contests where values and morals compete for acceptance and articulation. So political opinions often arise out of an inner crisis of one sort or another. A difficult border crossing in Hungary gives birth to a militaristic nationalist. No matter what the personal crisis we bring to our politics, however, no matter how much our political opinions might compensate for the fundamental conflicts we confront deep within ourselves, it's probably impossible to resolve those conflicts through a devotion to public causes because public causes live in the hard-edged land of material culture, and our conflicts have about them an idealistic force that is at times debilitating, at times empowering, and at times just elusive enough to be damned near invisible. But these inner conflicts, and the forces they bring to the fight, are always convincing, and they will always find the political solution falling just short of their demands for resolution, for psychic wholeness. And at these times, the political sticker seems very visible, but deeply unrepresentative of who we are, and so we peel it off the book bag, and we hide it away.

Conclusion: I'm not enough of a political historian to know if the dangerous equation that lands politics and morality on either side of the equal sign is a new equation or an old one. Either way, it's riding roughshod over all our calculations, just now, both public and private, and I don't like it. A lot of my students, sometimes without knowing it, are doing all they can to avoid the equation's iron restrictions. Let me, as my students have done, be clear about where I stand. I'm sick to death of the words "good" and "evil," and "right" and "wrong," even as many of our politicians seem daily titillated by them. If we live in a community of shared burdens, then claim virtuousness for one social policy that might lighten the burden for some, and assign depravity to another policy that would lighten it for others, this is a form of partisan paranoia that verges on madness. So I believe there is a good bit of madness in our country nowadays, and although I am certain this madness is simmering away in other countries too, I find that my inability to do much about it right here in my own arena compromises my ability to worry about it over there in the larger arena. I'm becoming a committed localist on his way toward being an impassioned inwardist.

III.

I was rereading George Orwell's essays recently as a thunderstorm moved in from the west and as Wolf Blitzer was interviewing one of my senators, a Democrat ensconced in a Republican state. I don't take these kinds of coincidences lightly. "Do you support the use of federal funding," Blitzer wanted to know, "for embryonic stem-cell research?" My senator said that he'd have to read the bill that was currently making its way through Congress and then, whenever it became feasible, he would formulate a response that took into account the enormous complexity of the issues involved as he and his voters back home went through the process of gaining clarity on this timely problem. Unfazed, Blitzer asked the question again. Equally unfazed, my senator reshuffled the words of his previous response, added a few more phrases, smiled, commented on the complexity of the issues involved, and the interview was done.

No hard information had passed between the two of them except this, which flew in just under the radar: my senator comes from a state that went solidly Republican in the presidential election, a state where a volatile and complex issue like stem-cell research calls up a number of equally volatile and complex issues like abortion, the constitutional rights of the unborn, in vitro fertilization, and women's rights. So he's forced by his political environment into brandishing the language that will slip past the censors crowding his airwaves, sniffing out the word or phrase that will reveal him to be the liberal he's sometimes accused of being. Many of us have become, by necessity, very adept at reading this code, and my senator knew this, and counted on this. Liberal values in the South are now on an extended survival hike, and this sense of commitment and struggle are evident in my senator's adroit use of a survivalist language.

The two sentences I'd just read in Orwell as the interview proceeded and the storm arrived were: "I think one must continue the political struggle, just as a doctor must try to save the life of a patient who is probably going to die. But I do suggest that we shall get nowhere unless we start by recognizing that political behaviour is largely non-rational, that the world is suffering from some kind of mental disease which must be diagnosed before it can be cured." He wrote this in 1945. The lights in my house flickered as the storm hit, the place went dark for a few seconds, blinked momentarily to life, darkened again, and then after a few more seconds in darkness, the electric hum and light of a living house returned for good. The lamps were on, Blitzer and my senator were gone, replaced now by a panel of chattering experts, and Orwell was still in my lap. This, I felt deeply, was as it should be. I am a literary creature by nature.

We probably need Orwell now more than we have ever needed him. We need his eye, his line of thought, and his prose style. They were all of a piece for him, and working together, they account for the sense of well being I have whenever I read him, even when I disagree with him. Orwell can at times seem wrong-headed, but he always seems trustworthy because he insists on being crystal clear about the motives that lie behind his argument. Revealing motives: it is not a liberty often allowed our politicians. Here is what Orwell has to say about nationalism. I liked it immediately, and when I reread it, I found myself making up the word "party-ism" and substituting it for "nationalism"; and for the word "national," I plugged in the word "party:"

> By "nationalism" I mean first of all the habit of assuming that human beings can be classified like insects and that whole blocks of millions or tens of millions of people can be confidently labeled "good" or "bad." But secondly—and this is much more important—I mean the habit of identifying oneself with a single nation or other unit, placing it beyond good and evil and recognizing no other duty than that of advancing its interests.

As my student said, "people are a little too complex to place in two or three camps of political persuasion," but as Orwell reminds us, it is resolutely our "habit" to do so. In Arkansas there are far more red insects than blue ones, and because I am a blue one, I ought to feel overwhelmed. Or threatened. Or even on the verge of extinction, as a dwindling population of insects might feel. But I don't. Why?

I don't because a political party, when I examine it closely, remains to me an abstraction, and while I'd like to believe that certain abstract principles like liberty, justice, and equality govern my life, I know that I am perfectly capable of going through an ordinary day without once considering those principles. I also know that not thinking about these principles is a luxury—it is only because these principles are already in place that I'm able to disregard them. When asked in 1965 to write on the subject of morality for *The American Scholar*, Didion eschewed the traditional notions of right and wrong that often attend the term, and came to rest instead on what she called a "fundamental loyalty to the social code," a sense of what is acceptable or unacceptable to the immediate community that each of us calls home. Here, it's often not about right or wrong, but about compromise and relinquishment. That is where I live on a daily basis—mired in the social code, compromising on this, relinquishing that, in hopes of exchanging this for that.

But Orwell put his finger on a profundity of sorts when he singled out the "habit of identifying oneself with a single nation or other unit," because an allegiance to a political party, which seems so natural as to be genetic, is in fact a habit that we must acquire, and it is the duty of the politicians to make certain that we acquire it. But the simplicity of the organizational scheme—red, blue, Republican, Democratic—doesn't reflect the complexity of even our dullest days. And yet we are bombarded daily in the media with every sort of reason to fashion our identities, to create the habit of self-identification from a range of . . . two options. In certain moods, I find this deeply insulting, but realize there's nothing to be done about it, and so recline and watch the storm pass with Orwell in my lap. In point of fact, I find that in this country our beliefs and opinions, those abstract realities that ride shotgun somewhere in our heads, don't always separate us in meaningful ways, or cause disharmony among us, until some larger organization or event, like a political party or an advocacy group or an election, asks them to do so. And then we line up across from each other, raise our voices, and take stands that we will have often forgotten by the time supper rolls around. So while I confess that living blue in a red state is hell now and again, it is largely an abstract hell, which considerably lessens its heat.

My students know this at an instinctive level. For them, the Facebook question that asks them to delineate their political preference resembles more a game of Texas Hold 'Em than it does the kind of political affiliation we traditionally associate with membership in the two parties. Political affiliation represents for them a series of fluid options that changes as they meet new people, encounter different ideas, and go about the business of living day to day. Most of my students look at a traditional political designation as one aspect of a much larger social identity, and some of them confess to changing their political designation in order to attract or repulse certain members of their community—*realpolitik* of the highest order, and one that honestly reflects the level of importance they'll naturally assign to anything as abstract as a political party. They have not yet, to recall Orwell, created the habit of the party. And I am trying to unlearn it—a consequence, I suspect, of living blue in a red state.

I do not want to advocate political apathy nor suggest that what goes on in Congress is irrelevant to my life. In fact, I regard my lawmakers as I regard the sun: they are necessary, they daily influence my life in ways I am unaware of, I take them for granted, but I care very little about understanding their innermost workings because I believe that understanding their innermost workings will do little to affect their influence on me. To bring Orwell back into the picture one final time: I do feel now and again as if the patient I'm trying to resuscitate with my vote is terminal, and yet, like the good doctor, I know I must continue my efforts and cast my vote. And so I do. I can't say that this is an optimistic view of things, but it's my view.

I believe that the court-decided presidential election of 2000 has had a tangible effect on the way in which many of us view the workings of our government. And it lay bare how little the average citizen has to do with the massive federal machine that oversees our elections and ultimately our lives. "Two weeks after the election," Didion writes in *Political Fictions*, "according to the Shorenstein Center's comparison of polling conducted just before the election and that conducted in its immediate aftermath, the number of Americans who answered 'none' to the question 'How much influence do you think people like you have on what the government does?' had increased from one in ten to one in four." That's a harsh statistic, and yet a predictable one. Washington DC remains for most of us a remote planet whose natural laws, we imagine, descend from the kind of avarice and greed that will only be satisfied by the wholesale acquisition of power. Max Weber once asked himself what could "politics as a vocation" possibly offer "in the way of inner satisfaction," and he answered, "first of all the sense of power." We suspect this, but seldom have we seen this bare and barren acquisition of power, and this greed, so publicly displayed as it was in the days following the election. It was a sobering moment, one in which all of the idealistic rhetoric about our forefathers and their grand legacy clanged and clattered as it was tossed into the wastebin and the real business of governing was transacted.

I live in a state that voted overwhelmingly for Bush and work on a campus that voted overwhelmingly for Kerry. I'm guessing that many liberal arts faculties in the South showed up on the charts as blue islands in a red sea. As I indicated earlier, I've voted in nine presidential elections and been on the winning side only twice, and since I've always worked on one of those islands, maybe I've become acclimatized to island life. There *is* something exotic, rare, even alluring about being continually cast into the misunderstood minority. I confess, too, that Clinton's election arrived on my shore as a kind of message-in-the-bottle: we never had stopped thinking about tomorrow, and so at last, we believed, we were going to be saved. And for a time, we were—or at least that's how it seemed. But the salvation many of us felt then turns out to be just as abstract as the dissatisfaction we feel now. If the people I care about were more hopeful then, they are less hopeful now; that's about all I can say. Whether that means the overall sum of hope in the world is greater or lesser or the same, I don't know, but when Irene Khan, secretary general of Amnesty International, announces in the annual report for 2004 that "the detention facility at Guantanamo Bay has become the gulag of our times . . . [and] evokes memories of Soviet repression," I have my suspicions.

Unlike death, which I wait for, and taxes, which I work for, the reality of the parties tends to vanish unless I cultivate the habit of identifying myself as belonging to one or the other. Yet, why bother? Because the politicians and the commentators who dominate the cable news stations insist that I do so if I am to call myself an American? But I don't believe them, and neither do my students, because the reality they offer us is often engaging, but finally not engaging enough. In America just now, selecting a coffee at Starbucks requires a more analytical mind than choosing a political party. I suspect that it has always been this way, and yet because our politicians must periodically ask our permission to continue with their difficult work, they seem constantly to be reminding us that whatever it is they are doing is valuable and noble. And about half of us, in a good election year, get ourselves to the polls, and tell them to keep on doing whatever it was they were doing. Then, when the polls close and the results are in, half of that number are glad they have done so, and the other half are left to wonder why they bothered. Thank goodness I don't have to ask the politicians for permission to do whatever it is that I do.

So I've got my own political team now, and its charter members are Oakeshott, Didion, Orwell, and my students; I'm pleased to say that we've reached consensus on this issue: a very large part of our political reality is a vast and compelling abstraction. And as with all such airy ideals, we have to be careful when they come calling—which means whenever we turn on the television, listen to the radio, read a newspaper, flip through a magazine. These ideals and abstractions, they can be very seductive. At times, we live for them, we walk under their banners, we make loud proclamations in their name, and a lot gets accomplished. And when our politicians are there to lead us, we will rain blessings on their heads. But the other part of that political reality, the reality that fires the Facebook, sees politics as lying much closer to hand than an ideal or a principle. Those politics chart a way of walking through the crowd, taking care of whatever and whoever shows up in our path. They are part of the social code, immediately arising from the immediate need. "Rescue the drowning," Henry David Thoreau wrote in response to the grand ideals of the philanthropist, "and tie your shoe-strings." Often, although many would have us believe otherwise, that is the most that we can do, and because nearly all of us, regardless of our party affiliation, have almost drowned or tripped over our own shoestrings, that is often the most that we should do.

16. *P* Is For . . .

Stephen Corey

Do I dare to eat a peach . . . ?
—T. S. Eliot

"Cheraw, ma'am."

Of all the words I've heard spoken in my life, few others—excepting some from loved ones—have stayed so clearly in the foreground of my mind and ear: the foreign-to-me sounds emitted from the white-coated druggist via these three (four?) syllables are difficult to capture on the page, though I can still hear them so perfectly in my head nearly fifty years after they were spoken: the strong *Shh*, heavy even though unaccented; the lower-toned but loud-struck *row* (as in *clown*) where my young Northern ear expected the higher-pitched *awe*; and the double oddity of *maym*, with its *a* of almost—*may* rather *ham*, to say nothing of its simple existence—this form of polite address rarely showing itself in my native western New York state.

The druggist's words came in response to my grandmother's probably dumb-seeming question, "What's the name of this town?"—which she asked because we had seen the name around, on signs here and there, but weren't sure what to make of it.

The year was 1960, mid- to late April—spring break time where I grew up. My paternal grandmother and I had walked about in that small South Carolina town, a dozen or so miles below the North Carolina border southeast of Charlotte, in search not of food or souvenirs or adventure, but Kaopectate.

My father lay suffering in our motel room on the edge of town, only able to move enough to get to the bathroom for another round of misery. My mother tended him and kept an eye on my two restless though still-healthy siblings. (I was in fifth grade, my brother in first, and my sister just about to turn five years old.) By the next day my parents would exchange roles, and the day after that we would finally continue our drive to the Atlantic coast of Florida—a place none of us had ever visited, and much farther from home than any of we young ones had ever traveled.

Aunt Fern, my grandmother's older sister, was living there in a trailer close to New Smyrna Beach, near Cape Canaveral. Years before, Fern had left Conneautville, in northeastern Ohio, with her second husband, whom I had never met and whose name I cannot now recall for certain. Harold, perhaps, or maybe Jerry. The morning after we arrived, Aunt Fern put something disgusting on my breakfast plate that I'd never seen during my almost-twelve years—grits—and later in the day I learned that the kid from the trailer next door possessed another revelation, this one submerged in alcohol in a Mason jar in his tiny bedroom: an alien being he had killed himself in his own yard—a coral snake.

This South would be no Kansas, Toto.

Virtually no one driving today from Jamestown, New York—about 75 miles south of Buffalo, 150 miles north of Pittsburgh, and just 10 miles above the New York–Pennsylvania line—toward New Smyrna Beach would pass anywhere near Cheraw. In 1960, however, President Eisenhower's dream of an interstate highway system had just begun its translation into reality, so as-the-crow-flies routes were still much more likely to be the most efficient. Examining a 2006 atlas state by state—New York, Pennsylvania, Maryland, Virginia, North Carolina, South Carolina, Georgia, Florida—I find that much of the route my father may have mapped out, or had mapped out for him in an American Automobile Association TripTik (MapQuest for the Stone Age), is recoverable only as guesswork, and I see no need to lay out even my best guesses here. The point is that every road then would have been what is now thought of as a back road, or at best a "secondary road," with small-town slowdowns and stop-offs the rule. No slipping past the regional details. No "rest areas."

By late in the second day of our journey I saw dual restrooms and water fountains, just as my teachers and textbooks—and the local newspapers and national magazines I was already reading regularly, among the latter *Life* and the *Saturday Evening Post*—had said I would, but I was nonetheless stunned, hot-faced, confused, and indignant, bearing with me that nascent ethical/moral sense of the preteen mind. Sure, the living arrangements were mostly segregated in Jamestown, with our 4 percent black population living primarily along the stretch of Washington Street just north of downtown and on a dozen or so numbered streets—roughly, Tenth through Twenty-fourth—perpendicular to that main thoroughfare. And there were several churches in that same neighborhood—Covenant AME comes to mind—where nearly all of those sixteen hundred blacks worshipped (the city population was forty thousand), though the only time I noticed this was when I was in high school and played in the local church basketball league. All of us were in school together and in the movie theaters together, and we—the white kids, at least—didn't think of the living or churchgoing arrangements as anything necessary, anything somehow arranged or enforced. We were racist by complacency rather than action, so whether or not this was truly less harmful, it *did* leave me with a mindset that saw, and knew, overt discrimination to be deeply wrong. Little could I think, stranded in Cheraw with those foreign words of the druggist bouncing around inside my head (with what would prove to be a sort of vacuum effect, whereby the bouncing would go on and on and on), that at the age of twenty-seven I would intentionally move to the South and end up staying there to this day.

In the 1950s and 1960s, before and after my only southward sortie prior to my move to Gainesville, Florida, in 1975, I really was taught about the South as if it were some other country—no, *the* other country—set within the borders of the United States. The histories of slavery, plantation economics, the Civil War, Reconstruction, racism, segregation, lynching, and integration—as well as all the key individuals involved therewith—were not given to us in any two-sided way at our Governor Nelson Rockefeller–rich public schools. Our textbooks, our teachers, and our fledgling television programs all seemed to be

"Northern," which to us was the equivalent of "American." The nation was large and included many different regions, but we learned that only one of those regions was different enough to be cast in a negative light, different enough to have its differences defined as wrong. New England was just that—the birthplace of our democratic nation. (Never mind those Spanish missions in St. Augustine and California.) The West, hugely if misleadingly defined, was explorers and forts and gold and mountains (with mountain men) and Indians and buffalo and settlers and ranchers. The Midwest—no, we didn't keep our chronologies straight in grade school—was corn and the Chicago stockyards and some Laura Ingalls Wilder. The South was slavery, war, and other troubles.

In the late 1980s I wrote "Town and Country Losses," the only poem in which I have tried to deal directly with the tremendous influence of the Vietnam War on my life, and I ended up including there the lone reference in any of my work to these childhood senses of the South. The poem's heart involves the wartime death of a young man from my hometown, which I learned about one morning from the local newspaper—a moment of discovery that, in the poem, threw me back further to my days as a delivery boy and to some of the stories and headlines I had come across, time after time after time, as I readied the papers each morning:

> As a paperboy I'd folded and tucked
> eighty copies in the pre-dawn dark,
> creased the same stories
> over and over, thrown them at all
> those quiet, undisturbed doors.
> My arm cocking and aiming and releasing:
> strange marches in the faraway South,
> Wilt Chamberlain's 100-point game,
> my own brother's birth.

This compression of a huge, complex region of the country into one quick phrase of avoidance ("strange marches"), along with an admission that that region was in a "faraway" relationship to my daily life, came long after I had taken up residence in said "faraway"—and the moments I was recollecting in the poem transpired *after* I had vacationed in the South as a fifth grader. In other words, neither visiting nor living below the Mason-Dixon Line seemed to have altered its foreignness for me.

I have been in the South now for more than three decades—five years in Gainesville; three in Columbia, South Carolina; twenty-three and counting in Athens, Georgia—but I do not and never will feel myself to be other than a visitor/observer/interloper who deeply appreciates the weather (from growing up near Lake Erie in the too-accurately nicknamed "snow belt"), and who was fortunate enough to find employment he loves and is unwilling to surrender. Of course, one could make a strong argument that I, like many another Northern transplant, have never lived in "the South" at all, but rather have political-and-cultural-island-hopped from one large university campus to another. For instance, the combined governing unit of Athens/Clarke County, home of the University of Georgia where I now work, has been the only Democratic stronghold (excepting portions of Atlanta) in the northern third of the state, and one of only a few these days in all of Georgia. Further, the cosmopolitanism bred by a major educational and research institution of more than thirty thousand students serves to make Athens almost an anti-Southern Southern city—as the University of Florida radically alters Gainesville, and as the University of South Carolina (somewhat, though to a much lesser extent) alters Columbia.

When my then-new family and I lived in Florida (1975–1980), we traveled to visit our relatives in Jamestown twice yearly, during the summer and at Christmas. We drove I-75 from Gainesville to Cincinnati, caught I-71 toward Cleveland, and then followed I-90 east to the back roads south of Buffalo that would bring us home. Eisenhower's interstates were much advanced from their fledgling life in 1960, but the now-much-more-efficient I-77 (via I-85) through North Carolina, Virginia, and West Virginia was not complete.

As a result of our route, on a couple of our summer trips we— I with my wife, Mary, and our two young daughters—stopped off in Norris, Tennessee, northwest of Knoxville, to visit a high school friend of Mary's who had landed there. The first time we made this social detour we got "confused" on some dirt roads near the Norris Dam, and at one point we came around a curve to see, near the edge of some woods about fifty yards from the road, a classic backwoods Southerner standing atop a five-foot mound of slag or rubbish. He wore dirty denim coveralls, a gray (and maybe also dirty) long-sleeved flannel-looking shirt, a wide-brimmed floppy hat, and boots of some kind. Resting in the crook of his arm was a long-barreled rifle. He was staring toward those woods, and in the ten or so seconds he was in our sight he never moved or looked our way.

This was in the late 1970s, only a few years after we and much of the country had had the shock of the film version of James Dickey's *Deliverance*, and I can say without hesitation those cinematic images came to mind when I saw that man—whose appearance made him quite unlike anyone else I had ever come across along any road in the years of my growing up. We drove on, not yet knowing for certain we were lost. Then the road ended, and we had no choice but to backtrack . . . I, at least, nervously. The mound was empty when we passed it again, but that didn't keep my heart from pounding, however baselessly, for the next few miles: I had seen poor Drew pitch forward from that white-water-running canoe in *Deliverance*, shot dead by the mountain man perched somewhere atop the high cliffs that enclosed Dickey's fictionalized but all too real river. From that Norris day onward I have felt a tension, even a fear, whenever I find myself on out-of-the-way Southern roads—an attitude I never developed in the North, where serenity and related pleasant feelings would come to me if I ventured far into the countryside

But if the writer James Dickey—a born-and-reared, lifelong Southerner—had to put distance between himself and his region at the same time he hugged it close, had to be (as he claimed repeatedly, in conversation and in print) both the novel's wily, bow-hunter survivalist Lewis *and* the gentle, intellectual narrator Ed, then how could I ever feel surprised by my need to look askance upon my at-best-adopted home? There *are* more guns here than in any other region of the country, and there *is* more day-to-day obsession with history—usually history as it has disappointed both those within and those without the South, though of course for very different reasons. (As a boy I neither saw nor heard of men periodically dressing in historic battle regalia and conducting mock warfare as a weekend ritual.)

Dickey's 1979 poetry collection *The Strength of Fields*, whose title piece he read at the presidential inauguration of fellow Georgia native Jimmy Carter, includes a favorite poem of mine, "False Youth: Autumn: Clothes of the Age." The speaker, at the least a Dickey-like figure, enters a barbershop in Columbia, South Carolina, and quickly removes his denim jacket and a fur hat bearing three foxtails. The locals in the shop immediately know he is not fully one of them, and shortly they begin the baiting: "Jesus, if there's anything I hate / It's a middle-aged hippie," says one, and then another asks, "When're you gonna put on that hat, / Buddy?" To the first the narrator replies (after swallowing), "So do I So do I," and to the second he answers—already having decided to pack up and get out—"Right now." Then, carefully pulling on the as-yet-undescribed jacket so that nobody in the shop can see the back of it, he heads out but pauses in the doorway to reveal the hand-stitched but unraveling eagle perched between his shoulder blades—and, embroidered beneath it, the rather ignoble bird's

> One word, raggedly blazing with extinction and soaring loose
> In red threads burning up white until I am shot in the back
> Through my wings   or ripped apart
> For rags:
>
> Poetry.

Dickey revels in the reactions he knows he will draw forth—and with double venom, no doubt, since his culturally charged final word is here aligned with a literally degraded version of our country's most cherished patriotic emblem. But he also would have carried the knowledge that to a significant extent he *was* one with his detractors: born in Atlanta—a far more out-of-the-way city in his birth year, 1923, than it is now—Dickey in his blood was one of those "Buckhead boys" he searches for elsewhere in a poem of that name; and when he or his poetic doppelganger spoke in that barbershop, however curtly and provocatively, he would have been known instantly to be a Southerner, however gone astray. That "Cheraw, ma'am," spoken a short hundred miles northeast of Dickey's Columbia, and grating in my head for nearly half a century now, would have flowed easily into his ear and almost as easily off his tongue.

I find it both exhilarating and depressing that *poetry* is often a fighting word that can elicit discomfort, mockery, anger, and other negative responses—but I have come to know, especially because of my years in the South, there is another *P* word that, were I to blazon it on my own denim jacket, would cause me far more trouble: *Pacifism*.

Few things disturb a greater number of Americans more than the suggestion that our country's ideals are not worth literally fighting for, or—an even worse intellectual sin—that we ought not to bend over backwards to bow down in honor of those fellow citizens who have "defended our rights and freedom" by "making the ultimate sacrifice" in one or another theater of armed conflict or war. To be a poet in America is to work near the farthest margins of what, practically speaking, passes for ordinary life; to be a poet *and* a pacifist, and to have made a lifelong commitment to both roles, can make one feel as if he were living on another planet—and this estrangement pertains and persists, for me at least, despite my internal faith that each of my commitments is deeply logical, vitally life-affirming, and ultimately necessary to any fruitful survival of the human race. (Yes, all belief involves egotism.)

I have written elsewhere about the complex of people, events, thoughts, and activities that brought me—I still lived then in the North—into the pacifist camp, and led me thereby to declare myself a conscientious objector when I came of age during the war in Vietnam. My time in the South began about a half-dozen years after I had taken this stand, so I won't rehash the preliminaries—except in so far as to note directly what some readers may have inferred from what I said just above: the development of my beliefs in poetry and pacifism were inextricably linked.

This was true in ways I did and didn't understand at the time, with "the time" spanning a solid handful of years—call it 1962–1968. I didn't know that the poems I was reading, mostly in high school, were preparing me for the poems I would begin to write—at first haltingly and sporadically toward the end of that strange, increasingly disrupted time in our country's history, then more regularly while 1970s America played itself out as the culmination and aftermath of a series of political assassinations and an especially questionable war. Neither did I know that poems—the many I had read, and the few I had attempted to write starting in 1967—were a crucial part of the thinking processes and the feelings that would lead me to become one who refuses the option of institutionalized warfare and violence in a world persistently and (it seems) increasingly devoted to both.

However, the mostly gradual emergence of my poetic vocation and my pacifist morality occasionally took a quantum leap—as when Professor Christian Gruber walked into our Harpur College freshman lit-and-comp class one day in his World War II parade uniform, climbed up onto the desk, and began to declaim e. e. cummings's "i sing of olaf" with the fervor of the convert he would subsequently tell me he had become:

> i sing of olaf glad and big,
> whose warmest heart recoiled at war:
> a conscientious object-or . . .

I was still gathering inklings rather than answers, and disturbing new prospects rather than a philosophy, and I was still innocent enough to be shocked and pruriently thrilled by a poem in which a character informs his tormenting superiors that "I will not kiss your fucking flag," and then goes on to declare, "there is some shit I will not eat." But in the months following Professor Gruber's performance, cummings and "olaf" were central pieces in the complex puzzle I put together—and then cemented in place: art affirms life, and particularly human life; the written arts, to which I was being incontrovertibly drawn, affirm what biologist Lewis Thomas and others have deemed the key distinguishing element of human existence—language; committing oneself to being a poet, which for me means attempting to explore the possibilities of life and language in a distinctive, individualized way, is ipso facto diametrically opposed to notions of doing intentional harm *and* of allowing others (whether individuals or political organizations) to make one's moral decisions.

This string of fundamental assertions is not offered according to Socrates Robert's Rules of Logical Order, but drawn from an internal well that I know is far too deep ever to be fully plumbed. Not all poets (by a long shot) are pacifists, even though I think they ought to be, and I've had some especially painful arguments with a few who are not. Those pains were emotional, however, and I was never in fear that they might turn into the physical kind—the fear I do have, as I've said, when I think of having my heart's core laid bare in the presence of the majority of Southern men. I've read too many local newspaper articles about the nearby Moore's Ford lynchings, and I've watched— at the tail end of the twentieth century—hooded Klansmen passing out leaflets along the main street through Athens and burning crosses beside a main highway not fifteen miles away.

So I have a strong tendency to keep quiet about my beliefs, to let myself be "practical" by reasoning that since I know I can't change the world anyway—especially the Southern world—I must be content with consistently but privately carrying through on my philosophy. I'm aware of the irony here, aware that I could be justifiably charged with smugness, weakness, and even self-delusion. What use is a belief if one does not act upon it? A good question, but one dependent upon—among other things—the assumed definition of *act*. The most important thing a pacifist does is to refuse an entire category of actions, day after day, and that refusal *becomes* his vital action.

No organized religion's tenets ever took genuine hold of me, so as soon as I was old enough to stop heeding my mother's requests that I attend our Methodist church's Sunday school, and then its services, I did so. In the nearly four decades since, my faith in the failure of codified faith has only increased. A while back, at my wife's behest, I gave the Unitarians a chance; a great bunch of people they were, in the Athens, Georgia, branch at least, but even they seemed to call on me to render external some things that I believe are only internal, and so I had to step away. However, they did sometimes sing one of my favorite old hymns, the one with the refrain, "Let there be peace on earth, and let it begin with me"—a pacifist credo if ever I've encountered one, and some days enough to make me trust that I've done what I could by making that beginning a crucial end in my life.

Early in 2006 I went to hear Arlo Guthrie play when he passed through Athens on his "Alice's Restaurant" Fortieth Anniversary Tour. I'm a sucker in general for nostalgic moments, even those with campy overtones, but this one maintained an immediacy for me that most cannot (and no doubt should not), since that particular song had been one of many elements in that rush of pivotal things helping me clarify my thinking about conscientious objection in the late 1960s. The ongoing relevance of "Alice" that Arlo pitched during his concert, by making certain side remarks and by rewriting a few of the original lyrics, was absolutely there for me already since, as I've just said, an antimilitaristic outlook has been in my daily regimen across the decades.

I'm not much of a slogan T-shirt buyer, but after Guthrie's concert I found that I had to have his "Not moral enough to join the Army" offering, nicely printed on military fatigue camouflage fabric. Interestingly, though, I then had some trouble leaving the house wearing it. I found myself thinking about where I was going to be: walking across the University of Georgia campus, or in the heart of downtown Athens? Sure, then—wear the shirt. In the men's locker room at the YMCA, or at Normaltown (an old section of Athens) Hardware when I know I'm going to need some assistance from the owner? Well, then, maybe not. Out with my wife and daughter for the Wednesday evening potluck supper at the Unitarian church? Absolutely—and with every expectation of eliciting some direct verbal responses of a laudatory nature.

Shall I wear my Arlo and go looking for that side road in Norris, Tennessee, where I wandered, lonely as a cloudy Northerner, all those years ago? Not hardly, as the armed man on that faraway slag heap might have said. But . . . shall I drive out that way again at all? If I do, this time I'll be in my pale blue Subaru station wagon—to the back of which I affixed, in the summer of 2005, the following special-order "vanity" license plate, courtesy of the state of Georgia: DR POET.

I'd thought for years about getting some such plate, something poetry-related that had the state's requisite seven letters and spaces. The extra money held me back, and then when I worked up the checkbook balance and the gumption, I asked for POETRY but learned it was already taken—as if I should have been overly surprised by that fact, even in a Southern state. No two plates in the state can be the same, which I suppose makes *all* of them poetic on some level, but I couldn't come up with another I liked well enough—I considered IAMBICP and DACTYLS, among others—until I learned about the allowable space, the non-letter letter. Combining my professional and artistic identities amused me, as did the thought of other drivers' possible reactions to the plate; I suppose some egotistical nervousness was involved as well—people thinking "That figures" when they see me and my plate making some foolish driving maneuver—but if DAWGGUY and HOTGIRL can survive, surely I can as well.

But would I dare display a PACIFIST plate, even if Georgia allowed eight characters? Or how about ANTIWAR? I know that state anti-obscenity laws wouldn't allow me such messages as FUCKWAR or WARSHIT, or probably even WARSUCK, but I don't know whether political stances would also be squelched—though that isn't really the question here. The question is, as stated, would I dare . . . ?

I don't think they'd let me have POLITIC, either, free speech always being more relative than we want to admit, but PACIFIC might make a nice compromise. The etymologists among the commuting crew could be piqued to speculation, and nearly everyone could think ocean thoughts and wonder what I'm after. Or how about the fifth-column PASFIST, which would borrow a typical Southern pronunciation of my identity and would also indicate what bodily part many folks might like to apply to me as a response to my position.

Okay, let's come back around to the real point: the United States, like the world, is too large to achieve the unanimity of purpose it needs to thrive, or even to survive. The sad thing about the American Civil War is that even though its sociomoral cause—slavery—was so despicable, its political impulse toward smaller governing units was right. No president or Congress can serve and appease the expanse that is our sea to less-than-shining sea; given how our people and their beliefs have evolved in the past three hundred years, if we were five or six countries, then maybe . . .

Or maybe not. We needn't be in Oz to assert, wonderingly yet obviously, that we're not in Kansas. Georgia would do. As would Tennessee, or New York. There's no place like home because home is what we learn to negotiate, learn to think of as "real" and "normal," as "better." And yet, as Voltaire showed us in *Candide* so laughably and grimly and so long ago, there is no better place, nor even a good one, because there are no absolute beliefs or Goods. (Now there's *another* position that would get me in really good with a lot of Southerners. And Northerners. And . . .) Only very recently, in the new age of rampant political terrorism, have I been forced to concede that not even respect for human life is a human value—so how could I ever expect a true antiwar stance to be one?

Living blue in a red state. Perhaps the real blue is oneself, the real red the rest of the world, with the real test and problem always each of our attempts to "come down where we ought to be"—in a *where* beyond the reach of, and at the same time exactly in, any Athens, Jamestown, Oz, or Cheraw one might see or hear or imagine.

17. Minority within Minority
Dynamics of Race and Culture
in the New South
Anthony Kellman

Midsummer came like an armed man, sudden and violent. The door-bell rang. Not long afterwards, my wife, Malaika, shouted up the stairs, "Gordon's here!" I caught up with Gordon on the last step of the staircase. He put his left arm around my shoulder, and we both stepped onto the oak floor. He slapped me briskly on the shoulder. Then we vigorously shook hands.

"What's happening, Gordon? Good to see you." He was a real estate agent, a six-foot redhead with a rugged demeanor. Shaved, lined, rustic face. We had met at the Family Fitness Center nearly a year ago, some months after I had moved to Augusta. He was unable to persuade me to purchase a home instead of renting one. I knew this presented a challenge to my tenacious friend.

"Look at this," he pursued as ever. "Do you know what a profit you could've made on this baby, if it were yours?" He paced the den, gesturing toward the walls. "Doesn't matter now, does it?" I said. Then I began singing an impromptu calypso, a habit from my musician days, designed to tease the life out of a victim.

> *I'm leaving this place come Monday,*
> *I'm leaving, no matter what you say.*
> *Over to Savannah, Gordon'll follow me*
> *With his old worn-out song: "Buy Your Own Property."*
> *Oiiiieeeeee!!*

I waved my hands in the air and gyrated my hips to an imaginary calypso rhythm. Just then Malaika entered the room. She'd been making tea. She smiled, shook her head, and looked at Gordon with a don't-you-be-bothered-with-him look. Gordon tried to be serious and said, "Funny. Real funny."

I said, "You like it? I know you do. Here's another one for you . . ."

You real estate fellas are all millionaires,
You make twice as much as we engineers.
So, don't mock me, don't lock me, 'cause if I buy a home,
It'll be one made of island limestone.
Oiiiieeeeee!!

"How you like me, Gordon?" I said. "How you like me?"

"Pleeeeeeease, Tony. This *can't* be the way Barbadians behave. You're a disgrace to your country." Gordon seemed as if he was desperately trying to repress laughter. "Darn," he said, trying hard not to give in, "you're wasting your life renting instead of owning. Think of the write-offs, will yuh? Granted, it's not the best time for selling, but it's a helluva good time for buying right now. The buying market's on the upswing, my man." By now, Gordon had conquered his urge to laugh. His intense brown eyes shone with the confidence of a salesman.

"I'm just not ready yet," I sing-sang. "When I am, you'll be the first to know. Trust me."

"Boy, have I heard that one before," he said, turning to Malaika. "Is this man of yours so hard-headed in everything?"

"Yes. I'm glad someone else thinks so. Keep on him, Gordon. Deep down inside, he knows he wants to own a home, but he pretends differently. Keep working on him, y'hear?"

"What is this?" I cried, raising my hands in mock surrender. "Two to one is murder."

"Correction," Gordon said, pointing a forefinger quickly back and forth at me and himself. "One to one is murder."

"What? This can't be true. Is this the same guy talking who couldn't do twenty French curls a few months ago?"

"OK, OK, men," Malaika said. "Now don't we start a fist fight now. And, besides, the tea's getting cold."

I'd met Gordon the first evening I worked out at Family Fitness. I had completed three sets (each of twenty-five reps) of bench presses, flys, lateral pull-downs, long pulley rows, leg curls, leg extensions, and French curls. When I went over to the bicep machine, it was occupied by a tall sweating redheaded man wearing brown boxer shorts. I stood next to the machine awaiting my turn. After completing one of his sets, the man gestured for me to use the machine. We continued in this way, exchanging the equipment with alternate sets, until we had each completed all of our sets. In between the iron pumping we must have said things to each other, and, when we were through, Gordon Donovan formally introduced himself and asked, "Where're you from, man? Ethiopia?"

I laughed and said, "You know, since I've been in the States, several people have asked me that same question. My pre-slavery ancestors must be from there. I'm from Barbados. Now, that's way down South. And it's the nearest of the Windward Islands to Africa, too—as the slaves fly."

Gordon laughed loudly, seemingly impressed by my curious wit. He slid off his weight gloves and bent down to put them in his duffle bag.

"I love you music, mon," he said in a bubble gum voice and looked up at me. "Especially reggae. Don't have any of my own, but I love it when I hear it. It has the omphf."

"The what?" I asked. I had never heard the expression before.

"The oooommmmmmmmmphf," Gordon said with greater relish. "It's hot, mon. Hot."

Although he had said the word "mon" before, I suddenly flushed at the way he said it. It was as if he was trying a little too hard to identify with me, or as if even (consciously or unconsciously) he was ridiculing my culture. I put my own gloves in my duffle and felt a growing anxiety to zip my rummaging thoughts. Unsure of the dual echoes in Gordon's tone, I drew the zipper and said, "Hey, Gordon. Remember one thing . . . I'm not you mum." We headed out of the fitness center and strolled across the parking lot with his loud laughter ringing like a gravel rain.

"I'll remember that," he said. His laughter erased the implications of his tone and allayed my fears. Forgetting my initial response, I started laughing as well, and we shook hands. It was the laughter of self-recognition that would form the basis of our friendship: mutual verbal mischief the way brothers, close in age, often are, playfully giving each other a hard time.

It wasn't long before we were shooting pool together once a week. One Friday evening, we'd arranged to meet at Gordon's house three miles away on Myrtle Drive. He'd earlier suggested we go to a nearby pool hall and bar and then, later, take in some live music. When I arrived at his tree-shrouded, two-story, red-brick house, the six o'clock May sunlight mildly waltzed over beds of yellow daffodils and pink azaleas. Several dogwoods surrounding the house frothed with joy.

I pulled into the wide driveway and parked next to a red Corvette. I got out the car and looked up at the canopy of pines, oaks, and ash that sheltered the dogwoods. The blue eyes of the sky peered through the taller trees, some of which must have been at least sixty years old. The large double-pillared house looked like old Georgia money. I wasn't surprised nor was I intimidated. It was the kind of house I secretly dreamed of owning. This had something to do with what I regarded as historical justice or leveling. There had been many houses this size in Barbados, but made of coral stone instead of red bricks. Even before I emigrated to America, affluent blacks were living in such homes purchased from the children of the planter class. The Barbados prime minister lived in a house three times as large as this on at least three acres of land.

Gordon's wife answered the doorbell. Brunette, blue-eyed and conservatively dressed, she held open the door in a tight-lipped manner. He had spoken of her, but this was my first time meeting her. She was clearly expecting me.

"You must be Tony," she said. I nodded. She introduced herself as Jennifer and swung the door open. "Well, come on in. Gordon will be down soon. Have a seat. May I get you something to drink?"

"No, thanks. I'm fine," I said, sitting down on a blue floral couch. Her cordiality made me uncomfortable. I looked up into the ceiling to find an escape. A magnificent chandelier, like crystal teardrops, hung there and allowed me the gratification of some partial distance, some partial relief. I looked down again to see a little redhead girl of about ten pass in front of me, seemingly headed toward the dining room. Like Hamlet to Ophelia, she kept her eyes glued on me until she passed out the room. Gordon appeared with a loud, "How're you doin'?" I got up to greet him. The little redhead passed by again.

"You're black," she said. She stopped right in front of me and folded her arms.

"Elizabeth," Gordon mildly scolded, "this is my friend, Tony. He's not from here. He's from Barbados. We'll look it up on the map a little later, ok?"

"Oh," the girl said, accepting her father's suggestion with a giggle.

"Elizabeth," I addressed her while wearily putting on the social mask. "That's such a pretty name." But even as I said this, I felt a mixture of hot and cold water run underneath my skin. I had heard that some Americans treated foreign blacks with greater respect than American blacks. The girl's acceptance of me following Gordon's distinction of blacks along geographical lines seemed to confirm this view. Or was I being oversensitive? Was the scenario at Gordon's home all innocent? Was I overreacting to what was an honest inquiry from a child who, for the first time perhaps, had seen a black person in her home? Was the child's comment an innocent attempt at conversation with a stranger? Was Gordon's statement simply information given so as not to confuse his daughter? given to educate his daughter?

I have never been able to come to terms with all the nuances of race in the United States. That is why such questions flood my senses when situations like this occur. I resist easy labeling, easy categories of black and white, but I cannot escape the existence of such thinking, particularly here in the South. It is evident wherever you turn, at school, on the job, in the media. When different races meet, the first thought is always color, the first sensation always a consciousness of color. I can't escape this cultural reality however much I abhor and reject it.

We left in Gordon's Corvette and headed for the pool hall and bar over in the Plaza. We arrived there in about twenty minutes and went into the bar area. The bartender smiled broadly at us and said, "How're y'all doin' today?" Gordon raised a hand in response. I indicated I was doing fine with a firm nod and simultaneous opening and closing of my mouth.

It was a typical bar: the subdued lighting, the monitor on the wall (now emitting a news update) installed primarily for the viewing of ball games; the constant subterranean hum of conversations punctuated by the howl, the raucous laugh. We ordered two draft beers. Gordon insisted on paying for them. After collecting our beers, we walked the length of the bar and then headed down a hallway to the poolroom at the rear of the building. Several pinball machines stood like sentries at the sides of the poolroom, and I heard the launch of intergalactic voices. One man with large tattooed arms clutched the handlebars and grimaced with the intensity of real war. Every now and again he hollered, "Gotcha!" and slapped his right hand against the machine's thigh. The hall was much less crowded than in the bar area. There must have been about fifteen people in all. It seemed that when the tattooed warrior had looked at me, all other eyes in the room immediately followed suit. The alien eyes fastened on me and, for a moment, all went dead calm. During that moment, my thoughts scurried like the striped and solid balls on the lawn-green tables. The dead calm emphatically stated that I was the only black person in the room. As Gordon and I approached the table, the balls in my head scurried faster when a middle-aged man, wearing blue jeans and a sweater, and carrying a pool stick, swished toward us.

"Hey, Gordon. What's goin' on?" the hefty man said. "Still selling all those houses?" He was right next to us. Flesh seemed to settle on him when he came to a stop. The collective eye divided into pairs and refocused on their respective tabletops. The clanking of the balls resumed.

"You're kidding me, Greg," Gordon said. "Don't you see all those For Sale signs up everywhere in Augusta and over here? Nobody's buying. I wish you'd send some business my way."

"Woah, woah. Just a minute now. That's not what I've been hearing."

All this time, Greg never acknowledged my presence. He looked through me as if I weren't there. Gordon seemed unaware of this. He addressed the other man as if everything was normal and in place.

"Well, actually, I'm survivin'. But just barely now."

"Sure. Sure. I know you are. I guess every little bit really adds up, eh Gordon? Well, take care y'self. Good seeing you."

"You bet."

The man headed toward the table at the far corner of the room. Normally, I would not have come into a place like this alone. But I was with a white man whom I regarded as a friend, so let them stare, let them not see me. As long as none of them bothered me, I intended to enjoy my game and my draft. And who knows? Maybe my friendship with Gordon might contribute in some small way to more racial tolerance in these parts. But I was aware that this could only work both ways if Gordon, in his turn, visited some of my haunts as well. I intended to later put all this to the test.

We spent a few hours in the poolroom and then went over to the Red Tiger, where we listened to a folk guitarist play and sing his heart out to an audience that grew progressively drunk and inattentive as the night wore on. We left the Red Tiger around one o'clock, filled with beer and merriment. On the way to Gordon's house, he said, "You know, Tony, you're not like other blacks around here." In spite of the alcohol, an uneasy feeling started creeping over me. It was the same inching unease I had earlier felt at Gordon's house.

"You have a sense of humor," he bubbled. "You don't carry around a chip on your shoulder all the time. You got the oommmmmmmmphf, mon. And I like that."

I was unsure of how to respond, so I said nothing. What was it that troubled Gordon? Or was it me who was overreacting? Why did I have this uncomfortable feeling Gordon was trying too hard to identify with me? And why didn't he introduce me to Greg? Was it merely a cultural attitude that bore no conscious judgment at all? Or was Gordon an accomplice (whether consciously or unconsciously) in the psychology of exclusion that some whites meted out to blacks and which I had experienced before in Louisiana and South Carolina? I strained not to think of him in this manner. I liked Gordon.

Next day, I raised some of these issues with Malaika.

"Let me tell you somp'n," she said, sitting cross-legged on the sofa and sipping a cup of herbal tea. "Gordon respects me 'cause I'm your wife, OK? But he's still typically White American (let me tell you what

I mean)." She paused momentarily. I knew that I could count on her support in matters such as this, whenever any threat or echo of threat came from the outside into our lives. Her lips opened into a vowel of protection. "ok. Some of them can't really deal with black Americans 'cause we remind them too directly of their ancestors' crimes, ok? The ones who still have some sensitivity, hook up with someone like yourself (a West Indian or an African, right?), so they can tell themselves: 'I have a black friend, so I'm no bigot.' But, in the end, it all smacks of patronage. There's still some line drawn as to how far they'll embrace you . . ."

"He's always telling me I'm not like other blacks here," I said, and leaned against the archway that separated the living room from the den. I sensed that some revelation was in the air. Malaika's shortly cut and tapered hair seemed to bristle with it. My right foot involuntarily began rubbing the instep of the left foot like a lonely or hungry cat scratching on the outside of a door. I starved for some clear answers. Even though I'd been in America all this time, I could never fully grasp the black/white dichotomy in race relationships. When it was overt and obvious, I understood it intellectually. But I only understood racist subtlety and nuance emotionally. It gave me a headache to try to figure it out. It simply wasn't my nature to think in such terms. Perhaps, too, it was a reality that I didn't want to accept, another cultural norm that might distance me further from my past, which I loved and feared in equal measure. But as much as I might have wanted to overlook the specter of racism, yesterday's memory of the hot and cold rushes under my skin made it impossible for me to do so.

"That's exactly what I'm saying," Malaika said. "What he means is that you're no threat to his deep-seated prejudices, because you're from another country and not right in his yard. He don't have to go through the discomfort of real change (change means work; takes a whole lotta effort). He don't have to deal with that, while at the same time he has you as a buffer for his conscience. You see what I'm saying?"

"It was the same way in Louisiana," I said. I didn't like where the conversation was heading, or my growing discomfort, but I was determined to see it through. The telephone rang. I walked over and answered it. "Who?" I asked and hung up. Then I walked over and sat on the black leather recliner and said to Malaika, "Alfred, the phone is for you."

"Silly," she said and smiled. But she quickly aborted the levity. She seemed anxious to get some beast off her chest. "But as I was saying . . . I'd be careful if I were you. It's not that I don't like Gordon. I do. He's funny. The kids like him. And you obviously fill a need in his life and vice-versa. But it's not Gordon all by himself. He's a family man, so that includes his wife, his family, and other friends. You see what I mean?"

"Yes, I see."

"Fancy his child looking at you and calling you black. Of course, you're black. Already the racial consciousness is in that child. All I'm saying, Tony, is don't put your expectations too high, 'cause I know how seriously you take friendships. I don't want you to get yourself hurt."

These were the kinds of conversations I remembered us having during college days: earnest, intense, penetrating, and supportive. They had bound us together like love vines. They were a wall around any alien force. Her pragmatism had done its job. I felt both disturbed and enlightened. I got up with a sigh and said, "I hear you."

I went into the kitchen, opened the fridge door, and took out a Heineken, uncapped it, and drank a third of it in one gulp. This calmed me some. When I returned to the living room, Malaika was sipping the last of her tea. She laid the blue china cup on to its saucer and looked at me.

"It's funny," I said weakly, retaking my seat on the black recliner, "most of the black guys I've met here so far seem just as provincial as the whites. The only difference is one type of segregation's racial, the other's cultural. But, at least, there's no legal segregation now. At least people can choose. I don't know. Perhaps sticking to one's own is the best thing to do, after all. I don't know."

"For blacks, the safest thing to do. It's called self-protection, Tony. Protection from abuse."

"I guess I can understand why blacks here stick to themselves," I said. "Historical mistrusts have a way of forcing people into a reverse provincialism, I guess. But how do you explain segregation in a place like Barbados, where the blacks are in the majority?

"You tell me."

"Barbadian whites don't get involved in the social and cultural life of the place, but, unlike minorities here, they can afford to. Financially, I mean. Whites still control most of the wealth in Barbados, you know. Emotionally? Personally, I think white Barbadians are all quite mad. Money can't buy them peace. They live in fear, like hostages in their own country. The segregation there that harms blacks emotionally is along class lines within the black community."

When Barbados became independent from Great Britain in 1966, blacks had been content to have political power, whites content to retain financial power. Racial coexistence had been established along these lines. I could not recall a single major racial incident in Barbados during my nineteen years there. Black middle-class people, many of whom worked for white-owned companies, had been the most visible source of irritation for the majority of other black Barbadians.

Malaika said, "You get that here, too, but certainly snobbery's not as valid a reason to perpetuate separatism as racism is."

"I don't think any kind of segregation's good, mind you. And I don't think black Americans should separate themselves from other ethnic groups because of their bad experiences with whites. But you're absolutely right," I said, warding off what I sensed was a gathering odor of argument. "And the results are the same. Always the same. Every crab in his own hole."

Malaika smiled her protective smile and slowly shook her head from side to side.

"I like that," she said. "And it's so true. Every crab in his own hole."

Gordon and I maintained our boys' night out and, after a few weeks, I decided it was time to put my plan to the test. I invited him to go with me to Super C Night Club. As much as Malaika had penetrated my consciousness with her theories on race, theories that had mangled yet enlightened me, I was still unprepared for Gordon's response. I extended the invitation one Wednesday evening as we were leaving the fitness center.

"No way!" was Gordon's instantaneous response. He appeared

horrified. "That's over in South Augusta. You don't want to go into that part of town." His voice had reached a cry. "You won't want to go in there with those expensive suede shoes. Someone could kill you for them."

He said all this in almost one breath. His horror was real, earnest, even well-meaning. A friend's warning? His response simply ratified how Americans saw the world starkly in terms of black and white, them and us. And it was more than this. Battle lines were drawn. It was war. Malaika's words banged in my brain. Caribbean black was more acceptable than American black. It all seemed so ridiculous. I couldn't take it anymore. I stopped walking and said, "Look, Gordon. I go to your pool halls, your clubs, your bars. I've seen men and women in them who looked like hardened criminals, so don't give me this bullshit 'bout 'that part of town.' If I can hang in your joints, you should be able to hang in mine, otherwise this friendship ain't worth a damn. I mean, if you feel that way 'bout black people, why bother with me, man?"

"I already told you, you're different . . ."

"I'm sick of hearing that crap, man. My socialization may be, but the history's the same, slavery, the whole lot. I don't have a chip on my shoulder (as you say) only because where I'm from 95 percent of the people are of my race and blacks have been ruling since the '60s. I see people as people. But, maybe, if I were socialized in this country, I'd probably be just like 'those other people' you talk so much about!"

"ok, ok, ok," Gordon said, his voice lowering to almost a whisper. "You've made your point."

We stood in the middle of the parking lot, just a few yards from our cars, which were parked next to each other. A few passersby observed our altercation with momentary curiosity. Others increased their walking pace. Dusk had gathered around the buildings of the plaza, and the headlights of cars on the neighboring highway were speeding fireflies. We stood there flushed, silent, and tense. Then, without any further words, we strode toward our respective cars, not once looking back.

Two weeks later, Gordon called.

"I have a confession to make," he began. I said nothing, still in a state of mistrust. I waited for him to speak again. He told me about his extreme conservative upbringing; how, in high school, he too, was guilty of racial intolerance, participating in racial jokes and such like. He had married his conservative childhood sweetheart. And then the shocking disclosure: his grandfather's associations with the Klan. His grandfather, a councilman, had risen to the position of Cyclops, which meant he was a leader of the local KKK organization. At age sixteen, Gordon remembered attending a huge Klan rally in Plains, Georgia. He described the scene as if it were happening at that moment. He described the large field behind a farm where the hooded members and the nonhooded guests had gathered. The cars had come slithering down the dirt road next to the farm and were parked, in hedgerow fashion, around the field. Huge oaks, curtained with Spanish moss, bordered the expanse like guards. The area wasn't completely level. Gordon described walking through patches of grapevine and palmetto in order to get to the clearing where a platform had been erected. In front of the platform, mainly old men, women, and children sat in plastic chairs arranged in semicircular format. Everyone else stood up. His grandfather had made him sit in a front row seat, and he remembered having to endure a pelvic itch for the length of the meeting. Much to his relief, the meeting was aborted when, halfway through, a man, hoping to disrupt the proceedings, rammed a Jaguar sports car into the speakers' platform, injuring a few bystanders and sparking a melee. Later, at home, he would discover a tick in his underwear.

"I'll never forget what a local farmer said to me on the way out from the meeting," Gordon said. "He asked me: 'Why have you brought all this trouble to Plains?' That made me think real hard. Real hard. I never went to another meeting and vowed, there and then, that I'd try to be different. It wasn't easy. When I was in college, I joined the Reserves and worked under black men."

I began to feel somewhat disarmed by Gordon's confessions, as if I were being drawn into some strange purgatorial web. All these experiences, he said, had made him more tolerant of blacks, but he was not perfect. No person was. He was still a product of a particular upbringing and culture. It seemed to me as if he had his own historical burden, and now I fully understood what Malaika had meant by me filling a need in his life. It was hard work shedding the skin of one's old nature. People needed help in that regard. Maybe I was unconsciously helping Gordon deal with his past.

It seemed he was seeking to absolve himself of some curious guilt. He had broken down and was big enough to share his ghost with me. "We're going out on Friday night," he said.

"Where?"

"Super C."

"You're on, man," I said.

18. Theater of Operations
Donald Morrill

Tampa, Florida, January 1, 2006

1.

The teenaged Roman emperor Elagabalus (AD 218–222) sent minions forth into the empire to gather people with the biggest hernias. These unfortunates were then made to compete in athletic events at the palace baths. For his pleasure.

See, the leadership isn't so bad in America at present.

Now close your eyes and get back to work.

2.

All those checks on governmental power in the U.S. Constitution and yet little or no concern there about overbearing private power, no intimation that such a thing could tyrannize while perhaps retaining the outward forms of the Republic as an inspiring camouflage. Though the framers were skeptics and realists—and more than one was deeply schooled in the burgeoning technologies and economies of the time—none could envision, apparently, something like oil cartels or media combines (not to mention their nineteenth- and eighteenth-century predecessors) dominating the People, with hands on the levers of the public till.

Or was there no way to admit such a thing and keep everybody in business who mattered to ratification?

Also, not the slightest alertness in the Constitution to the powers of the image (though Ben Franklin—media man that he was—surely understood it well, urging administrative unity, for instance, as early as 1754, in the *Pennsylvania Gazette*, through a woodcut depicting the colonies as a chopped-up snake, with the caption, "Join, or Die").

Alas. Perhaps it is true that during the Enlightenment people still wanted to believe words mattered more than pictures, and that words would control pictures and would be controlled, in the end, by reason.

3.

Last October, I presented the following hypothetical "deal"[1] to a class of first-year writing students at the university where I teach (in response to one agitated student's demand to know why the world was "so fucked up"—why it seemed few, if any, in Washington cared much about, say, the suffering inflicted by Hurricane Katrina, or about child poverty in the United States—or the vast poverty beyond our shores—while billions in tax cuts and rebates were pouring into the coffers of the richest 1 percent of the U.S. population and billions more, on credit, were disappearing into the national security pork barrel and the Iraq fiasco): *A million dollars, tax-free, will be deposited in an off-shore bank account in your name; all you need do is write "yes" on the blank piece of paper before you. But if you write "yes," a third-world peasant will be liquidated—with no legal consequences for you, of course. Simply write "yes" on the sheet . . . or "no" if you reject the bargain. Nothing else.*

Seven of nineteen wrote "yes."

I'm tempted to leave off my report of this incident with that last sentence. But I'm already far too sentimental about the obvious—about how certain phenomena are so overwhelmingly the case most everyone can acknowledge them; I forget how often wishes deface the facts.

So: only two students remarked on the ethical implications of the class response, though the others—given their peculiar silence (the silence of disturbing recognition?)—seemed to sense how it illustrated one way ordinary people might become monstrous.

At last, one student did pluck up her courage and declare only a fool would not take the money and run.

When asked, no student could offer a cogent definition of "public interest" or "social contract." None could distinguish government from enterprise, not having heard of such a distinction, apparently.

4.

"Oh, come on, they let 9/11 happen!"—how often we hear it, or a premise more or less similarly paranoid and/or aggressively knowing (and yet not always so far-fetched). Those who demand such conspiracy theories—the world run by an international camorra or an invisible regime-within-all-regimes—must find consolation (and perhaps aesthetic satisfaction) in the assertion of a malignant order. Better an awful purpose, they seem to be saying, than what appears to be chaos.

> *What but design of darkness to appall*
> *If Design govern in a thing so small . . .*

—Robert Frost, "Design"

5.

Me? Raised in a blue-collar family. But I'm neither blue state nor red, and I resent this misleading binary imposed for its high-contrast tele-value. (It's intractably typical of the current political derangement and cultural stupefaction that so many millions who a generation ago would have slugged anyone calling them "red" now accept the adjective as common shorthand for their virtues and programs; the moment abounds in perversions and inversions of meaning—hypocrisy extolled as morality, greed selflessness, ignorance strength, privilege not an example of social promotion but an ordinary, down-home fact of nature).

JOURNAL: FRIDAY, DECEMBER 1, 2000

The election recount continues. Bush is forming his cabinet and claiming he has won. Gore is trying to keep the public interested in having all the votes in Florida counted. The clock is ticking, giving appropriate charge to this horrible, sleep-inducing outrage. No matter who finally prevails, he will look like he stole the election. The few people on both sides of the situation seem unwilling to say much. We all hurt, because of the indecision and because the usual rottenness of the system is impossible to ignore. I dangle over the spike of contempt for George W., a man who's never accomplished a thing on his own and has the blankness of his arrogance to prove it. His voice is a room decked out in what the decorator suggested and what he held over from his fraternity house. This is justice for us. He'll be worse than Reagan, run by his advisors and unable to keep up with the cue cards. But he'll have most of Reagan's advisors, who are now appearing in public like insects when the lights go down. No one voted for them, but there they scuttle. Gore is only a little better, but he's intelligent and he works hard. The country wants the status quo. (It would keep Clinton four more years, if it could.) Gore's conservative and shifty and tiresome; he even adopted the Reagan head-wagging in the debates (which didn't soothe people, apparently), but he aspires to seriousness. He speaks of seriousness, and unlike his opponent he can form a complex sentence. He can hold two ideas in his head at once. Fifty million voters were more concerned with Clinton's peccadilloes as they somehow applied to Gore than with whether the new president could name the countries on a map of the world.

We're hopelessly at the mercy of organized mobs—parties of any sort, whether they advocate green issues or spreading the green around. Nader is being vilified by Democrats: he stole the votes, they say, that would have given Gore a victory. It's true. Nader would have had a tremendous effect on the election—and the country—had he been allowed into the televised debates. That would have been excellent for the country. But no one in power wanted anyone fucking with the national agenda. So he was shunted out the door, into a dim, echoing tunnel of threats about lawsuits.

What is there to say of public life, since there is an industry of commentary? Agony and sleepiness . . .

In the days just before the election, realizing how improbably close it was turning out to be, I'd begged one of Nader's young supporters, now contrite, to go for Gore.

"There's a real choice here, in policy and character," I said, hoping blandness would be read as gravity.

With a flush of excited idealism, he assured me, "Things have to get worse before they get better."

Even after the selection, there were some here in my neighborhood (an absolutely Republican precinct) who—troubled by the outcome and, even more, the means—could hope the office would be bigger than the man and maybe even somehow bypass him.

"That boy might still amount to something," one quite elderly lady opined over her hibiscus, the only comment she's made on the situation.

Certainly Gore and company would have bombed Afghanistan after 9/11. The global financial system would not have permitted perceived inaction. But Iraq? The false cries of yellow cake uranium and WMDs? Or the big belt-buckle swagger? How about the Dr. Strangelove pronouncements from sneering Uncle Cheney? Or the last prop of integrity, Colin Powell, testifying before Congress with his reconnaissance snapshots of truck and tubes, kissing his presidential aspirations adieu?

Then, just beneath this high drama, not really out of sight but mostly out of mind, there's the dismantling of environmental protections, the naturalizing of no-bid contracts, the aggressive secrecy, the retrograde economic and social agendas—met with, well, astonishing acquiescence.

It makes one wonder what kind of political opportunism 9/11 would have inspired in Gore and company—Gore the avowed internationalist, proponent of Internet globalism and new policies on greenhouse gases. What might he have done, facing, as Bush has not, a legislative branch in the hands of the opposition party?

6.

Tocqueville's *Democracy in America* is cited by pundits of every stripe—almost like the Bible in certain arguments—but he made several observations about the nation pertinent to an understanding of its burgeoning imperial dilemmas and present impasse:

- In America, there exists a tyranny of the majority: anything outside the broad circle of opinion is ridiculed

- In America, there is an almost religious belief in majority, that it can't fail, that it is as infallible as a king

- The more equal the circumstances of Americans the more inward-looking and insular they are

- The American press doesn't do good but it can keep us from evil and preserve civilization

- There is much talk in America but little independence of mind

- Americans mostly read short books about self-improvement

- A flourishing Democracy is rooted in local administration

- Democracy requires the opportunity for people to join associations and to have broad access to the press, to speak to the world.

7.

Well, for more than a decade, the '80s, I was a monster in the eyes of one of my brothers, a disaffected Catholic turned fundamentalist Christian who believed I embodied the deadly Western Secular Humanism—which, I admit, I did, with an equally fundamentalist zeal. (How quaint that demonizing now seems—like Dan Quayle, in '92, arguing in the press with a character from the TV show *Murphy Brown* about the state of the family in America, revealing himself to be, as far as the audiences were concerned, not only a fool and an ignoramus but nearly as much a fiction in most people's lives as the TV character with whom he contended, who at least understood, as most every fellow American would, that single-parent families were commonplace.)

Anyway, my zealous brother eventually came out, divorced after nearly a decade of marriage, changed churches and went into therapy, where he began to see that—as he liked to reassure me in that trans-formative period, when we first began to talk again—"things are not black and white."

Has he become a monster, now, in the eyes of those with whom he worshiped but who would deny him who he is?—a sensitive, fragile person (as he was even at his most fearsome and blinkered), a hard-working guy (twenty-six years at the same company) with one son married and the other on the dean's list at college, a middle-aged man looking to settle down again monogamously, worried no one will want him and he'll grow old alone.

"I used to pray so hard," he sighed, recalling his life in the closet, "for God to beat those wrong feelings out of me . . ."

But he lives in Iowa (state motto: "Our liberties we prize and our rights we maintain"), a purported red zone somewhat different from Florida . . . or the Floridas, I should say.

8.

Lines from "Old Europe":

> Thieves who steal from private citizens spend their lives in bonds and chains; thieves who steal from public funds spend theirs in purple and gold.
> —Cato, *Praeda Militibus, Dividenda, XI, 3*

> In daily life we are more often liked for our defects than for our qualities.
> —La Rochefoucauld, *Maxims*

> It is no longer a single historical world—as it has been from the beginning of the nineteenth century onwards. Nor is it any longer ours. We, in the culture of commodities, are living our crisis; the rest of the world are living theirs. Our crisis is that we no longer believe in a future. Their crisis is us. The most we want is to hang on to what we've got. They want the means to live.
> That is why our principal preoccupations have become private and our public discourse is compounded of spite. The historical and cultural space for public speech, for public hopes

and action, has been dismantled. We live and have our being today in private coverts.

—John Berger, *On Keeping a Rendezvous*

Understanding does not inform our morality, our morality informs the ways we have of understanding. The language of pleasure and the language of justice are inextricable. By being a new way of saying this, psychoanalysis can be recruited to consolidate our prejudices or to show us what our prejudices are for.

—Adam Phillips, *Terrors and Experts*

Men owe us what we imagine they will give us. We must forgive them the debt.

To accept that fact that they are other than the creatures of our imagination is to imitate the renunciation of God.

I also am other than what I imagine myself to be. To know this is forgiveness.

—Simone Weil, "Void and Compensation," *Gravity and Grace*

Power wears out those who don't have it.

—Giulio Andreotti, six-time Prime Minister of Italy (later indicted and acquitted)

9.

In May 2005, at a large travel agency here in Tampa, the man behind the desk—Mr. Green Tie, I'll call him—mentions that South America is now a preferred destination over Europe, "except Brazil, of course . . . Yes, we're seeing people coming back from Europe now and they say 'never again!' . . ."

Kicking me under the desk, my wife, Lisa, replies cheerfully, "That's OK. We hate our president. We'll fit right in with the Spaniards."

Green Tie shakes his head wildly, as though fending off a blow of cartoon amazement, and pushes hard on his pen, scratching across my international driver's license. He finally looks up and says, "It's good that you can say something like that here and not be shot for it."

Lisa laughed later, "You could see he wanted me to be shot for it."

"Yes," she replies to him, "If we're lucky, we'll make it through the next few years without losing our rights."

Green Tie leans hard on his pen, trying to maintain the demeanor of a good customer consultant.

"I'll think about that as I drive home to the gulag tonight," he says, finally, shaking his head again, as if to clear it of some noxious ether.

10.

For the ancient Athenians, free speech was not a right but a "mark" of a free man—a characteristic behavior.

The longer the crime the more challenging it is to say there has been wrongdoing. The longer the lie the more difficult it is to remember the truth it tried to conceal.

The most successful ideological effects are those which have no words, and ask no more than complicitous silence.
—John Harvey, *The Condition of Postmodernity*

11.

TO THE SECRETARY OF DEFENSE, PREPARING FOR THE DAILY PRESS CONFERENCE DURING *OPERATION IRAQI* FREEDOM (5.22.03)

Rumsfeld I saw a man in the KashNKarry parking lot
    wearing the humiliating hairnet hat
    Maybe you know it   the kind food service personnel have to wear

He's from Russia or one of those *Breakaway Soviet Republics*
    we heard fondly of so briefly
    former enemies of our nation in the Cold War decades
    you were making policy in   remember

He's unfalteringly friendly this guy
    because of course he's glad to be in Tampa Florida

slopping pails in the deli though he's middle-aged

though he's got to know by now that smoking like that
    even if just a habit
    is some kind of Old World provocation that will end him up with
    not enough insurance
    in a place where they can't treat him very long

It's a useless toughness he probably doesn't intend
    because his poor English will repeat that he's happy and

he is happy to start life again like this to be the start of a family
    in a new country
    his mind gray with nonsense the nostalgia of his parents
    for Stalin ignoramuses a perfect focus group

It's the mop pail he leads or if promoted the cold cuts
    as he did back in his shit burg
    where men like you don't appear but on Occasions

He's staring across the lot waiting for his ride
    because he doesn't own a car or even have a license
    yet
    He's just happy to be in America mop pail and some day
    cold cuts
    Though tired he looks dignified in his demeaning hat
    because he doesn't have to hide it

His grandkids or someone like them may work hard
    or charm a connection and rise to power like you
    and then lie as you do each day for your position

That's if you and your owners don't dismantle The American
    Chance
    for this man's progeny to become corrupt in a way
    that affects so many

Come to the podium Rumsfeld
    Brief us just once on the true theater of operations

12.

Almost since our high school days, I've been the object of generally tender—and half-smug—ridicule from two of my oldest friends, red-staters back in Iowa. Behold me in their eyes: the "self-righteous liberal," "the guy who wants to give it all away to the lazy welfare cheats," the "feminazi" . . .

We've argued ferociously, sometimes, concluding eventually with beer and cheer. They don't believe in "big government," (often a euphemism for taxes) except, of course, when government serves their interests. Though they call themselves conservatives, they aren't conservative enough to defend flag burning as free speech. In many ways they simply want to be left alone, to send their kids to schools in the better-funded districts and complain occasionally about the decline of moral standards perpetrated by Hollywood.

The events of 9/11 drove fear and the yearning for an unquestioned innocence deeper into them. They would hear nothing, it seemed, but the same tribal consciousness, the same "us and them" roar that is the first fallacy of fanatics everywhere. Two decades of imagery—beginning with the seizing of the American embassy in Iran in 1979—had prepared them to believe they understood who the terrorists were. (The countenance: young, male, unshaven, Arab in aspect—a face, in its effect, not unlike the young black in the blurry mug shot offered, for years now, by the evening news.)

Like most of the citizenry, we moved to the centers of our circles of opinion, and our circles hardly overlapped. These were always quietly religious men, slightly paternalistic, convinced that I was, finally, an apostate destined to return to the fold. These men love me, and I love them. But history had to lean on us only a little, and we all grew more strident about "values," their arguments cresting on the nearly unspoken assumption that those gathering in the pews on Sunday possessed them for us all. (They'd despised Clinton's personal failings and subsequent evasions, perhaps because these so faithfully mirrored their own. They may admire Bush for the same reason.) In the end, however, the more embattled of the two simply grew tired of my polemics and turned up the volume on his family radio program—to underscore the announcer's invective against such dark forces as Ted Kennedy and the dreaded Hilary. I finally withdrew when, during the closing weeks of the 2004 presidential campaign, one of them emailed me that jpg file (surely, you saw it) of John Kerry's face emblazoned on a piece of North Vietnamese currency. Yes, it was just another typical inversion—the decorated veteran as traitor (running for office against a toy soldier). But only one of us had served in the military (and not in Vietnam), and now none of our children were risking it all among the occupation forces in Baghdad. My friends seemed to have accepted so many lies—and many of them much more serious than a campaign smear—in the cause of what greater truth?

On hearing my grievances—and grief—about these matters, an energetic left-wing acquaintance in California sweepingly assured me that, compelled by the appropriate circumstances, my old friends were the kind who would surely give me up to the executioners, if not perform the liquidation themselves.

Absurd. But all around I see how desperately our species needs new moral mythologies and metaphysical fictions—new languages and images—that reflect the reality of civilization and the universe as we understand it now. Such inspirations take centuries, of course, if we're allowed them. Meanwhile there are many across the globe who would kill me for promulgating heresy, since every day they kill for the supremacy of their godly metaphors, fervent that these metaphors be literal.

And then there's Mrs. Darwin—who is us, any of us viewed from the future. How touching and futile that she was full of trepidation that her husband's studies might prevent them from sharing eternity together.

13.

Errol Morris's recent documentary on Robert McNamara and Vietnam, *The Fog of War*, suggests how the current managers of folly may indeed manage their own misunderstanding of their actions. The former Secretary of Defense under Democrats Kennedy and Johnson— now ultimately defending himself against himself—justifies the initial U.S. involvement and disastrous escalation in terms often echoing any number of Pentagon press briefings on the Iraq invasion.

Morris shows us file footage of a younger McNamara, the technocratic epitome of the "best and brightest," pointer in hand, explaining, summarizing, mastering the information for all in attendance. We see him interviewed about his reputed arrogance, smiling primly in those black and white days when TV was new—less than a decade after Nixon's Checkers speech amid the laughably stilted campaign ads of Adlai and Ike. His excitement abounds as it is impressively restrained.

The McNamara of today is impressive, too. Articulate, as always, and emotional to the point of tears, yet nuanced of notion, formidable in his grasp of the details. With grace and verve, he recounts his rise and the circumstances he confronted along the way. (When he speaks of Bobby Kennedy and Sargent Shriver contacting him on Jack's behalf about a cabinet post, you begin to understand the furious paranoia of those who felt the government had fallen into the clutches of an Irish family mob, reprehensible just beneath its suave style—this, of course, before the martyrdom in Dallas disallowed such discussion.) As McNamara proceeds, you also start to understand that his stories are shapely because he's told them often—and they are mostly stories of the dead, who cannot dispute. At their edges lie the vaster wilds of self-knowledge entered only with the greatest caution. One of the gifts of the film, however, is that you find yourself rooting for him, this old man, still possessed of his substantial faculties, questing for insight, it seems, into his own errors and misdeeds. With a hunger whetted on Sophoclean epiphanies, you want to believe time bestows sufficient truth in exchange for all it takes away.

What we discover—once this teller's charm has receded into the distance of cooler regard—is a man who can recall his pay rate sixty years ago but who says he cannot remember whether he authorized the use of Agent Orange. A man who recounts history in admirable particulars but finally conflates World War II, Korea, and Vietnam—attempting to veil the vague or venal agendas of the latter two conflicts in the unmistakable moral purposes of the first. (Such misdirection flourishes today. Recall the 2005 Super Bowl salute to "the greatest generation." A stadium propaganda event worthy of the Chinese in Mao's day, it purported to honor those who have served the cause of freedom. But as the aged World War II veterans, followed by ever-younger veterans, were marched out to triumphant cheers, it was clear the audience was not supposed to wonder why this country has warred so often but, instead, should savor the painful yet glorious certainty that all the invasions and incursions were as noble as the midcentury struggle against the Axis powers. The event was, in effect, a state advertisement for American innocence, that most venerable of infantilizing myths, an announcement to the world that the Iraq occupation, too, was of the same righteous order, and our resolve would remain firm, etc. There they were, our fighting men and women, us, used again.)

McNamara admits the United States did not understand the Vietnamese—this error he can acknowledge. (But isn't such ignorance always a precondition of war?) With a confidence resonant of Eichmann, he insists the responsibility for the woeful policies rested with Johnson, implying that he, serving at the president's pleasure, merely followed orders. Of course, Johnson's own Oval Office recordings—aside from showing how often all concerned had decided to deceive the public—reveal a complicated entwining of roles: McNamara as advisor, sycophant, organizational turf boss, and game player. His tears, though at first touching, are ultimately disturbing—tears for instance, then and now, about being given the Medal of Freedom as Johnson showed him the door. This from a man who implies his guilt is mitigated because when he left the defense department not quite half the total American casualties had occurred. At best, the tears are displaced and more damaging than none at all.

"The fog of war," McNamara himself calls it, but much of the misting is his own. He didn't resign his post in protest, and he didn't speak against the war even after he left the Pentagon. He was loyal, most of all to his love of power. So there was knowledge he had to forsake, thought he had to forego. In order to keep, or stay as near a possible, to it: the power . . . the illusion of power.

14.

Lines from North America:

The domesticated animal is unable to welcome doubt, let alone assume it. Human strengths—language, imagery, memory, character—are therefore converted into burdens. These tools, which promise virtue and knowledge, become a fearful prison.
    —John Ralston Saul, *Voltaire's Bastards*

Human art and language (as opposed to institutional art and language) *always* cite the exception, and it was Norman Rockwell's great gift to see that life in twentieth-century America, though far from perfect, has been exceptional in the extreme. This is what he celebrates and insists upon: "normal" life, in this country, is not normal at all—that we all exist in a general state of social and physical equanimity that is unparalleled in the history of humans. (Why else would we alert the media every time we feel a little blue?) Yet, we apparently spend so many days and hours in this state of attentive painlessness that we now consider it normal—when, in fact, normal for human creatures is, and always has been, a condition of inarticulate, hopeless, never-ending pain, patriarchal oppression, boredom, and violence—while all our vocal anguish is necessarily grounded in an ongoing bodily equanimity, a physical certainty that we are safe enough and strong enough to be as articulately unpleasant as we wish to be.
    —David Hickey, *Air Guitar*

Sometimes when I am reading a Greek text I force myself to look up all the words in the dictionary, even the ones I think I know. It is surprising what you learn that way. Some of the words turn out to sound quite different than you thought. Sometimes the way they sound can make you ask questions you wouldn't otherwise ask. Lately I have begun to question the Greek word *sophrosyne*. I wonder about this concept of self-control and wonder whether it really is, as the Greeks believed, an answer to most questions of human goodness and dilemmas of civility.

I wonder if there might be another idea of human order than repression, another notion of human virtue than self-control, another kind of human self than the one based on dissociation of the inside and outside. Or indeed, another human essence than self.
—Anne Carson, "The Gender of Sound"

15.

The personal isn't enough to be political.
The personal is all there is.
The personal is only a story.
Reality will always be given a face by story,
But only one face at a time. And that's not enough.
You want statistics over narrative?
But showing a face simply turns real life into a movie—usually a stupid one.
The failure of imagination is the great tragedy of life. It's the enduring problem. Once you get some food you have to imagine others who don't have any, and we don't do that very well.
You mean we don't worry so much about whether our actions are right or wrong, or good or bad, but whether we might feel good or bad about them. Or we start to view events from some high, mythic balcony, hoping for detachment.
That's always a kind of consolation, isn't it?
If you focus only on changing yourself, the world will never be made better.
To an extent unimaginable to previous generations, we witness the workings of the world, every day. And we can't do a thing about most of what we see, especially the suffering.
That's what it's supposed to make you believe.

IT WASN'T ALL BAD

When Israeli soldiers accidentally shot to death Ahmad Khatib, a 12-year-old Palestinian boy, his family didn't vow vengeance. Instead, they donated his vital organs, which have been trans-

planted into six Israelis. Ahmed's lung, kidneys and liver went to Israelis between the ages of 7 months and 58 years; his heart now beats in the chest of Samah Gadban, a 12-year-old girl. Her mother, Yusra, hopes to speak to Ahmed's family, especially his mother. "I will ask her to receive us for a visit," she said, "so I can hug her and kiss her and thank her."
—*This Week*, November 18, 2005

16.

Daily, Florida is neither red nor blue—purple is more accurate, if one must keep to the metaphor of color. Earlier I used the term *Floridas*—suggesting the many states within this state, a beautiful and often defaced region, strenuously mythologized, whose population has increased eightfold since World War II and whose burgeoning cavalcade of the provincial and the cosmopolitan, the profound and the fatuous, has often made it a stage for the nation's political dream life. Tampa Bay is typical of it.

Last spring, for instance, believers of every sort stepped to the microphones outside a hospital here to inform the world of the unfortunate Terri Schiavo's true mental condition, which, not surprisingly, each spokesperson claimed was in conformity with his or her understanding of persistent vegetative states, the right to die, the will of the Lord, or the limits of medical know-how and funding. Of course, no one—not even conservative congressional chiefs like Dr. Frist, scrapping for personal advantage via a medical diagnosis delivered from Washington—could know the accuracy of their claims without an autopsy performed on Ms. Schiavo, and the truth was, finally, revealed. For all the rancor and media plundering, the matter of what to do when the health care wishes of an apparently brain dead person are not manifest remains unresolved and has receded from view, for now.

Then there's Sami Al-Arian, a University of South Florida computer science professor, recently acquitted on eight charges relating to the terrorist organization Palestinian Islamic Jihad. As of this writing, he remains in jail while the authorities decide whether to retry him on other counts that had resulted in a hung jury. Demanding his release, Al-Arian's supporters assert his case has now moved from the legal realm into the symbolic, where it will have profound effects on how American Muslims view their faith in the U.S. justice system.

There are also the struggles of Mickie Mashburn, a gay Tampa police detective whose domestic partner of ten years, Lois Marrero, a veteran Tampa police officer, was killed in the line of duty. Mashburn has been seeking the death benefits paid to surviving spouses but has been denied them by the pension board. And there's Joe Redner—libertarian city council candidate, notorious owner of Tampa strip clubs and the Bay Area's most frequent defender of the First Amendment—announcing he is gay and suing the county over its policy barring the government from acknowledging or participating in gay pride events. One of the county commissioners, Rhonda Storms, has exerted herself this last year advocating ordinances many consider antigay—and she is merely the most recent in long line of such activists. Yet this is a city that one friend tells me a major gay publication recently named one of the ten best in which to be out and under thirty.

It's a holiday destination, our Tampa, and a clean industry metrohub that sought to host the 2012 summer Olympics. Migrant Northerners continue to diversify it, all the while the Spanish spoken, even by ATMs, reminds us we live at the northern edge of the vaster South. Here, you can now open the newspaper to find—as we did this last September—a society column on the nuptials of a wealthy white widow to a prosperous black businessman and longtime family friend—an October–August marriage, but with the radiant bride the more senior in age and declaring happily, "He's the head. I'm the neck, and the neck turns the head."

Of course, in south Tampa, you can still hear a Republican media consultant—perhaps your neighbor and casual friend—sigh at a cocktail party, "I'd rather be a Taliban fighter at the bottom of a cave than a pregnant woman." And as ships come and go to the port, they pass the point of the south Tampa peninsula where CENTCOM is housed at MacDill Air Force Base, the site from which the nation's wars, prior to the Iraq occupation, have been directed. (It is the only precinct in this part of town, it should be noted, that went for Kerry in 2004.) Repeatedly, thousands of us protested the current war at MacDill's gates. And

for months thereafter, hundreds—and then an ever-diminishing number—waved flags and yellow ribbons in support of the troops at what
city authorities came to officially designate "Patriot's Corner" on Bay-
shore Boulevard. (Curious it is, the symbol of the yellow ribbon, since
the song from which it derives is about a man just released from prison
after three years. His crime is unspecified though presumably victim-
less—perhaps of the white-collar variety?—and it's not clear how he is
like a soldier returned from a tour of duty. But he's done his time, as the
song says, and so he's welcomed home.)

JOURNAL: THURSDAY, MARCH 20, 2003

Missiles into Baghdad last night (morning, there). And W announces the start of the war. The missiles were aimed at some
target in the southern part of the city, a "target of opportunity,"
said my sister (How quickly we adopt the terminology of the
machine.) Supposedly, the missile was aimed at Saddam himself
but hit, maybe, one of his body doubles.

Night before last, dining at a sidewalk restaurant in St. Pete
with K and his two brothers, one a Mennonite minister, we were
interrupted by a Frenchman from a nearby table who wanted to
tell us that he thought our conversation was the most intelligent
he'd heard lately. He said he has had to keep silent these past
weeks, and when he has spoken, he is dismissed for his accent.
(A professor from Maryland, he was in town to interview for
a job at USF. I reminded him of the Al-Arian case.) We all felt
more hopeful and proud, and parted in that little gold light. Just
up the street at the cigar bar, we encountered the screaming sub-
pundits on Fox, MSNBC, etc. They were damning Tom Daschle
for suggesting that Bush and his cronies had acted in bad faith
with the UN. They were demanding complete allegiance to W.

"What if Tom DeLay had said that?" the proprietor of the
cigar bar asked me.

"Tom DeLay says many things I find repulsive," I replied, "but
he has a right to say them."

The man slapped down an address book-size copy of the Declaration of Independence, well-curved from having been sat upon.

"Tom DeLay is my cousin," the proprietor said. "I've read that document. Not many people have."

He was furious the UN hadn't complied with W's wishes.

"So the UN should be a rubber stamp?" I asked.

"No. But . . ."

"So the UN does have authority, and we're in violation?" K said.

"No . . ."

"So the states on the security council have authority?" I said.

"Oh yeah," the proprietor replied. "Cameroon. They're a superpower!"

"If we're going to follow resolution 1441," K said, rising on his stool, "shouldn't we also follow all the UN resolutions about Israel?"

I tapped him on the arm. "Don't bother. That bolt's rusted on."

Perhaps the most telling of current local phenomena is *Bodies: The Exhibition*, now on display at the Museum of Science and Industry here and at several other museums across the country. As the sign at the entrance explains: "The specimens you are about to see are real. They have been preserved using a process called polymer preservation. In this process, all tissue water is replaced with silicone rubber to the deepest level. This creates a preserved human specimen without changing any of its structure, allowing you to experience a connection to your own body, the organism closest to you."

The exhibit literally incarnates the dominant mode of our public life: obscurity by apparent transparency, the obvious willfully obscured. "To see is to know," one of the exhibit signs exhorts. But what does one know from what one sees? These "specimens"—whole, sectioned or composed of a single organ or limb—are Chinese, younger, perhaps three-quarters of them male. They come from Dalian Medical University, and the promoter of the show, Premier Exhibitions, claims all died of natural causes and were unidentified and unclaimed. Yet there are unanswered questions about where and how they were acquired. (Were they prisoners? Perhaps political prisoners?) There are also concerns about how the bodies are displayed and for what audience they are truly appropriate. The Florida State Anatomical Board, which oversees the use of bodies for education and research, voted 4-2 to deny approval of the show. It asked the Florida Attorney General to enforce its ruling, but he (a gubernatorial candidate) declined the opportunity. As a friend from one of the Tampa Bay newspapers told me, "We pointed out these problems, but the story never got any bite."

No. As elsewhere, unprecedented, profitable throngs jam the exhibition rooms, peering into the lamplit tissues and vessels and nerves. Here an entire body, partially flayed, kicks a soccer ball, or cheekily hitchhikes, or raises a conductor's baton (as the person certainly never did in life). Here the musculature of a man holds hands with the skeleton it once encased, as though both were about to jitterbug, or spin like kids in a game of All Fall Down.

Public education is the pretext for all this, with a little national hygiene thrown in. (Nearly all the lungs on display are blued from smoking, though given industrial China's air pollution, one not need light up to do damage.) But the crucial product here is the Real, packaged for the consumer self, "the connection to your own body, the organism closest to you." Aside from pausing at a few of the more disturbing displays—not quite carnival curiosities or grisly wonders from the pathologist's cabinet—one drifts along, finally, encouraged to let the appearances accumulate around a still point of meaning: *This is how I look inside.* And this is supposed to be the truth beneath the naked truth.

Yet everything presented here could be reproduced as a model. Others have done it (and have been sued successfully for infringement of copyright by the originator of the plastination process, Gunther von Hagens, an artist-anatomist based in Heidelberg). But who would come out—who would pay—for mere models? One wants to touch the spinal nerves bundled like uncooked spaghetti, or the hardtack feathering from a shoulder. One wants to meditate on ruins and the durability of the body. But only because the body is real—real!—and we the audience profess to crave reality.

Yet how much of reality is denied in the very mounting of the exhibition, in its dubious necessity, in how our complicitous desires are served, and also excused, by it. We've paid to see, the logic goes, and that gives us a right to pretend not to know too much about the forces and motives that bring us the goods.

At a party recently, a woman whose son is currently serving in Iraq—a woman slowly deciding that even a so-called left winger like myself may share her desire for freedom and peace—summarized the effect well:

> I had some problems with the exhibit at MOSI, she said, that they were not claimed bodies, they were homeless ... But this was the greatest achievement, really, in their lives, more than they could ever have expected ...
>
> It was a veneration ... The body with the veins showing, that was the most beautiful thing ...
>
> How could you harm another person after looking at that? ...You see how you would prick yourself anywhere and you would bleed?

17.

Last night, CBS's *60 Minutes* ran a segment on how Hill and Knowlton, the PR firm, had been hired by the Kuwaiti government to convince the American people to go to war against Iraq. One of the features of HK's attack was the testimony before a congressional committee of a young Kuwaiti woman who claimed to have seen Iraqi soldiers committing innumerable atrocities, the most spectacular among them the yanking of infants from hospital incubators. *60 Minutes* showed how this detail focused the emotions of the country, how congressmen and the president repeated this detail—and how Amnesty International, after research, asserts that no such atrocity occurred. The VP at HK who talked to CBS—a young black woman whose eyes clarified willfully as she spun the story—claimed that her company was merely acting as an advocate for the Kuwaiti government. It "had a message it wanted to get out" to the American people, she said. She had coached the young woman who testified. When asked what her firm would have done if Iraq had come to it for some PR help, she said that these things are decided by a committee, that she didn't know. Of course, the war was sold like soda pop. Interesting as this was, the real story was why CBS took so long to pursue the use of this PR firm, etc.

18.

Another year begins. And political scandal has, again, shown its familiar face in our capitol, a corrupt place, almost by definition, though at present immoderately so. The magazines of opinion are detailing for us how the dishonesty among the presiding party has operated—detailing it too well to have just learned of it. Improbably, Tom DeLay has been forced out as House Majority Leader and must content himself behind the scenes. Perhaps more indictments are forthcoming, as various officials find themselves snagged in their networks of favor. Perhaps there will even be an impeachment one day, since the president admits he has authorized unwarranted electronic surveillance of U.S. citizens—the same action that brought Nixon's demise.

But we live by different lights now. Compared to those in charge, Nixon, in some ways, resembles a dangerous social progressive. (After all, at the time of his resignation, he was at work on a national health care plan.) And the country-at-large still teethes daily on fear and boredom and distraction. In the main, Bush and Company appear to be seeking unprecedented power for the executive branch, perhaps even the prerogative to set aside acts of Congress in order to protect the country during a conveniently open-ended, remarkably vague and mostly counter-productive war on terror. A constitutional crisis seems likely—at least one hopes for such, should Bush press on unabated, as he will (why not?), ready to accept the path to greater authority widened when (not "if," as we are often told) the next terrorist attack occurs. (Indeed, dear leaders, we know it's a dangerous world. Don't we worry about it on our streets? Don't we see it in your faces? Haven't we witnessed the premise purveyed on TV for three generations—where it competes with sex of the product variety, general inadequacy masked as superiority, irony that quickly tames each advance of satire, and indefatigable and interchangeable celebrity?)

In the meantime, the actual war in Iraq—mostly un-televised, as is the nightly delivery of troop caskets to Dover Air Force Base—will continue to preoccupy the airwaves here in the form of the same story of bombings and continuing civil progress, repeated daily as though it were the same story, and all. It will continue to draw attention away from so much damage here at home (damage plainly visible to anyone who cares to notice) and from the serious, little-examined and rarely discussed policies that spawn terrorism. Why? In the end, I can only assume that even so-called liberal institutions like the *New York Times* have pushed the war and, in the main, given the Bush regime a free pass because the elites who run it are privy to information revealing an infrastructural fragility that will not allow for the journalistic work of preserving civilization as, say, Tocqueville might have imagined it. Perhaps, with countries like China building cars and highways at a fantastic rate, the world has begun the first true global struggle for resources, as the deep ecologists envisioned decades ago. Certainly, the 2000 presidential election was, as much as anything else, a battle for political power between old and potentially new energy paradigms, and between old forms of media and new. Big oil needed to ensure it could sell every drop under lease and that alternative energy technologies, championed by the likes of Gore, should remain primitive and marginal. The TV networks—long a consort of government—needed more time to reposition themselves in the burgeoning Internet marketplace. What else explains the huge effort of mainstream media to puff up Bush—far beyond the usual tactic of stimulating narrative tension in an election season—and to thereafter ignore or minimize almost every deception, blunder and possible crime?

My old friends in Iowa and I have known each other too long to remain mutually abandoned, and so, finally, we have made amends, with delicate patience and some daring. Just the other night, one of them even admitted it's all wrong with Iraq, but we're there now so let's try to make democracy work for them—lemonade from lemons, right? And the other one tells me just today: "Bush wants his face on Mount Rushmore, and so does Osama . . . They want a place in history. They've made their bets." For once, I didn't press either of these guys to think further. They've been able to do that all along—just like my friends here in Tampa who recently attended a large Halloween party (the theme: "Oz") garbed as genies in green shears. "Emerald City Extremists," they billed themselves, complete with glowing, dirty bomb fanny packs.

"Maybe people will finally start waking up," another of my friends here in Tampa said wistfully—meaning the majority of the electorate, dissatisfied with Bush and Company before 9/11 and again now, but who remain generally inert, uninspired by a Democratic party that appears innocent of alternative ideas. Her wish, framed in that venerable cliché, suggested we were entering the next phase of a predictable myth cycle. I wondered what the waking would look like, should it occur. Would it resemble our collective manner and mood in the days immediately after 9/11? Or was that state of emotion the beginning of a new, shocked sleep? Were greater monstrosities ahead? Or perhaps the reemergence, however slight, of representative, enlightened government, and an acknowledgement of the rest of the world? Could we, the people, discover in ourselves a more courageous moral imagination—one that would subdue and replace the fanaticism posing as faith, and challenge unchecked authority and ignorance?

I thought, too, of that blessing of the Dyula, a Muslim people from Côte d'Ivoire, Burkina Faso, and parts of Mali and Ghana: "May everyone here wake up one at a time."

Only generations of tribal warfare and colonial invasion, destruction, diaspora, and imminent alarm, could inspire such a vision of paradise. It is, of course, our Eden of relative freedom and peace, here at home in Empire America—where, for the most part, our shrewdly unscrupulous rulers (our employees, remember?) and those they control rise all at once, day after day, for the enrichment and empowerment of a very few, at the expense of the rest of us.

Note

1. This exercise is not my invention. I learned of it from the poet Stephen Dunn some years ago, and thus I credit him here—though, misremembering the assignment Dunn described to me, I most likely have altered the particulars.

19. The World Loves New Orleans, but America Has Not Come to Its Rescue

Mona Lisa Saloy

Before Hurricane Katrina, New Orleans was laced with tropical greens—ferns, banana trees, palms of every sort, rugged grasses like St. Augustine or crab, and ornamental grasses like monkey or blue sliver, plus enormous oaks and evergreens tall and bushy, swamp cypress hanging with grey moss. The city was punctuated with begonia and bougainvillea from pinks to purples, with azaleas painted every color from passionate reds to pinks to purples and even yellows. There were roses of every imaginable size, shape, and shade, and towering, flowering magnolia trees, or shorter crepe myrtles lining sidewalks in a parade of color from white to beet red, from pale pink to bright fuchsia. Post-Katrina flooding killed everything. Every blade of grass, all the magnolias, more than half the stately oak trees, every bush, every banana tree in sight is dead in at least half the city. The historic Vieux Carre, the French Quarter, built—as instructed by the native Houma people—along the Mississippi crescent, was virtually untouched, like the Garden District and Uptown neighborhoods where life continues as it did before the storm; downtown New Orleans past Canal Street remains devastated, many places still without electricity or phone service: homes are broken or abandoned, like the ghost towns of the old West. The United States of America poured forth massive economic aid to tsunami victims in Asia, to 9/11 families of New York's twin towers' tragedy; yet ten months after Katrina's destruction, the American character is absent from New Orleans. New Orleans, beloved by the country and the world for its architecture, culture, history and music, now stagnates "with three-fourths of its homes uninhabitable, with 8 million tons of debris stacked or strewn in yards and streets."[1] America prides itself on being a benevolent land of the free, its arms open to the tired and huddled masses; yet it now ignores its own treasured, unique city, New Orleans.

New Orleans was the New York of the nineteenth century, perhaps the most important port-of-call, and its international population reflects its enterprises, its travelers. Of course there was the steady flux of French, Spanish and Italian, but the Irish were the first English speakers, and the resulting accent is a Brooklyn-sounding brogue. Many people know of the importation of slaves from the Caribbean, and after that the continuing stream of Cubans, Puerto Ricans, Hondurans, and so on. But how many know that for centuries the New Orleans area boasted the oldest Filipino settlement in America? (It is only in the last decade of the twentieth century that scholarship documents Filipinos landing earlier, specifically in Morro Bay along the central California coast.)[2] Anyone living just over the Orleans Parish line, in St. Bernard, is aware of this historic community and knows that Filipinos gave us dried shrimp and had houses on sticks, just like in the Philippines, until hurricanes broke them down. Filipino "Manila Men," who jumped galleons while fleeing Spanish domination, were fierce warriors and later intermarried and remained a permanent part of the panorama of cultures in the swamplands just below the Crescent City.[3] After Hurricane Katrina, some two hundred Filipino families evacuated to the Houston area, and others moved inland closer to places like Violet, where I have extended family.

Despite this great—and sometimes unacknowledged—diversity, New Orleans is often characterized by the media as "sin city." Whole Mardi Gras montages focus on tourists baring their breasts on Bourbon Street and drunks performing debased acts. In reality, every neighborhood in New Orleans is littered with churches. Many are Catholic, but the large variety of houses of worship include Baptist, Presbyterian, and Greek Orthodox churches, a Jewish Temple and Synagogue, and a strong Muslim presence. True, there are more small neighborhood bars than grocery stores, but it might surprise folks that New Orleans is and has always been a city of families, great families; it is those people who create and continue the many cultural traditions—the food and music—that repeat visitors and convention goers celebrate and enjoy. And before Katrina New Orleans was "the busiest port in the world. Sixty percent of our grain exports, 20 percent of all exports, 40 percent of our natural gas supplies pass through the port."[4] In addition, "two of the largest refineries in the United States are there. Ask Cargill, General Mills, Xcel or Center-Point whether there's a national interest at stake here."[5]

So where is the aid? Why is half the city still dead? Thanks to our national media (owned by only five multinational corporations[6]), during the immediate aftermath of Hurricane Katrina, the same footage of a few blacks "looting" food and clothes from downtown stores aired daily (literally all day long) for weeks. Since the federal government ignored Mayor Nagin's and Governor Blanco's pleas for emergency aid, flooded residents were left on their own. Hungry, thirsty, and desperate mothers and sons, fathers and daughters waded through stale, putrid floodwaters for clean drinking water and food—which could spoil at any time—and shoes to protect their feet from snakes and broken glass. Yet when the media showed white families performing the same acts, they were said to be searching for food, an acceptable action under the circumstances. Moreover, when word arrived that aid was indeed coming, many black people moved to the higher ground of interstate ramps or overpasses (many elderly in wheelchairs); some of those people died of dehydration and lack of medical care while waiting. The scenes of the huddled masses of blacks at the Superdome—where bathrooms failed, where clean water ran out, where large numbers of prisoners from the city jail were sent, where waves of people went asking to be helped—recall images of the holds of Middle Passage slave ships, where blacks were sandwiched like sardines in a can.

Switch from these images to the flattened and flipped-up debris of homes in the Lower Ninth Ward of New Orleans, largely inhabited by New Orleans's poor people; these were presented like reruns of TV sitcoms. Why did the media not show the huge areas of middle-class white homes broken in half,[7] the debris piled over twenty feet high along the boulevard medians (what we call the neutral grounds)? This biased reporting creates a national perception that only poor black areas were hardest hit, and are therefore expendable and should not be rebuilt. Welcome to the televised American version of New Orleans post-Katrina; far too many gaps occur when presenting the extent of losses for both blacks and whites. Is this really America after the Civil Rights Era?

Yes, there were thousands of blacks who did not evacuate as ordered, who remained in the city due to lack of transportation. Why? Well, the New Orleans public transportation system was already working twenty-four hours a day, seven days a week. Many working-class blacks did not own cars, although they probably owned an enviable wardrobe of clothes, several TV sets, music players and music; perhaps they didn't have credit cards either, and no way to book a hotel or no relatives outside the city. Where could they go? This was the first-ever mandatory hurricane evacuation in New Orleans history. And, after all, it seemed like just another hurricane.

Let me explain.

Hurricane season is annual, like spring or winter, for the Gulf Coast. Oh yes, we prepare. We stock up on canned food, get the grill ready to cook whatever is in the freezer before it spoils, load up on clean water, line up movies and music, along with plenty of flashlights, batteries, and candles—the Blessed kind, or Voodoo candles for protection. We have holy water to bless the house. We even fill the bathtub in anticipation of the sewers being out of commission. If that happens, one fills water in a bucket to pour or flush the toilet. *Voila!* We are then ready to quiet down, listen to the wind roar, the rain bullet our roofs, and pray that the windows hold. The eldest daughter of a Baptist minister, my mother converted to Catholicism to marry my Creole father; this was no easy matter, especially the catechismal study the devout practice required. The result was that my mother became more Catholic than my dad. Especially during hurricanes, we—Mother and I—prayed the rosary together under the light of Blessed candles. When the wind wailed, our prayers grew more intense. For children, this was an exciting prospect: the preparation, the angst of our parents, the news broadcasts warning residents to take care, to remain inside our homes. In fact, other than the great flood of 1928,[8] New Orleans had continually escaped massive damage until Hurricane Betsy.

As a kid in 1965, I lived through Betsy. Always, before the blowing of such a natural force, Mother Nature prepares as well. The normal sounds of New Orleans disappear. No birds chirp. No dogs bark. No cats meow. No bugs fly—none. The city goes from semitropical, mini-jungle-like sounds to total quiet. Betsy was my first horrible hurricane. The wind beat everything in its path, and after the eerie silence, the blowing debris blasted against our house with enough fury to scare hell. The odd thing about hurricanes is that when the eye, or center, passes over, all the rain and winds halt; even the sky clears for however long it takes the eye to pass. During this break, people peep out to see what's occurred; we did. My dad opened the front door, so swollen with rainwater it required significant strength. Then Mother followed, then each of us siblings. The silence was deafening; the whole world was still. Just as quickly as the sun appeared, it disappeared, and Daddy rushed us inside before the wind began again. Suddenly, another roar startled us all; as we looked, water rose quickly down the streets, rushing toward us. This was not a movie; this was our neighborhood, our street, flooding before our eyes.

After the winds and rains abated, the sky remained dark, but the water was almost four feet high. We, and all our neighbors, were trapped in a sea of water. My brother and I, fierce swimmers, thought it a great opportunity, so we dove off the front porch and swam because the weather was heavy, humid, and hot. Our parents were furious, for they saw the water moccasins, then the dead bodies floating.

Hurricane Betsy was nicknamed "Billion-Dollar Betsy" since she was the first storm to cause billions of dollars worth of damage. Less than a hundred people died; but when you see corpses in the water, the numbers somehow are irrelevant. When levees failed, the Lower Ninth Ward was hit hardest with massive flooding. It was the first time we saw media images of people on rooftops waving for help. Finally, when the water receded, no one was the same. The two weeks of stagnating water (a total of three weeks for things to begin to get back to normal) were a harsh lesson for families, for businesses, for the city. Rumors spread that the Ninth Ward was flooded purposefully, the water surge diverted to save better neighborhoods. In any case, Hurricane Betsy's damage was so profound that the name Betsy is retired from the list of Atlantic hurricanes, and it was her devastation that ushered into being the Army Corps of Engineers' Hurricane Protection Program. The promise was that such a tragedy—the deaths, the destruction, the flooding—would never happen again.

At home, at first, we cooked anything thawing in the freezer on the little grill, then leftovers, then canned food, then finally peanut butter sandwiches while rationing the bread. Remember, stores are closed. The water is not fit to drink. We gathered the dirty standing water in buckets to flush the toilets. What was once an imagined event, an exciting adventure, gave way to a primal existence with few creature comforts, though that turned out to be good for us. We appreciated everything, especially the first baths when clean water ran through faucets. What joy to wash our hair!

Although Hurricane Betsy diminished from a category 4 to a category 3 hurricane when she hit the city, we all considered it a great training ground for the next time. In all these years, New Orleans has had many near hits and many misses, but we never evacuated. Hurricanes are a part of the landscape, like the rainy season itself. We stock up on necessary items to prepare, go on as usual until it's time to hunker down, and let it pass. Most people remain at home and ride it out.

The attitude about the impending Hurricane Katrina was no different. I had no intention of leaving town. Besides, where would I go? In what direction? Even with the best predictions of the National Weather Service, hurricanes have minds of their own. Like Betsy, Katrina ravaged Florida and struck straight for the central Gulf of Mexico, then somehow she turned, aiming for the central coast. The range of possible hits covered half of Texas, all of Louisiana, Mississippi, Alabama, and the panhandle of Florida. How does one decide a direction, let alone a destination?

Because of such uncertainties, many residents pray a lot. In particular, Catholics believe with fasting and prayer—prayers of the faithful, that is—anything can be changed, the course of history or a storm. There are numerous altars to the Blessed Mother, particularly where the Mother of Jesus is known as Our Lady of Prompt Succor. The statue of this title remains in its original home of the Ursuline Convent, considered a holy place in New Orleans. Numerous miracles are traced to prayers to Our Lady of Prompt Succor: the saving of the Ursuline convent from fire in 1812, the success of the Battle of New Orleans, and intervention against many hurricanes. No wonder then, when Hurricane Katrina began her rise to Category 4 strength, on many Catholic lips a familiar invocation echoed: "Our Lady of Prompt Succor, hasten to help us."

A cradle-Catholic, armed with prayers, Holy Water and supplies, I slept soundly my last August 2005 Saturday night in New Orleans, confident that this storm would surely pass us again, as had so many.

Sunday morning, while securing yard tools, chairs—anything that might become a projectile had to be stored or tied down—my cousin Connie called. "Are you packed? When are you leaving?" she asked. I never leave, and she knows that. Her husband, Dwight, remains too; we always laugh about how best to ride out the storm, sober, drunk, or dancing.

"Dwight is taking us," she said. I was shocked. "Didn't you hear the news? Turn on the television." Connie was as serious as a heart attack. Reluctantly, I clicked the TV, and almost every local station flashed bulletins. When I checked the Weather Channel, the size and scope of Katrina was staggering. I was still not convinced, but Connie was insistent. The next words out of her mouth changed my mind. "Mona Lisa, I had a dream last night; I had a dream that this one is bad. You have to go. You have to leave now. Don't wait. Please don't wait." With each word, Connie's voice cracked. Rarely does Connie dream anything of an ominous nature. I didn't have to be told twice.

That was it. There was no plan, no intention, no preconceived destination, just the sincere urging of Connie's message.

My elderly neighbor, Ms. Ruth, was also planning to ride out the storm, confident that I and my sixty-six-pound dog, Jazz, were next door. Reluctantly, she readied herself when she heard about the severity of the hurricane. Because it was hurricane season, my gas tank was full. I loaded my red Toyota 4Runner with my dog, enough snacks and food for a few days, two changes of clothes and pj's, papers to grade, and Ms. Ruth.

From New Orleans, in any direction, one must cross water. To head north, we had to cross Lake Ponchartrain, over the Bonnet Carre

Spillway, the route the interstate takes toward the next largest city in Louisiana, Baton Rouge. Normally, it takes fifty-five minutes to reach Baton Rouge. We were encouraged that the contraflow—that is, the use of all interstate lanes to head north—was working. In every lane alongside of us were whole families piled tight with babies, dogs or cats, and the elderly. We were further encouraged that we were not the last to leave the city. At one point, we saw a caravan of cars containing my other cousins: Carol, Marlene, Herman, and their families, including their mother, my aunt Mary. We switched radio stations for news, but cruised on the Gospel Music Praise Station, singing along with Kirk Franklin, Yolanda Adams, Donnie McClurklan. It seemed like going on vacation at first. Then the lines tightened, stopping traffic for twenty to thirty minutes at a stretch, and we made little progress.

A full seven-hours later, in bumper-to-bumper traffic, we were just inside the Baton Rouge city limits. We were closest to the home of my longtime friend, the writer Dr. Cindy Lou Levy (her writing name is Cindy Lou Levee, changed after Betsy, in honor of the broken levees' wrath). I called her and explained that we were willing to sleep outside in the car, but we needed some relief from the lines of traffic parked on the interstate.

Cindy and I were classmates in graduate school. We met in Kathleen Fraser's workshop, in that first fall of 1979, in the San Francisco State University Creative Writing program. Cindy was from New Orleans, Uptown, but she was white. I was a native, too, but black and from downtown—light years away in economic class, race, social status. As kids, in Jim Crow times, we would not have met; but across the country in California, we began a conversation that continues today. Cindy welcomed us and we huddled in her living room: Ms. Ruth; Jazz; Terry, Cindy's husband; BJ, her son; and me. We tried to sleep, but the storm raged. We held court in front of the TV until the electricity went out. Finally, exhausted, we all slept off and on, the wind screaming outside.

The next day, Monday, debris was everywhere, but Cindy's home was intact, and so were we. We gave thanks together. I helped Terry pick up the large tree branches, and we worked all day clearing the yard. I walked Jazz a few times. She was not used to being with strangers; she was not an inside dog, and she gave Cindy's cat and dog hell the entire time. Cindy's parents were forced to leave their hotel due to overbooking, so they needed to join their daughter and her family. Cindy felt horrible, but we were so happy just to land safely; it was no problem. We rode the storm in shelter with friends. We were blessed. I called another girlfriend, Jackie Jones, who was glad we were safe and readied rooms for us.

Jackie was the interlibrary loan librarian at Louisiana State University when I studied for the MFA. We, too, became great friends. We love learning, especially about black people anywhere. We are always sharing research, news, and cultural facts and entertaining queries about what really happened to blacks out West—her specialty—or in the Deep South—my special interest. We spent a peaceful couple of days with Jackie and her husband, Selwyn, glued to the TV news, the first we had seen or heard since the storm cut power in much of Baton Rouge. Jackie's home escaped damage; but her cousin, Gina, who was severely immobile due to diabetes, lost the use of her hydraulic household. Gina is more like a big sister to Jackie than a cousin; in fact, Gina raised Jackie for much of her life. Gina joined us; and while Jackie had space for us even with Gina, I did not have the heart to put her out. Gina needed substantial care, from help with bathing and clothing to eating and everything in between. Jackie had her hands full, and the additional three of us were too much.

It was at Jackie's that we saw the repeated images of so-called looting. It was also at Jackie's that I located Ms. Ruth's family in Atlanta and arranged for her to join them by plane. Jazz was settling into being an inside dog. When Mayor Nagin said it would be some months before we could begin returning to New Orleans, I knew I needed work and a place to live. I began with the classified ads, using the library for Internet access.

After calling, searching the want ads, and driving around, it was clear that there were no rentals available, not even places for sale (not that I could afford to buy, but like many I was desperate). It was my hope that my friends Dr. Joyce Marie Jackson and her husband, J. Nash Porter, had a little room for us. They had taken in numerous families, in their primary home, and at Cultural Crossroads, an apartment building turned workshop, gallery, and studio space. One couple was expected to leave, and I was told to act fast; I did, and we moved there by the Friday after Katrina hit.

Nash turned one space into an apartment for me. Exhausted from the stress, Jazz and I were happy to be with friends again, to have shelter, to feel safe. There was no TV and no phone, so the weekend brought rest, then other friends visiting. We saw Dr. John Lowe, Hurston and Wright scholar and my former dissertation chair; current Louisiana Poet Laureate Brenda Marie Osbey; her mother; James Borders, an arts administrator; plus other friends of Nash. Nash hugged us all and brought great red beans and rice—our signature dish next to gumbo—along with lots of hospitality.

Because Katrina was a category 5 hurricane, a direct hit, the electricity was out in half the city, and many phones were down; even cell phones did not work. Baton Rouge was overcrowded; the locals felt invaded with over-long lines for gas, bread, water. Tempers were short, and opportunities were limited. I wrote to everyone I knew, explaining that I needed work. My friend and University of Washington alum, Jeanette Martin, brought me to Chair Dick Dun's attention. Renowned poet Colleen McElroy and National Book Award Winner Charles Johnson, both my former professors, recommended me. By the grace of God, President Emmert, Dick Dunn, and Jeanette's good wishes, I landed a visiting associate professorship at the University of Washington in the Department of English.

However, I knew I had to return home first, or wonder what I was leaving behind. I needed to salvage my research, as I was scheduled to be in Alexandria, Louisiana, in early fall for a residency at the Arna Bontemps Museum. I shipped my 4Runner north and rented a car; and with the aid of my Dillard University colleague Gayle Duskin's husband, Richard, I drove to New Orleans. I was grateful to have mature male companionship on this trip. We were not sure when we left if we could gain access to the city, as the Mayor was allowing only businesses to survey the damage.

The trip on the interstate was smooth, until we entered the city. The devastation was unimaginable. As expected, we were detained by military guards. I insisted that I must retrieve my research. The guard warned us to be careful, as there were no traffic lights, but some live lines down in areas. There was no drinking water, no phones, and no one to call for help. We continued.

The smell was sickening; and if the wind blew, I did all I could not to puke. We drove east to the Ninth Ward, toward Richard and Gayle's lovely brick home. Along the way, we saw middle-class black family homes broken in half, bricks strewn like Lego play pieces. Trees, flora, grasses—all dead. The stench was pervasive. Gayle and Richard's home was flooded to the ceiling. We took pictures; and when done, we used disinfectant to clean the sludge off, but the smell remained. We drove further east toward their daughter's home. We saw a ghost town. There were whole streets not fit to enter, the water still stagnating, the houses crushed as if by a giant.

As we neared my neighborhood, the Seventh Ward, I was still hopeful that my home, already four feet off the ground, was not flooded. When I saw that my own neighborhood had fared no better than New Orleans East, a rush of tears flooded my eyes. I felt sick in my gut. Not in my wildest imagination did it occur to me that I would see my recently renovated, lovely shotgun home water-soaked (five feet high in some rooms) and filled with sludge, my library drenched and destroyed. All my books, my computer, my printers, my unpublished book-length poems, my research on kids' lore and adult male toasts, my unused dissertation chapters—all gone. The sludge was thick brown, loaded with snakes and bugs and slime and the smell of death—and this was three weeks after Katrina's flooding. Outside, the green grass was burned brown by salt water; inside, the salt water corroded pots, pans, anything below the water line. Into triple plastic bags, I loaded some clothes I thought might clean. Many things just disintegrated: dresses, shirts; shoes curled up. It would be easier to board a plane to Seattle, knowing that not much more could be done for now. My chest was too heavy. I had not felt such pervading sadness since my dear mother had died, the year after Hurricane Betsy.

The heat in Baton Rouge was oppressive; and with no air conditioning, the lovely studio apartment was a better resting place in the late evenings. Luckily, I was able to retrieve some film of my kids' lore; and from that, I reconstructed a talk for my residency. I worked most days at the air-conditioned library. At other times, I shopped for housekeeping items. By this time, Hurricane Rita was bearing down on Baton Rouge. Jazz and I caught the last flight out before Rita hit.

Seattle was cold and rainy, as expected. I was welcomed at the airport by my brother, Anthony, and his lovely wife, Penny. It had been years since he had been home to New Orleans, but when I saw him, I knew everything would be all right. He was there for me the way good brothers are. If I just needed a hand, or an arm, he'd give his. What a blessing and a great feeling to be loved.

Penny and Anthony helped me get Jazz home to Donna's place. Donna Kimbrough is another longtime girlfriend from my undergraduate days at the University of Washington. Since Anthony lived across Lake Washington in Redmond, and my sister Barbara's home had no room, Donna welcomed Jazz and me for our first weeks in Seattle. From the lovely picture window in her living room, one has a view of the south end of the lake. Her yard accommodated Jazz during the days while I was at school. At night, Jazz slept in my room. Donna made us feel right at home in spite of Jazz's cranky nature; we'd had too many addresses already.

As was my practice when in Baton Rouge, I beat the pavement daily, looking for a place large enough for the two of us, which means a house. None of the places I saw worked out. They were either too expensive, too small (one can not get a closet in Seattle for six hundred dollars a month), not conducive to a pet, or already taken. Finally, I found a little World War II bungalow on the north end, dog friendly, and within my budget. A few weeks later, I had to leave for my residency in Alexandria.

Once in Alexandria, I wanted to kiss the ground. I was in Louisiana again. The Arna Bontemps Museum experience was rich. My writing experiences were paved with residencies earlier; but this time I would be signing my first book, *Red Beans and Ricely Yours*. Finally, this was my turn, except that I was not home in my beloved Crescent City, to share my joy with the people who inspired the collection. Because my poems paint layers of New Orleans culture, audiences were curious and interested in the subject. They seemed pleased; for that, I was thankful.

The Bontemps residency completed, it was back to teaching at the University of Washington. Before long, another trip was planned for

Truman State University and Kansas State University. I read my poems to receptive audiences. My heart was full, though my strength was fading. I felt so fortunate to have such opportunities; all the while, there was just not enough information coming out about New Orleans.

Finally, I was invited to give one of the keynote addresses at the "Rebuilding New Orleans" conference at Tulane University. This would allow me another trip home, to check on the house, to lend my voice to the rebuilding process, to gain much needed information.

The conference news was sobering. Policy makers, designers, architects, builders, artists, clergy, academics, folklorists all presented. Designers and public planners spoke of five-to-ten years before New Orleans would bounce back to normal and maintained that it would require effective planning and participation. Architects urged residents to consider "first-floor elevations" so that no homes would sit below the water line in case of future flooding, as it would take years to repair the levee system to adequate protective strength. Residents felt ignored and uninformed. Many were angry and let it be known.

Since Katrina, I've made ten trips home. My roof is repaired. My house is gutted. I am awaiting the cost of elevating, and I am utilizing only local contractors. I want my money to be spent on local labor, and I am confident in the quality of New Orleans craftsmanship. I have great faith in the goodness of God, and I count my blessings daily. Yet after these many months, I remain in shock, moving from one event to another, from one responsibility to another. There have been no breaks, no rests, only work, and I thank God that I've had meaningful work. Still, and only recently, there are days when I grieve, when the sadness is so heavy I lean over as though weighed down by boulders. I was fortunate to have left in time, fortunate to have landed safely, and fortunate to enjoy the hospitality of friends. Eight addresses later, not once was I in a shelter.

My family is strewn from Arkansas to Texas; we call and email, encourage one another. Some cousins are home now, waiting for phone and other services. Some acquaintances are resettled elsewhere, still angry, waiting for more information, wondering if they can or will return. My neighbors are all elderly—we just cry together; we miss our home, the sweetness of life we enjoyed, our Creole dishes and ingredients, from crawfish to merliton. There is no place like New Orleans in the world.

New Orleans survived Katrina; it was the levees that devastated us. One levee crumbled under Ponchartrain's surges. One levee was damaged by a barge that was not supposed to park near the Ninth Ward streets. We paid for a seventeen-foot-deep levee, but we got ten-foot-deep levees. Who has all that money—the hundred of thousands earmarked for the people's protection?

Our streets are brutalized by neglect. Our homes are segregated by broken promises. Our hearts, like our voices, are hollow now in the aftermath. Did we not work hard, pay our taxes, vote our leaders into office? What happened to life, liberty, and the pursuit of the good? Oh say, can you see us, America? Is our bright-burning disappointment visible ten months later? Are the baked-on sludge of putrid water and your empty promises all we are to receive? Where are you, America, when the citizens and the city of New Orleans need you?

Notes

1. Rick Heydinger and Curt Johnson, "New Orleans Revisited," *Minneapolis Star Tribune*, May 30, 2006, p. 1 (available at http://www.startribune.com/563/story/457994.html; accessed June 7, 2006).

2. See Eloisa Gomez Borah, "Filipinos in Unamuno's California Expedition of 1587," *Amerasia Journal* 21, no. 3 (Winter 1995–96).

3. Veltisezar Bautista, *The Filipino Americans (1763–present): Their History, Culture, and Traditions* (Warren MI: Bookhaus Publishers, 2002), p. 100.

4. Heydinger and Johnson, p. 3.

5. Heydinger and Johnson, p. 3.

6. General Electric, AOL Time Warner, News Corporation, The Walt Disney Corporation, VIACOM INC (source: Project on Media Ownership).

7. Particularly West End Boulevard right next to the Jefferson Parish Line, or Canal Boulevard all the way to the Lakefront.

8. Legendary "Hurricane Okeechobee struck the Leeward Island, Puerto Rico, the Bahamas, and Florida in September 1928, and was the first one recorded to reach a Category 5 strength, killing 4,075 people, causing $100 million ($800 million in 2005 USD) in damages" (http://en.wikipedia.org/wiki/1928_Okeechobee_Hurricane, accessed June 8, 2006).

20. Louisiana's New Political Landscape

Angus Woodward

A glamorous nine-year-old named Garland got up in the window of Mona Lisa, a funky French Quarter restaurant, and belted out a passionate rendition of Carole King's "Natural Woman." She sang every word of every verse, throwing herself into the high notes, closing her eyes and holding one hand up. Amused, slightly inebriated tourists passed by outside, glancing up at her. The place was almost empty by then anyway, and we had already made a nuisance of ourselves. Garland's parents, Andy and Carmen, had quizzed the waiter on the content of salads and salad dressing to guarantee preservation of their vegan diet. Various custom dishes had been requested for Garland and our daughters, Geneva and Nina. We had lingered over the table, talking long and loud, eventually allowing little Nina to wander the dining room on her own. Garland and Geneva left the table and conferred secretly between potted plants in front of the window. After all of that, what harm could there be in letting Garland indulge her diva tendencies?

This was early August, three months into a brutal five-month summer. We had gotten together for what would turn out to be a last hurrah. All of us but toddler Nina were former New Orleanians. Andy, Carmen, Jalan, and I had spent formative early-adult years in New Orleans. Garland and Geneva had been born there, ten days apart, and spent their toddler years in the Crescent City. Jalan, Andy, and I had paid our professional dues teaching freshman composition at Delgado Community College. Carmen had painted a whole slew of ambitious pop-art oils in her studio. Andy had written most of his poems in New Orleans, and I had labored over hundreds of pages of fiction. Garland and Geneva had slobbered on one another and fought over toys. Now here we all were again, seven years after leaving the city, two families reunited for two days on our way to visit parents in other states.

Andy, Carmen, and Garland had wound up on the west coast, but we had simply moved eighty miles up Interstate 10 to Baton Rouge. Politically and culturally, New Orleans and Baton Rouge were much more than eighty miles apart. In New Orleans you could find restaurants with mismatched chairs and hand-painted tables, the walls obscured by images of the Mona Lisa—as a cow, with a mustache, à la Matisse, and so on. In New Orleans people like Andy, who had a waxed mustachio and a pointy van Dyke, were easy to find (though like snowflakes, no two were alike). I think I can say with confidence, without having to consult the Statistical Abstract of the United States, that New Orleans had more fortunetellers, tarot card readers, painters, poets, and musicians per capita than any other city for hundreds—if not thousands—of miles. New Orleans had had a whole string of black mayors—Barthelemy, a couple of Morials, and Ray Nagin. Most wards consistently voted Democrat, with a very few exceptions. Gore and Kerry had carried New Orleans, despite losing Louisiana. New Orleans was a big blue dot at the bottom of our red, unraveling-sock-shaped state.

Baton Rouge is more typical of the rest of Louisiana. We live in a land of pickup trucks, Confederate flags, Cadillacs, fat cat politicians, football fans, and riding lawn mowers. Our voting precinct covers an enormous subdivision established in the early '50s, a neighborhood of ranch houses, senior citizens, and lawn sprinklers. In the 2004 Presidential elections, exactly 144 of us voted for John Kerry, 443 for George W. Bush.

A liberal living in Baton Rouge has to seek out pockets of liberalism. Jalan made friends at La Leche League when we first moved here. The Unitarian church has a lively, active congregation, several hundred strong. LSU has its share of liberal academics (and a good many conservatives). We found LSU art department functions comforting. Jalan and I are sort of stealth liberals, relatively conventional in appearance and lifestyle. Fortunately it has been possible in Baton Rouge to find friends like Gayle, who passes on particularly scathing articles from the *Nation*, and David, who ducks into my office once or twice a week to explicate the hypocrisy of Bush's most recent speeches.

Louisiana is a red state, but it's as much Confederate red as Republican red. Up until the 1990s, Southern states could be counted on to vote Democrat, but not because the south was liberal. I was baffled when I moved to Louisiana in the late '80s in the middle of a fiercely contested governor's race. None of the billboards, bumper stickers, or roadside signs I saw identified the political party of the candidates they endorsed. Perhaps that had something to do with the strength of the Democratic Party in Louisiana back then; it went without saying that you were a Democrat, and if you were a Republican you didn't want people to know. Maybe it had more to do with Louisiana's open primary system, which continues today. The top two vote getters in a multiparty gubernatorial primary go head-to-head in November, no matter what party they belong to. Democrat versus Republican, Democrat versus Democrat, or Republican versus Republican.

A Southern Democrat was not necessarily a liberal. A textbook example is Edwin W. Edwards, who governed Louisiana from 1972 until 1980, then from 1984 until 1988, and yet again from 1992 until 1996. During his third reign, he became very pro-gambling, almost single-handedly bringing casinos to Louisiana. All along, EWE was very pro-EWE. In the mid-80s he was indicted (but not convicted) of a whole slate of corruption charges. In 1998, he was indicted for essentially selling riverboat gambling licenses. This time he was convicted, and began serving a ten-year sentence in 2000. From my point of view, Edwards was a villain who had exploited his position to enrich himself and his friends, diverting resources that could have gone to improving the state's education and health care—someone who got what was coming to him.

And yet the vast majority of Louisiana's liberals voted for EWE at least once. During the gubernatorial campaign of 1991, "Vote for the Crook—It's Important" bumper stickers had proliferated throughout New Orleans, and I had gladly voted for him. I still remember the sick feeling I had when I saw that the incumbent Buddy Roemer, a straight-shooting Democratic reformer, had placed third in the open primary. Edwards had come in first, two percentage points ahead of David Duke. David Duke was the reason it became important to vote for Edwards in the runoff. Duke, of course, was the "former" white supremacist who had managed to get himself elected to the state legislature. He ran for governor pretending not to be a racist, making frequent use of the phrase "youthful indiscretion," and got hundreds of thousands of votes from people who pretended they didn't believe he was a racist (and just as many from voters who didn't pretend). The district Duke represented in the state legislature is right next door to New Orleans, separated from it by the 17th Street Canal. Those were tense times. Duke supporters' big blue and white signs popped up all over neighboring parishes, though I don't remember seeing many in Orleans parish. The *Times-Picayune* ran a big color photo on the front page of white men in the back of a pickup truck shouting and giving the finger to anti-Duke demonstrators above them on a highway overpass.

Louisiana's political history is a little embarrassing for self-proclaimed liberals who live here. So is its political reality. It isn't easy to live in a place where the *legal* emission of pollutants is annually measured in hundreds of millions of tons, where race relations are strained, where the frequency with which police officers are convicted of felonies is alarming. What do you do when the man cutting your hair casually trots out the N-word? Did it make sense to keep living in New Orleans in the mid-'90s, when two NOPD officers were convicted of murder? One was Antoinette Frank, a former Delgado Community College student, who collaborated with her boyfriend to rob a Vietnamese restaurant, shooting and killing three people in the process (including a fellow officer), then returned to the scene in her capacity as a cop to ask what had happened. When doubts creep in, I find it helps to remember that Mardi Gras is not just an opportunity for college students to get drunk. Once a year the streets burst at the seams with people of all colors and classes and ages, who mingle and chat and compete for the millions of pretty plastic baubles that rain down upon them. Seattle tried to get in on the Mardi Gras thing in 2001, and it turned into a riot that had to be dispersed by 350 armed police.

The morning after the 2004 presidential election, I slid the newspaper out of its plastic sleeve still hoping the early returns of the night before were misleading. No such luck. However, I found a consolation prize. Kip Holden, a black Democrat, had defeated the incumbent Republican mayor of Baton Rouge. With the election of Governor Kathleen Blanco, Democrat, the year before, and the reelection of Senator Mary Landrieu, another Democrat, in 2002, Louisiana was starting to look relatively progressive. I had not voted for Blanco in the open primary, instead voting for another Democrat who seemed less pro-industry, but had voted for her in the election and had seen good signs during her first year in office—she had held a big summit meeting on Louisiana poverty and had begun serious reform of Louisiana's juvenile justice system, generally considered among the most Draconian in the nation.

We didn't talk much about Louisiana politics with Andy and Carmen that night at the restaurant. With a war on in Iraq and a straw man in the White House, most of our political discussion focused on national politics. I think I told them the good news of Holden's election. Not long after Garland's performance, Geneva tugged at my sleeve and asked me to escort her to the restroom. She was nine at the time, perfectly capable of going to a restaurant bathroom by herself, but this was Mona Lisa, where you go out the back door and use the facilities of a neighboring apartment building that shares a courtyard with the restaurant. I led her to the back and pointed to the restroom door. "I'll wait right here," I told her, and then she opened the door. Inside sat a young man with long hair and a miserable expression on his face, pants around his ankles. He frowned at us. "Oh," said Geneva, and let the door swing shut. We looked at one another for a moment, eyes wide. "Let's come back later," I suggested, and we hurried back to the table giggling.

Four weeks after our dinner with Andy and Carmen at Mona Lisa, I went out into the withering heat to put the patio furniture into the garage, tie down a couple of kayaks, and move a potted Satsuma tree to the patio along with a couple of wheelbarrows full of last year's firewood. Hurricane Katrina was said to be headed our way. I pulled scraps of plywood out of the garage and tried to puzzle them together over the bay window in the front of the house. I do all of these things at least once a year, and by now it is a familiar drill. One year earlier, Hurricane Ivan had come barreling out of the Gulf, seeming to target southeast Louisiana. Ivan was a big storm, 140 mph winds driving its howls to high pitches, and New Orleanians took it more seriously than they had taken any storm in years. Baton Rouge filled up with cars, some of which had taken twelve hours to get through an eighty-mile evacuation traffic jam. Ivan ended up veering to the east, becoming just another bullet that New Orleans had dodged. After Ivan, the state police drew up contraflow plans (in which traffic on both sides of a divided highway flows away from the storm) to speed up the evacuation process. But almost every year some storm had come along and headed towards New Orleans, and every year there was much discussion of the devastation a direct hit could wreak upon the city, and every year the storm turned to the west or east. In 1992 Jalan and I sat in our living room in New Orleans and saw television images of the destruction wrought by Andrew in Florida and heard them say that Andrew was headed our way and that New Orleans could get twenty feet of water. We spent one frenetic hour putting tape on our windows and moving books from the lowest shelves, packed up the cat, gave our spinet piano a last, wistful look, and jumped into the car to speed up to Baton Rouge, where Jalan's mother had a brick house that seemed like a mountaintop fortress compared to our little raised wood-frame bungalow. Andrew obligingly followed us, turning to the west and roaring right through Baton Rouge, knocking out power and depositing a tree on the house we would buy six years later. The rain came in sideways and the trees flexed wildly while the wind moaned almost musically. "What was the weather like here?" we asked a friend, after returning to New Orleans. "It was kind of breezy. No rain," she said.

As Katrina made her way toward New Orleans, television news organizations sent reporters to stand outside in the least bit of wind and rain, making dramatic statements in rugged, colorful rain gear. Wild-eyed locals who had decided to ride out the storm were located and duly interviewed on camera. Wild-eyed locals who had decided to evacuate were located and duly interviewed on camera. Diagrams and maps were displayed. Alarming stock footage of past storms made its annual appearance. Hurricane experts provided updates and presented hypotheses on the strength and path of the storm. Hurricane experts made disclaimers to let us know that the storm could end up just about anywhere. Anchormen and -women promised to stay with us. Surfers were shown taking advantage of storm-generated waves that had traveled hundreds of miles. More diagrams were displayed. We saw people buying water, batteries, and generators from under-stocked stores. For Gulf Coast residents and newshounds everywhere, the whole pre-game show was a rerun.

Ten days before Katrina, Jalan and I had hired some men to take down a big water oak fifteen feet from the house because it was showing signs of deteriorating and we didn't want the next big storm to blow it onto our house. As I battened down the hatches, piles of sawn-up tree lay all over the lawn. It looked as if the hurricane had already passed through. Adding to the post-hurricane illusion was the failure of our central air conditioner the day before. "I'll bring you a replacement on Monday," the repairman had said. "Unless that hurricane comes."

While Katrina's wind and water lashed New Orleans, Jalan, Geneva, Nina, and I hunkered down at my mother-in-law Jackie's house, where the A/C was fully functional. Baton Rouge, being to the west of the storm, didn't get more than a few inches of rain. The wind blew all day, gusting to forty or fifty over and over again. The power went out at Jackie's house for eight hours or so. Baton Rouge lost over seven hundred trees. Enough limbs came down around our house for me to make a pile the size of a pickup truck. Our power was off for five days. On the third day, I emptied our lukewarm refrigerator, tossing out meat, cheese, butter, pickles—everything. Baton Rouge had instantly become the largest city in the state, doubling in size the day before Katrina. It was suddenly hard just to get from place to place on roads choked with traffic.

At Jackie's we kept the news on almost all of the time for five days, struggling to grasp the scope of the disaster. We rotated between CNN, Fox News (cringe), and a local station where the anchors and reporters had let their hair down and rolled up their sleeves to provide wall-to-wall coverage with the help of New Orleans telejournalists who found themselves homeless.

The storm itself was apolitical. For a day or so, Fox News was hardly distinguishable from CNN. Things changed when the looting started on Tuesday. It sure seemed like Fox News pounced on the looting and gave it a lot more play than other networks. A jerk on an Internet forum I frequent posted a thread entitled, "Why Are All the Looters Black?" The politicization of Katrina was off to a roaring start.

Despite Fox News's best efforts, the political question that got the most attention had more to do with the slow response of the Bush administration. As far as I can tell, the question started not in the newsrooms, but on the flooded streets of New Orleans. Desperate people waded through the streets, pausing to shout at the news cameras. "Where the hell is the government? Where are the troops? We need buses. We need water. Where's FEMA? Get somebody down here!" News commentators began asking why the response was so slow. Ray Nagin appeared on a local TV station on Thursday night and told the feds, "Now get off your asses and do something, and let's fix the biggest goddamn crisis in the history of this country." After a while it seemed as if the whole country was whispering, murmuring, screaming: "What the hell?!" And liberals nationwide began to see that Katrina had a spiral-shaped silver lining, because people were blaming George Bush, so much so that he took the extraordinary— nay, unprecedented—step of blaming himself. It took him about two weeks to get around to it, though.

Bush's supporters quickly came up with strategies to deflect the heat he was taking. One strategy was to criticize Blanco and Nagin. The *National Review* wrote of Blanco that "Her forte seemed to be crying" and that Bush should have "brushed [her] aside." In my neighborhood a scrap of plywood leaning on some curbside garbage cans bore a spray-painted message about impeaching Blanco. The *National Review* also said that Blanco's crying "nicely complement[ed] Nagin's ability to yell."

But most people blamed Bush in the immediate aftermath of the storm. In the weeks and months after Katrina, the questions of blame and responsibility have been examined more soberly. The evidence shows that Blanco's and Nagin's conduct before, during, and after the storm was not without mistakes. We've all seen images of the flooded

New Orleans buses that didn't get mobilized in time. But overriding any poor decisions on the part of Louisiana's Democratic politicians is the fact that FEMA had been weakened considerably by the Bush administration when it became part of Homeland Security instead of an independent agency. As I write this, Congress has just begun investigating the response to Katrina. Blanco has provided a hundred thousand pages of documents and e-mails to the press and to Congress.

I think every Louisiana liberal knows that our state's Democratic politicians have been tarnished if not battered by Katrina. Blanco has taken a lot of criticism for appearing confused, dazed, even "overmedicated" during press conferences after the storm. One of her aides made the mistake of speculating in an internal e-mail that Blanco may have been napping as Michael Chertoff, Secretary of Homeland Security, tried to reach her the day before Katrina's landfall. Commentators have pounced on that speculation, giving it more emphasis than it deserved. Among the first e-mails to be discovered by journalists were those regarding Blanco's image that passed between members of her staff—advice on what the governor should wear to appear more rugged, who she should be seen mingling with on the ground in New Orleans, and so on. Governor Blanco probably bungled the statewide mobilization of school buses for post-Katrina evacuation of New Orleans, and her reluctance to allow Bush to federalize local law enforcement and the Louisiana National Guard probably contributed to the delay in the federal government's response, but the media seem to be more interested in how her staff managed (or mismanaged) her image. I worry that Louisiana voters have decided they made a mistake in electing a woman to be governor.

Ray Nagin's public image was forged in the aftermath of Katrina. He was not especially well known outside of New Orleans before the storm. He beat former New Orleans chief of police Richard Pennington, who had brought community policing to New Orleans and made significant progress in bringing down the city's murder rate. A former cable television executive, Nagin left the Republican party and became a Democrat just a few days before his election. Now he's known as a plainspoken, straight-shooting voice of the people, the kind of guy who comes right out and says things like, "I don't know whether it's the governor's problem. I don't know whether it's the president's problem, but somebody needs to get their asses on a plane and sit down, the two of them, and figure this out right now." Maybe he's given to exaggeration, but I think when he estimated that ten thousand bodies would be found in the streets after Katrina, it was for a good reason.

As with Blanco and Nagin, a Louisianian's opinion of Senator Mary Landrieu depends on his or her political persuasion. "What's wrong with Mary Landrieu?" my mother-in-law Jackie asked us after one of the first post-Katrina press conferences. To me Senator Landrieu looked exhausted. "Her mouth keeps twitching," Jackie said, "almost like she's trying not to laugh. And look at her eye. Has she had a stroke?" Mary at one point expressed, on national television, a desire to punch President Bush. I think most Louisiana liberals had a good laugh at that. Some may have cringed, knowing what would happen next—conservative commentators nationwide pounced, calling on the Secret Service to investigate the threat of bodily harm to the Commander in Chief.

Louisiana has a reputation for political corruption, thanks in large part to Edwin Edwards. Speculation in the media that whatever money made its way to Louisiana after Katrina would be misused must have trickled down to my mother in Michigan, who told me on the phone that she had heard the state was so corrupt that it couldn't be trusted with money. I told her I didn't think that was the case anymore. Maybe I was wrong. I have been disappointed to read the ongoing story of a motorcycle dealership in River Ridge that managed to land a no-bid contract to supply FEMA with travel trailers despite not having permits from the state to sell them. What began as a $2.4 million contract ballooned into a $108 million contract (we can thank FEMA for the ballooning). The dealership at one point offered to pay the Louisiana Recreational and Used Motor Vehicle Commission a $10,000 fine to settle the matter. The fact that the owners of the dealership are the father and uncle of Gary Smith, a state legislator, hasn't helped matters. Representative Smith, sad to say, is a Democrat. The Baton Rouge Police Department has been somewhat disappointing as well. Large contingents of state troopers from Michigan and New Mexico came to Baton Rouge to assist BRPD in its struggle to cope with the city's inflated population. Within a few days, both states' troopers had left, refusing to work with BRPD. The out-of-state troopers claim that they observed police misconduct that would have been grounds for criminal prosecution back home: officers damaging cars, beating handcuffed suspects, and firing Tasers at people who were never charged with a crime.

On the other hand, I don't think Blanco has a reputation within Louisiana for corruption. The political cronyism behind the motorcycle dealership scandal is the sort of thing people associate with Edwin Edwards, more a lively vestige of the past than a case of business as usual. Of course, Louisiana Republicans and old-guard Dixiecrats may disagree.

Even Baton Rouge mayor-president Kip Holden's image has been tarnished in the aftermath of Katrina, at least in the eyes of Baton Rouge liberals. In general, Baton Rouge's response to the influx of evacuees was vigorously warm and generous. Once the Superdome and convention center in New Orleans were finally evacuated, shelters were set up in Baton Rouge to house thousands at the Southern University basketball arena and at the convention center downtown, and LSU's basketball arena became a temporary hospital and shelter for ill and injured evacuees. LSU's ag center turned into an enormous pet shelter for thousands of displaced animals. All of the shelters were swamped with volunteers and donated items from the community. After a few days, however, paranoia set in. Those televised images of looting, the rumors of murder and rape at the Superdome, and the reports of snipers firing upon police and rescuers hung in the air, and it occurred to Baton Rougeans that there could be a criminal element in the shelters. Four knives were confiscated from evacuees at the Baton Rouge River Center shelter, and BRPD received a false report of looting near there. (The chief of police said, "It wasn't looting. We had a problem with some of the displaced people going into businesses and asking for food.") Holden responded: "We do not want to inherit that breed that seeks to prey on other people. We want to send them this message: we are not going to let thugs walk around our street and intimidate people."

The next day, police got false reports of a riot near the River Center. In response, BRPD deployed a well-armed "Special Response Team" in front of the nearby governmental building. Upon noticing the police activity from his post in the city court building, the Baton Rouge city constable sent his men out with shotguns to join the police. The sheriff's office sent its "Special Community Anti-crime Team" to join the assembly. Government workers filed out of their buildings shortly thereafter and went home, cutting short their first day back to work after Katrina. A few days later, one of my students, Webb, was walking through the parking lot of a medical clinic on his way to class when a sheriff's deputy pulled over to talk to him, wanting to know who he was and what he was doing. Once the deputy learned that despite Webb's brown skin and dreadlocks he wasn't a thug, he backed off a bit and instructed Webb to go around any private property on his way to class in the future. "And I will," Webb told me. "So I might be a little late to class once in a while."

Blanco, Nagin, and Landrieu appeared on national television, separately and together, virtually every hour during and after Katrina and became the voices and faces of Louisiana after the crisis, which must have rankled certain kinds of Louisiana voters—not only the politically conservative, but also the culturally conservative. Two women and a black man on national television—all over every national network, in fact—speaking for the state, saying how Louisiana felt and what Louisiana was thinking. It remains to be seen if any of them will be reelected. It may be that the only political winners in the aftermath of Katrina will be those who challenge the incumbents.

The trivialization of Katrina began immediately after the politicization. A hair salon posted signs reading "Now serving Katrina evacuees" on the roadside within days. Car dealerships offered "Katrina Cash" rebates. The Baton Rouge newspaper runs a weekly bowling column, and twice in September its subject was Katrina: "Displaced Bowler Wondering How Things Are Going in New Orleans" and "Effects of Two Hurricanes on State Bowling Centers Vary." I couldn't help thinking of the aftermath of 9/11, when there was so much exploration of how the disaster touched every aspect of our lives. At least one writer, syndicated columnist Jim Hoagland, pursued the opposite extreme in a piece explaining how Katrina and Rita had helped the "axis of evil" nations.

On October first, four and a half weeks after Katrina, I returned to New Orleans for a few hours. I drove our new friend Cecile down to check on her apartment. Cecile had come from France to study law at Tulane University, arriving in New Orleans about a week before the hurricane. She had time to rent a room in a large apartment uptown, register for her classes, and buy her books before she had to evacuate. With only ten minutes to pack, she had left behind most of her clothes, her camera, all of her snapshots, and some important documents. She had bounced around the southeast for about a week with roommates who had cars, then landed in Baton Rouge, hoping to take classes at LSU until Tulane could reopen. Once we had tracked down all of our friends from New Orleans and learned that they had places to stay, we started looking for a way to lend our spare bedroom to the recovery effort. We found Cecile on the local Craigslist. She graced us with her presence for about ten days, then found a room much closer to the university.

The Uptown area surrounding Cecile's apartment had not flooded badly, but it had only been opened to residents the day before Cecile and I drove down in my truck. It was the first New Orleans neighborhood to reopen after the evacuation. Cecile knew her second-floor room had not flooded but had no way of knowing whether the roof had leaked, if her windows had broken, or if the apartment had been smashed by a tree or looted. As we sped toward New Orleans, I braced myself for long lines of traffic at police checkpoints, but the only police car I saw all day was the one sitting in front of a barricaded interstate off-ramp. We zoomed easily into the city along the elevated expressway, and then dropped down to street level near the Superdome.

Hundreds of flooded cars sat under the overpass. None of the traffic signals were functioning, though temporary stop signs sat at most intersections. Half the vehicles on the streets carried utility workers and debris-clearing crews. All along St. Charles Avenue staggering piles of brush and storm debris sat in mounds by the curb. Outside of many businesses and homes there was another kind of debris—carpets, carpet pads, books, trash bags, furniture, clothes, bedding. Just about everyone along St. Charles had duct-taped a refrigerator shut and muscled it to the curb. Someone had come along and written "Voodoo today here now 5" on most of the refrigerators—an imprecation, I guess. Crude, hand-painted plywood signs were the new mode of communication. They leaned on lampposts and trees bearing messages like "tree removal" or "storm cleanup" and a phone number, plus occasionally a comment like "fair prices." Many places still had boarded-up windows, some with slogans meant to repel criminals ("looters die").

Cecile directed me to park beside an old two-story blue building on Coliseum. It looked whole from the outside. She crossed her fingers and unlocked the side door. We trudged upstairs into the hot, stuffy, vaguely stinky apartment. A little water had leaked through her window and stained the blinds, but otherwise everything remained as she had left it.

We spent an hour or so packing up her belongings and finding a few key items some of her roommates had asked her to retrieve. I took one of the suitcases down to the truck, and when I reentered the apartment the smell seemed a little worse. "I made the mistake of opening the refrigerator," Cecile confessed. "It is full of black stuff."

Uptown New Orleans is one of the oldest parts of town, and as such it is on relatively high ground. Like the French Quarter and some other parts of the city, it was settled long before the advent of a comprehensive levee system. Some of the wealthiest streets in the city are uptown, as are some of the poorest. Pockets of white wealth lie next to pockets of black poverty. Sprinkled among them are pockets of Tulane and Loyola students, along with pockets that are mixtures of all sorts of people. Floodwaters don't discriminate, of course. Katrina flooded black, white, student, and black-and-white areas of Uptown equally. Whether cleanup and recovery from Katrina will accentuate the class and color differences between individual blocks remains to be seen.

Cecile had some books from the Tulane law library, and I suggested that we could probably drop them in a book-return slot outside the library entrance. We drove further up St. Charles, and I marveled that its famous live oaks had withstood the storm. The Tulane campus was a busy mess patrolled by a well-armed security force, a member of which waved us through a laissez-faire checkpoint. An enormous pile of university furniture sat outside the main library. We parked across from the law library and lugged the heavy law books up to the front door, stepping over big flexible ducting that led into the building from enormous, diesel-powered dehumidifiers. The door was open to let the ducting in and out, and with no book drop-off evident outside, we entered cautiously. The air was cool and dry, and of course the lights were off. I almost wanted to call, "Hello?" We saw no one, shrugged, and took the books back to the truck.

Tulane was relatively unscathed. Across town, Southern University at New Orleans suffered widespread damage, with floodwaters from the London Avenue Canal levee breach reaching the second floor of most buildings. Its ultimate fate is more uncertain than the fate of other New Orleans colleges. The editors of Baton Rouge's daily newspaper, *The Advocate*, published a column recommending that SUNO be abandoned altogether, its doors closed for good. They cited the damage, the university's low enrollment and its poor academic performance. SUNO is a historically black university, a former "shadow university" left over from the days of segregation, when Louisiana had a white university system and a parallel black system. Rather than a seeing SUNO as a reminder of a shameful period, blacks in Louisiana regard it as part of their heritage that serves low-income students. The column in *The Advocate* gave no credence to SUNO's role as an asset of the black community in New Orleans.

I drove over to Carrollton, thinking I would see if I could take it all the way up into Lakeview, where Jalan and I had lived for seven of our eight years in New Orleans. Doing so would be illegal, since only the Uptown area was open, and again I envisioned police checkpoints that never materialized. Several blocks up Carrollton, we began to see floodlines on the sides of buildings and on the cars parked on the street. Just a thin line or two of mud a foot off the ground, then two feet. Battered aluminum skiffs sat on the neutral ground or sidewalk or in front yards, having served their purpose and settled in place as the water had receded. Up near Claiborne, the burnt-out shell of a building covered most of a city block. The floodlines moved gradually higher the further up Carrollton we drove. By the time we got up past I-10, the cars parked along the street had been completely submerged and had spent the past couple of weeks baking in the blazing sun.

Our route took us past Xavier University, a distinguished private, historically black institution. It may be fairer to compare Tulane to Xavier, rather than SUNO. Tulane and Xavier are both private universities with sterling academic reputations; one is white, the other black. Both were flooded, Xavier more deeply, but both intend to reopen in January, just four months after Katrina. So does SUNO, though its offices and classrooms will be housed in temporary trailers provided by FEMA.

I took Canal Street over to City Park Avenue, and we came upon Delgado Community College, where I had worked for eight years. In contrast to Tulane, SUNO, and Xavier, Delgado is a vibrant jumble of all colors, ages, and classes. Dozens of pet carriers and cages sat in loose rows in the parking lot outside of the administration building. A table and a few chairs sat near the street. The college parking lot at the corner of City Park and Orleans Avenue was a teeming hive of tents and travel trailers, men with and without hardhats scurrying here and there. More tents and trailers were crowded onto the wide Orleans neutral ground. Dozens of idling semis towing open trailers lined Orleans, presumably waiting to be dispatched throughout the city to haul storm debris. I took a left and drove down Orleans, threading my way slowly through the chaos. Another left on Navarre—also lined with idling trucks—took me behind the college, and the second right brought us into the neighborhood Jalan and I had lived in, in three different houses, for seven years.

We found ourselves in a ghost town. The streets had been cleared, all of the brush and fallen trees mounded up between the sidewalks and the curbs. The floodlines on the sides of houses were eight feet above the ground. A haze of dried silt coated the streets, the dead grass, the sidewalks, every parked car and the lower half of every house. Every house had rescue-crew codes spray-painted in orange on or near the door, and most also had animal rescue codes in black ("Cat RSQ 9/25"). I drove slowly, and Cecile and I kept our eyes wide, watching the landscape slide by. Since residents hadn't been allowed to return to Lakeview yet, we saw none of the giant mounds of soggy belongings we had seen uptown, until I turned down one of the streets Jalan and I had lived on. A man crossed back and forth between his house and the curb, trespassing on his own property as he made a growing pile of ruined belongings. No one else was around.

I'm sure the carnage was more dramatic in other parts of the city. My old neighborhood was far enough from the 17th Street Canal that houses and cars had not been shoved around by the currents that had ravaged other areas. Presumably the water just seeped quickly in, rising steadily until it was over everyone's head. I remembered that sick wistful feeling I had when Jalan and I left almost everything behind for Hurricane Andrew, but I could hardly imagine the feeling I would have had if he had brought eight feet of water into my house.

In a lot of ways, Katrina was a great equalizer. Twenty-year-old K cars and brand new Jaguars looked equally worthless after being submerged in muddy water and baked in the sun. The 17th Street Canal levee breach hit Lakeview, a predominantly white area, just as hard as the Industrial Canal levee breach hit the predominantly black Lower Ninth Ward. It was the evacuation, not the flood, that accentuated divisions of color and class in New Orleans. Middle-class whites from Lakeview left for Baton Rouge, Florida, Texas, and points beyond as Katrina bore down on the city (as did middle-class blacks from New Orleans East). Poor people from the projects and the Lower Ninth Ward, lacking transportation and other resources, ended up in the Superdome. The vast majority of them were black.

It will take years to see if the process of recovering from Katrina diminishes or heightens differences in class and color in New Orleans. Five years from now, we can all go and tour the campuses of Tulane, Xavier, Delgado, and SUNO. We'll see who is still using temporary buildings, whose enrollment has recovered from the precipitous drops of the 2005-6 academic year. We can tour Uptown, comparing pockets, then tour Lakeview and the Lower Ninth Ward. I have to wonder if the middle- and upper-classes are less likely to return, since they have the resources to succeed elsewhere. Or are they more likely to return, since they have the resources to rebuild? So many of the city's poorer citizens went from the Superdome straight to shelters in Texas, Baton Rouge, Arkansas, even California. Who knows if they'll have the resources to return, to quit new jobs and move new belongings back to New Orleans? If New Orleans ends up being a whiter, more Republican city, Louisiana will be a solid red state with no blue dot on its big toe.

As we left the old neighborhood, I realized that I was experiencing a political landscape. Post-Katrina New Orleans has been compared to a war zone because of the physical damage and depopulated streets. And as in a war zone, every square foot has political significance. How could anyone see New Orleans now without thinking political thoughts? Katrina had turned it into a brutal testing ground for Bush, Chertoff, Brown, Blanco, Landrieu, Nagin, and dozens of other politicians on the local, state, and national levels. Its levees and floodwalls were primarily funded, designed, and built by the federal government, and many had pointed out that some of that funding may have been compromised by the expensive war in Iraq. Its citizens were for the most part Democrats, and now hundreds of thousands of them were scattered indefinitely, most of them to other states, altering Louisiana's political makeup for years to come. Vast areas, including the most impoverished neighborhoods in the city, were ruined, raising thorny political questions that will be debated for years. What should be rebuilt? Who should do the rebuilding? Who should pay? I try to imagine the old wood-frame houses of the Ninth Ward five years from now, and I don't know if they'll be bulldozed, gentrified, replaced, repaired, or abandoned. And of course the loudest political question about New Orleans is "Whose fault is this?"

The whole world watched New Orleans struggle with the storm, the flood, and the heat. The whole world watched Louisiana's leaders accumulate credit and blame for all that happened. Our poverty, our politics, our inadequate levees, our police misconduct, and even our pollution were exposed for all the world to see. Liberal or not, Louisianans can't help but feel like that young man in Mona Lisa's borrowed restroom. We left the door unlocked, and someone yanked it open while we were sitting there with our pants around our ankles.

December 2005

21. Summertime
David Starkey

1.

When I was growing up, the South was hot. Always hot. Day and night. You sweated in the morning, though a little bit less, and you sweated more and more as the day heated up. You didn't go out in the middle of the day unless—everyone in my family agreed—you wanted to pass out from heatstroke. You kept sweating in the evening, and if, as in my maternal grandparents' home, you slept with the window open, you were sure to sweat at night under your single sheet while the noisy fan clicked and ticked and pushed the humid air around.

Of course one of the reasons the South seemed so hot to me was that I was only there from June to August. From 1962—the summer I was born—until 1979—the summer before my senior year in high school, I spent the hottest months of the year in Beaumont, Texas, and Lake Charles, Louisiana. My dad's father had worked his whole life in the oil fields, and he and Grandma had a two-bedroom, one-bath brick house to show for it. By contrast—and the contrast seemed all the sharper in my young eyes—my mother's father, Pappy, had for twenty-five years been Superintendent of Schools for Calcasieu Parish (parish being the Louisiana equivalent of a county), and he and my grandmother lived in a two-story, white-columned home with a big front and back yard shaded by huge live oak trees. Beaumont was uptight, cramped, overly clean, and chilly—and not just from the window unit air conditioners in every room. Lake Charles was relaxed and comfortable. The kitchen, dining room, and den were kept air conditioned during the day, but the rest of the house was left open to the balmy air. It made you sleepy; it calmed you down.

My real life, my life during the school year, took place in suburban Sacramento, yet the South was clearly my family's home. Our California tract house had been thrown up just fifteen years earlier; six floor plans repeated themselves with slight variations throughout the neighborhood: living room on the right, living room on the left. People came and went all the time, unlike the South, where you hunkered down for the long haul. Foothill Farms was not a place where one belonged, but simply somewhere to live. Though I was born in Sutter Hospital, the South was where I was *from*.

This is not to say that my parents were unfailing champions of Southernness. They were clearly Southerners, still retaining traces of their accent, still using "y'all" for the second person plural rather than California's standard "you guys." But on the whole they weren't especially nostalgic about the South. While my younger sister and I were the only kids in the neighborhood who said, "Yes, sir," and "No, ma'am," otherwise we blended in well with our bland environment.

My father had joined the Air Force during the Korean War. After a year in the Azores, he was assigned to McClellan Air Force Base, and probably because he found his parents' influence so stifling, he didn't return to Texas after his discharge. He still loved to bass-fish and duck-hunt, but there were plenty of places to do those things in California. After receiving degrees from LSU and Vanderbilt, my mother married a Methodist minister, and for a year and half they tramped haplessly from one rectory to another in Louisiana and southern Mississippi. The marriage was traumatic, and after her divorce, she was ready for a change.

Joan Didion describes Sacramento in the mid-1950s as a slightly overgrown, but nevertheless quiet, tree-lined farm town. I imagine that when they began their new jobs as elementary school teachers and moved into a rented bungalow in Del Paso Heights, they felt right at home.

As a child, I often was so excited about my family's annual pilgrimage to see "the folks" for the summer that I couldn't sleep the night before our flight. Yet almost from the day we arrived, my sister and I complained of a lack of things to do. No kids—or, to be more precise, no *white* kids—lived in either of my grandparents' neighborhoods, so we were left to our own inventions. Dutifully avoiding heatstroke, my sister played elaborate, hours-long games of dollhouse and tea party in the living room, but I'd sneak outside.

In Lake Charles, I'd pretend to be an NFL quarterback and throw the ball to imaginary receivers in the vacant lot next to my grand-parents' house. I'd build forts and hunt for rats in the thick stands of bamboo that served as fences between backyards. Standing out there in my bare feet, insects singing, the air as palpable as another person, I'd often feel a frisson that was almost sexual in its intensity.

In Beaumont, I'd help Grandpa pick tomatoes and string beans, and I'd hang around as he tinkered inside the work shed he'd built behind his garage. It was a dark, mysterious place guarded by a thick padlock, and the few times he was ever truly angry with his grand-children was when we he'd asked us to retrieve a rusty wrench or a handful of nails and we'd forgotten to snap the padlock shut. Behind the garage grew a thriving fig tree that Grandpa fed daily with com-post. I wasn't supposed to pick the huge figs—most of the fruit was earmarked for canning, the rest for breakfasts of figs and cream with heaping spoonfuls of white sugar—but like Saint Augustine and his stolen pears, nothing tasted better to me than a sweet, sun-warmed fig, peeled and devoured in secrecy.

There were no computers, of course, no cable television. When I exhausted my small store of made-up games, I would occasionally have a chance to go bass fishing in the Lacassine Marsh, or I might be taken down to Pine Island Bayou to shoot crabs with a .22 pistol. Mostly, though, I was told to read, and that is was I did. I struggled through the leather-bound volumes in Pappy's library: *Leaves of Grass* and *The Iliad* and Keats's *Endymion*. I read dozens of *Reader's Di-gest* condensed versions of popular novels from the '60s and '70s: *The Taking of Pelham 123*, *A Woman in the House*, *Heartsblood*, *Of Good and Evil*, *The Headmaster*, *The Captain*, *The Artist*. I read dog-eared James Bond paperbacks and whatever bodice-ripper my mother had recently finished. When I was a young teen, I'd take my allowance to the classics section of the Walden bookstore at the mall. Gradually, ambitiously, I made my way through *Magic Mountain* and *Notes from Underground*; I read *The Death of Ivan Ilyich* and *Siddhartha* and *Hard Times* and *Pride and Prejudice* and *Black Boy*.

Often it would rain in the afternoons—big noisy thunderstorms. In Beaumont, I'd ensconce myself in the rocking chair in the guest room, right next to the noisy air conditioner. In Lake Charles, I'd sit outside on the screened porch in a chaise longue, the rain pounding like gravel on the aluminum roof, a spicy smell rising from the wet earth. If my sister moved out there with her dolls, I'd shift to Pappy's cool study, which smelled pleasantly of pipe tobacco and cigars. In a dim sort of way, I felt myself getting smarter, and I liked the feeling.

Getting through the summertime required adopting a rhythm—a Southern rhythm, I thought then, though it was also the rhythm of older, retired people. The South was comforting, like anything slow and unthreatening, although my sister and I—and my parents, too, if truth be told—were always eager to return to California when August rolled around.

The last year I went South for the summer with my parents, I was arrested by the Beaumont police. My grandparents were taking us out to eat at Luby's Cafeteria, and though I'd been to Luby's before and knew that it didn't require any sort of dressing up—dressing *down* was more like it—my parents insisted that I wear the good pair of slacks they'd just bought me, along with my new dress shoes. I felt ridiculous—I never wore anything but jeans and sneakers—and I argued with them until the last minute, when I finally capitulated and put on the hated garb.

With my long, awkward legs, there wasn't enough room in Grandpa's Buick for the six of us, so I followed behind them in the other car. Apparently, I was following too closely because a Beaumont police cruiser pulled me over. When the officer asked to see my driver's license, I realized I'd left it in my jeans. That excuse wasn't going to fly with him, however, and he had read me my rights and was putting me in the patrol car when my family circled back to see what had happened. They explained the situation, and the officer reluctantly let me go with them, although he gave me a ticket and a court date.

I can't think when I'd ever felt quite that upset: here I was, doing something I emphatically did *not* want to do, and now I was practically a criminal! At the hearing, the judge let me go with a warning, but during the week before my court appearance, I constructed a number of elaborate and horrifying fantasies about my life behind bars. When I walked out of the Jefferson County Courthouse a free man, I swore it was going to be a cold day in hell before I set foot in the South again.

By the time I was a senior in college, I didn't think much of the South, one way or the other. I'd pretty much succeeded in denying it had formed any part of my character. If you'd asked me for a quick impression, I probably would have said it was a place perpetually hot and muggy, where all the sidewalks were cracked by Bermuda grass, that it was mostly old people sitting inside by their air conditioners waiting, politely and patiently, for you to leave.

And yet I couldn't, or didn't *want*, to settle down in California. Some restlessness was urging me: *Leave*.

One day some friends and I drove from our central California university to the Napa Valley vineyards. Though we were all underage, a few of us had fake IDs, and we managed to sample a great variety of wines—swallows of Bordeaux followed by Riesling followed by Chablis followed by Pinot Noir. We were quite drunk by the end of the day and ended up sprawled out on a blanket in a field of blooming goldenrod, eating bread and cheese and pears. My girlfriend at the time, Cherry Carlson, was talking about going back to see her uncle in Sweden. Brian Flanagan had spent the summer before with cousins in Ireland. Galen Wong spoke of visiting relatives in Taiwan, maybe getting a teaching job there to support himself. At that moment I resolved, with all the force that comes from being twenty and drunk in a beautiful place, that I, too, would someday live in my own ancestral homeland. I could see myself lazing on a porch swing under a canopy of pine branches as clearly as I could see Cherry chewing on her last crisp bite of pear.

It didn't happen immediately, but at the age of twenty-five, I applied to and was accepted into the MFA program at Louisiana State University—my mother's and my uncle's and Pappy's alma mater—and I moved to Baton Rouge. When I finished my degree, all three of the teaching jobs I was offered were in the South. None of them were particularly appealing, but at one—a small university in South Carolina—I would be allowed to teach creative writing. So we moved: my wife—my *ex*-wife now—and our two children. She found a job with a mortgage bank in town. Eventually, we bought a house. Our third child, a son, was born. After our fashion, we settled down.

2.

When I moved to Louisiana in the summer of 1988, the Berlin Wall still stood, and being "red" still meant being a Communist, a particularly nasty accusation to make against any Southerner. In November, George Herbert Bush took Ronald Reagan's place as President of the United States, and the Right luxuriated in a well-founded sense of sense of optimism. Reagan had made conservatism chic all across the country, and now that all the white Southern Democrats were becoming Republicans, suddenly no one could win the White House without courting Dixie.

Indeed, the two Southern states where I lived, Louisiana and South Carolina, were both famous for politicians who had manipulated radical conservatism to their advantage. It was with horror that I realized during David Duke's 1990 campaign to become one of Louisiana's U.S. Senators that nearly half my class—many of whom were Catholic—favored his candidacy: this despite Duke's ties to the Klan, an organization that has excoriated Catholics since its founding. (Polls showed that Duke ended up receiving 60 percent of the white vote.) And Strom Thurmond, the Dixiecrats' 1948 segregationist presidential candidate, was an absolute fixture in the Palmetto State, a United States Senator for almost a half-century, retiring, finally, at age one hundred.

The list goes on, of course: George Wallace, Huey Long, Jefferson Davis, John C. Calhoun. Southerners even more than other Americans have relied on demagogues to lead them. In *The Mind of the South*, W. J. Cash explained it this way:

> the common white, as a matter of course, gave eager credence to and took pride in the legend of aristocracy which was so valuable to the defense of the land. He went farther, in fact, and, by an easy psychological process which is in evidence wherever men group themselves about captains, pretty completely assimilated his own ego to the latter's—felt his planter neighbor's new splendor as being in some fashion his also.

Boosterism was omnipresent. Once they'd hear my Yankee accent, it didn't take long for any new acquaintance to begin singing the South's praises. Granted, even as staunch a defender of the region as Fred Hobson resents the Southern "aversion to reasoned argument, . . . [the] distrust of analysis, reform, and social change," but most white Southerners I met rang a variation on the following statement by University of South Carolina history professor Clyde Wilson: "The South is a national asset, a priceless and irreplaceable treasure that must be conserved." (Wilson also said, in a 1998 piece in *Gentleman's Quarterly*, "We don't want the federal government telling us what to do, pushing integration down our throats . . . We're tired of carpetbagging professionals coming to our campuses and teaching that the South is a cultural wasteland.")

Ironically, conservatives—I learned later, after I'd extricated myself from the red states—had somehow managed to paint themselves as an "endangered species": they were only coming on so strong because if they didn't trumpet their values they would be swept away by the liberal deluge. In my seven years living in the South, I never saw even a trickle of this supposed flood, but—who knows?—maybe I was looking in the wrong place.

Frankly, I didn't care much for my new home, and it wasn't crazy about me. I sometimes wonder now, if I could go back and erase it all, would I? It's tempting. If we'd stayed in California, my ill-conceived marriage would certainly have broken up sooner, but my son would never have been born. And I did write some inspired poetry down there, wallowing in my increasing antipathy for all things Southern.

That vision I'd had in the Napa vineyards, however, began to seem like a visitation from the Great Deceiver. Religion, gender, race, and the environment: on an almost daily basis I was confronted by issues that were uniting white conservative voters and alienating everyone blue. The environment, race, gender, and religion: here they came again.

Astonishingly for people of their generation, none of my grandparents was very religious. I don't remember attending church a single Sunday during our summer stays, although my father's parents identified themselves as Baptists, while my mother's folks were nominally Methodist. My own parents picked up and passed on the knack for missing church, so I simply wasn't prepared for the onslaught of evangelism I faced when I actually set up house in the South.

Restless renters, my ex-wife and I moved often: twice in Baton Rouge, four times in Florence, South Carolina. Yet no matter where we went, as soon as—and sometimes before—we'd hauled the last box out of the Ryder rent-a-truck, they'd descend on us: Methodists, Pentecostals, Free Will and Southern Baptists, even the occasional Presbyterian, all trying to recruit us to their "church home." I wanted to believe that, in part, they were simply welcoming us to the neighborhood, but a hardy undercurrent of salesmanship always accompanied the greetings. "Can we count on you to worship with us next Sunday? Our new construction fund needs an awful lot of help."

Because my ex-wife and I were skeptics, we did not find it easy to mingle with our neighbors. Our daughters had an even harder time. Although we allowed, even encouraged them, to participate in church activities in the hope that they would make friends, our own disbelief clearly rubbed off. "My momma said I can't play with you unless you go to church," a seven-year-old girl once announced.

"So?" our eldest replied.

The friendliest child from a religious background was Tori, the daughter of a Free Will Baptist minister. A former member of a motorcycle gang—he still had the tattoos of Satan to prove it—he and his wife were of the "Praise Jesus!" variety, but seemed genuinely intent on evangelizing for the sake of souls rather than tithes. Unfortunately, their racially mixed congregation had constant financial troubles, and after they lost the brick building they were renting, they had to move their services to the preacher's mobile home, on a dirt road at the edge of a swamp.

At the other end of the financial security spectrum were the numerous Southern Baptists. A well-organized, almost militant denomination, the Southern Baptist Convention was formed in 1845 in large measure to ensure that *some* Baptists, at least, would not be corrupted by the burgeoning antislavery movement, and it seemed to me that a racist taint still clung to the sect. Yet the cheapest, closest (across the street), and most reliable daycare in our part of town was sponsored by Southern Baptists, so that's where our two daughters went during the working day. The two elderly women in charge of the center were nice enough to the girls, but it was impossible not to notice in the few minutes I spent dropping off and picking up my kids that the women were blatantly hostile to the lone African American child in their care. "Come here, sweetheart, let me wipe your nose," they'd say to the whites. But it was always: "*Michael!* What's that ugly stuff running down your face?"

In *Who Speaks for the South?* James McBride Dabbs, a champion of desegregation, concludes that "Southern history was God's way of leading two originally opposed peoples into a richer life than either could have found alone." I must admit that I never stepped foot inside the local Baptist church on a Sunday morning, but since I lived only a few houses away, I could, from my pine-shaded porch swing (Cherry Carlson, where were you then?), easily watch the lines of cars coming and going. I don't recall ever seeing a black face in any of those cars. Whether or not this indicates a sustained, systemic act of prejudice on the part of the congregation, clearly no progress was being made in bringing blacks and whites together in the worship that took place on my street.

How strange it was to come from politically correct California to a place where white people freely admitted, "Everyone's prejudiced, if they'd just admit it." While there may be some truth to that statement, saying it so bluntly also served as a kind of excuse for not trying to change: "You can't fault a person for being honest." But no matter how you justify it, racism is ugly, and it fuels white Southerners at their worst. I admit this is hardly an original thesis—Southerners have been denying it for centuries.

In an essay purporting to show why racial animosity is *not* at the core of Southernness, John Shelton Reed mentions an incident in which his "high school friends once ran the Stars and Bars up the school flagpole on the anniversary of Appomattox, but they'd have flown the swastika or the hammer-and-sickle, if they'd had one, with the same fine, thoughtless, apolitical desire to raise hell." I think Reed is partly right: I can easily imagine a group of white Southerners flying the Nazi flag, but I find it inconceivable that the same crowd would raise the Communist banner.

The Confederate flag, like the swastika, is a powerful symbol of Aryan hatred. Certainly, African Americans do not appreciate whatever glorious past the Stars and Bars is supposed to commemorate. Quite the contrary, most black Southerners vigorously object to the Confederate flag's official, governmental use. Yet when I listened to the radio news in the morning, I'd hear the voices of ancient white men denying that the Confederate flag should disturb blacks. The flag often featured prominently on pickup trucks that sported bumper stickers like the one reading, "If I'd have known, I would have picked my own cotton," a sentiment at once so historically absurd and so incredibly narrow-minded I would nearly choke with rage whenever I saw it. And in Florence I saw bumper stickers like that a lot. "It's Not Racial, It's Regional," said one defense of Johnny Reb's flag. "I'm Offended That You're Offended," said another. Incidentally, these same bumper stickers can now be purchased on the Ku Klux Klan's Web site, and I can't help but think that—no matter how much pride it inspired in them—conservative whites would have abandoned the Confederate emblem long ago if they didn't take such pleasure in the misery it represents to blacks.

Granted, the contemporary version of Southern racism is more often cloaked in genteel euphemisms, but I recognized it as a species of the prejudice I had witnessed in my childhood. I never saw my grandparents physically or verbally abuse a black person, but I remember how, in the 1960s and '70s, my father's mother would always scald the glass from which her black yard man had drunk his iced tea, because "You never know what diseases those people have." When I visited Beaumont in the early 1990s, I told my grandfather that I was thinking of taking my son on a walk around the block. "I wouldn't do that," he said. "There's nothing around here but burr-headed niggers." We looked at each other, and he seemed conscious that I found the statement extremely offensive. "Nothing but Japs and Chinks and burr-headed niggers," he repeated.

My mother's parents were a bit more well-heeled. Pappy, as the superintendent of schools for an entire parish, obviously had to take a more politic line. Nevertheless, as my sister and I sat on his knees, he would tell us stories about Little Black Sambo and the pickaninny who was nearly eaten by the rhinoceros. I suppose from his perspective the material was relatively harmless, but an African American child was always the narrative's victim. Even the animals of the jungle, we learned, were smarter than blacks. Not long ago, I asked my mother where Pappy stood on the issue of school desegregation. Though I never heard anyone in our family mention the subject, it must have been a hot topic in the Louisiana of my childhood. My mother hesitated for a moment. "I think," she said, "that Pappy tended to be on the conservative side of the fence."

So were most of the white college students I taught. Obviously, the South has no monopoly on prejudice, but the burden of the past, which many Southerners seem to enjoy shouldering—slavery, the Civil War, lynchings, Jim Crow, the violent resistance to Civil Rights—makes Southern racism especially noxious. "What about *white* history month?" half my class at Francis Marion University choroused every February, and when some brave, outnumbered African American student explained, "Well, y'all kind of have white history month all the other months of the year," many of the whites would look on in patent disbelief.

Southerners have always prided themselves on their good manners. The charming Southern belle is an icon, and travelers to the antebellum South often noted the graciousness with which their hosts treated them. However, many Northern visitors also noted the severity with which the slave population was treated; they came to agree with Frederick Douglass that Southern manners were really no more than the thinnest veneer of social courtesy: beneath was something at the very least insincere, at worst, horribly malicious. One South Carolinian I knew, scion of generations of large landholders, agreed. He believed that what differentiated Southerners from other Americans was a constant fury simmering just below the surface. He claimed elaborate etiquette was necessary to keep that rage from erupting. "Starkey, if we didn't say 'May I please be excused from the table,' we'd probably just take an ax handle and *explode*."

While there's nothing quite as spectacular as watching a Southern woman coming to a boil, more often than not the anger my friend referred to is directed by men at women. Novelist Anne Rivers Siddons contends: "The South is dreadfully hard on its women . . . I suppose this is true of other regions as well, but I think it is more true of the South." My ex-wife echoed that sentiment: "Discrimination against women is more pronounced. The only women who don't accept it are the ones who aren't from the South."

The South's conservatism, mostly an ideological aggravation for liberal white males, clearly has more substantial consequences for women. I remember being among fifty or so pro-choice protesters, mostly women, standing on the capitol steps in Baton Rouge. An anti-abortion bill was in the legislature, and we were there to prove that not every woman in Louisiana wanted to cede her reproductive rights. But things didn't look good. We were surrounded by hundreds, perhaps thousands, of evangelical Christians—so many that they could encircle the entire capitol while holding hands. The summer sun shone hard on the white marble building, on the front of which someone had spray-painted "ABORTION IS MURDER."

"Stupid Nazis," a woman next to me said. And indeed the hatred in so many of those eyes made me think of films I'd seen of Germany in the 1930s. (*Kinder, Kirche, Küche*, ran the Nazi slogan: children, church, and kitchen.) Most of the marchers were dressed in Sunday clothes, but a line of burly men in jeans and T-shirts and baseball caps stood, apparently impenetrable, at the bottom of the steps. "STOP

KILLING THE INNOCENT," read their banners. "ABORTION: THE AMERI-CAN HOLOCAUST." The image I retain is those men refusing to allow a slender woman to cross their line. "Excuse me," she kept saying with growing desperation, but their arms were locked in fury.

"The skies serene and calm, the air temperately cool, and gentle zephyrs breathing through the fragrant pines," William Bartram said of the Southeast in the 1770s. "The prospect around enchantingly varied and beautiful; endless green savannas, chequered with coppices of fragrant shrubs, filled the air with the richest perfume."

He wouldn't recognize the place today.

An ad campaign entitled "Don't Mess with Texas" did a great deal to curb littering in that state, and I often wished that South Carolina had come up with a similar slogan. The state's Anti-Litter and Beautification Organization did launch a "Palmetto Pride" effort in the early years of the new millennium, but I was tempted to call the rural back roads on which I drove to work the "Land of Litter." Several times a week I had to clean my front yard. I'd pick up cigarette butts, gum wrappers, beer and soda cans, whiskey bottles, crumpled advertisements, condoms: detritus thrown from passing cars. Evidently, for many Southerners defiling the land was an act of defiance: let somebody else pick it up, damnit. Indeed, a few of my neighbors had apparently given up; the edges of their lawns looked like strips of junkyard.

Of course, road trash was nothing compared with the chemicals that industry spewed out. Once, in Baton Rouge, the lead story on the ten o'clock news was about a kind of plastic snow that had fallen on the northwest part of the city. A reporter talked to the residents of the neighborhoods adjacent to the Exxon refinery. Everyone interviewed was black and, though they were clearly angry, they seemed to feel it was useless to complain. One teenager scooped a handful of the white flakes from the roof of his car, shrugged his shoulders, and threw the "snow" into the air.

Back in the studio, the anchorwoman laughed. "Christmas comes early to Louisiana," she said in her musical drawl, ending the story with a quote from an Exxon spokesman who assured the public that "the accidental release of these chemicals poses no health threat whatsoever."

The snow wasn't always made of plastic. Sure, summers were just as hot and miserable as I remembered them, but, on top of everything else, there was an actual *winter* to deal with. We were entirely unprepared when it actually snowed in South Carolina, and when the temperatures dropped into the single digits in Baton Rouge in the great "Arctic Outbreak" of December 1989, our pipes froze solid for two days. We skipped baths and used bottled water to wash the dishes. Later we learned that a mother and daughter down the street had fallen asleep in a small bedroom with their space heater on. It had baked their skins to powder, while outside the world was ice.

3.

If the final section of this essay had a soundtrack, I'd select George Gershwin's "Summertime," from the opera *Porgy and Bess*. But the singer wouldn't be Ella Fitzgerald, or even Billie Holiday. No, the only person for the job is Janis Joplin, from Port Arthur, Texas, a few miles south of my grandparents' home in Beaumont. And although, on the recording I am thinking of, Janis is accompanied by her first and sloppiest band—Big Brother and the Holding Company—she sings the song with the authority of a very old spirit. The music plays as the camera pans across Louisiana's Avery Island in spring, the Smoky Mountains in the fall. We see the curving streets of Charleston, the dignified squares of Savannah, the barely contained chaos of pre-Katrina New Orleans. Even the tacky working-class splendor of Graceland and the colossal Vulcan Statue in Birmingham are ennobled by Janis's voice, as we cross-fade to her high school yearbook photo: Art Club, Slide Rule Club, "B" Average Award; the bouffant hairdo, the big nose and crooked smile and suspicious eyes.

As Janis croons in the background, let me say, frankly, that I found it hellish to live blue in a red state, to always feel surrounded and outnumbered by people whose vision of the proper order of things was so different from my own. When a small liberal arts college in the western suburbs of Chicago offered me a creative writing job, I accepted it instantly and with no regrets.

While I was living in Dixie, white Republicans began pitching a

New South—relaxed and charming, yes, but also efficient and shrewd and business-savvy—and my secret curse was that the corporate model would eventually erase the South's distinctive regional character. So long, Darlene's Donuts, bring on Krisy Kreme! If Atlanta, "The City Too Busy to Hate," was the most Northern city in the South, then I thought, let the other cities be more like Atlanta. Let homogenization reign, let the malling over begin. In my angriest moments my wish for the South was this: may you become as tepid and safe as the California suburb I fled.

I say this, and yet, although my impression of the South is largely negative, I wouldn't really want it to become a giant mall. As so many of the contributors to this book have said, living blue in a red state can't help but turn one a little purple. Yes, V. S. Naipaul was right: this is "a landscape of small ruins." But even the crustiest blue stater would find it impossible to deny the South's beauty when the dogwood and tulip and magnolia trees are in bloom, when patches of daffodils grow wild along the roadside and wisteria drops its purple blossoms on the lawns.

Anyway—believe it or not—distance has blunted my angry edge. (I wrote much of the previous section of this essay while living in South Carolina. If this version seems vitriolic, you should have seen the earlier drafts.) Absence from the scene hasn't filled me with nostalgia, but it has given me some perspective.

I can no more dismiss my family outright than I can slice out my liver or spleen with a pocketknife and hope to go on as blithely as before. If Pappy didn't work for segregation in the schools, if he told racist stories to his grandchildren, he also taught me about extemporaneous narrative invention: every story must, in some important way, be made up on the spot. Grandpa, too, was a lover of words, an enthusiasm that manifested itself whenever we played card games like Pitch. If you put down a bad card, you were "nuttier than a peach orchard shoat," and he was going to "tear you up like a bale of hay." Get a run of trumps and you were "hotter than the hinges on a depot stove." That love of language and storytelling, of keeping an audience entertained, what raconteur would deny his heritage?

However unsavory his political leanings look to me from this distance, Pappy was nevertheless known around Lake Charles as a straight-shooter. One of his brothers had been killed in the Second World War; another had become a Methodist minister in South Carolina: they were a family that did what they believed was the right thing, and I still feel the thrum of that genetic calling to Be Good.

And what about Grandpa's surprising tolerance when two gay men moved in next door? "Them boys are queer, all right," he said. "I don't hold with what they're doing. But they're polite, they don't make a lot of racket, and they sure keep up their yard."

Maybe my hidden complaint is simply that the South I knew from my childhood summers was nothing like the South year-round. Childhood and memory being what they are, how could it have been?

Or maybe what I'm trying to do is reconcile the different parts of myself—the red and the blue, the bold and the meek, the agitated and the peaceable, the optimistic and the cynical, summer and winter—just as this country is trying to hold itself together, to see its many conflicting impulses not as a weakness, but as a source of strength.

When Hurricane Rita swept across Beaumont and Lake Charles in late September of 2005, I was living in Santa Barbara. My parents were down from Sacramento, visiting me and my new family. My mother had telephoned her friends: they were safe. My dad's sister had gone north to stay with cousins. My mom's brother had left Lake Charles years earlier. And their parents, my grandparents, were all dead.

Rita came so close on the heels of Katrina that just about everyone from the threatened area had been evacuated. Yes, there would be some property damage, but surely no one would die this time. In comparison to the disaster in New Orleans, this didn't seem like a such big deal—at least to me.

However, as the storm came closer to making landfall, my parents became glued to the television. Their four-year-old granddaughter, normally the center of attention, was playing alone in her room while Granny and Paw Paw switched from the Weather Channel to Fox

News to CNN. The newscasters' rhetoric of danger increased as the wind and rain picked up.

I left the room for a few minutes. When I came back, the TV showed images of flooded streets and uprooted trees. My father had an arm around my mother, who was weeping. "Look," she said, pointing at the screen, "look what's happening to my *home*."

Afterword
Writing the Personal Political Essay
David Starkey

Feeling Blue, Seeing Red

In "Living to Tell the Tale: The Complicated Ethics of Creative Non-fiction," Lynn Bloom writes: "the writer of creative nonfiction has to play fair. This is a statement of both ethics and aesthetics. The presentation of the truth the writer tells, however partisan, cannot seem vindictive or polemical." That's particularly challenging when writing about an area that's so charged. When were are "feeling blue," it's difficult not to "see red." Writing that heavily foregrounds emotion often comes up short in its appeals to reason. *Pathos* in short, can overwhelm *logos* and, as Bloom suggests, *ethos*. Nevertheless, I am convinced that the contributors to *Living Blue in the Red States* have acquitted themselves well in this area.

Indeed, reading and rereading so many fine essays, I began to wonder if what I came to think of as "the personal political essay" might be a distinctive subspecies of creative nonfiction. After they'd completed their chapters, I asked the contributors to help me define the genre in which we were working, and I received a number of intriguing replies, many of which are quoted below.

Before continuing, though, I should make it clear that what I am discussing is the *left-leaning* personal political essay. A book entitled *Living Red in the Blue States* published by, say, TimeWarner Books would be a very different collection than the one you hold in your hands. I imagine such a book would be thesis-driven and would stay relentlessly "on message." When someone like George Will cites personal experience, he typically does so not to examine the experience from all angles, but as evidence for his argument. However, most of my contributors recoiled from that strategy of argumentation. Instead, they occasionally waffle, they often take a while to make a point, they see both sides of a question. They discover and explore. This book is far more Montaignian than Baconian: it asks more questions than it answers.

Still, when I initially began soliciting essays, I did anticipate that a strong, central and often-repeated argument would be a feature of many of the chapters. It came, therefore, as something of a surprise to hear the vehement denunciations of personal political writing that is dogmatic or predetermined. David Case expresses this sentiment quite forcefully: "My essay definitely did not come from a thesis, and I doubt that many good essays do. As Nietzsche put it, every piece of 'systematic' writing is a record of what its author needed to believe." Most of the contributors would probably agree with Gil Allen's reformulation of Yeats's famous statement: "We make out of the quarrel with others, rhetoric, but out of the quarrel with ourselves, poetry." Allen advises, "substitute 'political debates' for 'rhetoric' and 'personal political essays' for 'poetry.'" The result is a piece of writing that is both inward-looking—occasionally metacognitive—yet also artfully crafted.

This is not to say that the *Living Blue* contributors thought of their essays as prose equivalents of Yeats's ideal poem, which was so carefully fashioned that it would "click shut at the end like the top of a well-made box." Far from it. Frank Soos dislikes "strong conclusions," preferring essays "that pull a reader into a question and get that reader stuck there in much the same way I have been as I've assembled my piece. Ideally, the essay will stay with the reader, be a means to a larger exploration." Soos admits, "I never have a plan. I tend to put an idea in my head . . . and let it rattle around." Lee Martin is also interested in "the exploration that allows me to know a little something about myself and the world around me that I didn't know going in." Tony Kellman works "from the particular to an implied truth. Writing the personal political essay is challenging in the sense that one needs to be direct without being direct, to keep both art and politics alive without undermining or blurring either one." And Jonis Agee begins an essay not to prove a thesis, but because "certain thoughts or perceptions or experiences are pressing on me for attention. My job in writing the essay then is to discover the unique connections that these elements possess and what that connection means."

Sometimes the "disquieting" struggle to discover these connections becomes part of the essay itself. Deb Olin Unferth notes:

> When I sat down to write my essay, I quickly had to abandon the idea of writing something "good." I knew I was incapable of that, partly because I have very few final thoughts or theories. Almost everything I accept is with qualifiers, hesitations. So instead I tried to write down simply what happened and how I felt about it. I tried not to add any insights or a thesis. As long as I stuck to very straight description and reaction, I felt I would be okay. But in fact even that caused a lot of trouble. I found it difficult to do, to write something compelling and honest and also factually "true." I have to admit I found the whole experience upsetting.

Like many of the contributors to this book, Olin Unferth is a fiction writer, and she believes that "the best personal political essays have the same qualities I admire in fiction: they preserve ambiguity and complexity; they unsettle, do not conclude." Not surprisingly, several other contributors praised judicious use of the elements of fiction as a way to strengthen nonfiction essays. David Romtvedt contends that "almost all writing is fiction in the sense that we shape our experience to suit the needs of what we believe to be a truth greater than chronology or biography."

Memoirists have long acknowledged that it is impossible not to do *some* fictionalizing, even when recounting the recent past. Memory is notoriously fickle, and artistic imperatives—the need to recreate conversations, to vividly describe scenes—sometimes trump allegiance to absolute fidelity. Yet as the *Living Blue* essays began to arrive on my desk, the boundary between nonfiction and fiction, which, presumably, all of us who contributed to this volume were continually skirting, if not actually crossing, suddenly became a significant issue: a spectacular controversy was brewing in the world of creative nonfiction, one that made the headlines of the national news. James Frey, author of the Oprah-endorsed *A Million Little Pieces*, a purported memoir, had been outed by the Smoking Gun Web site. Apparently, a great deal of what he reported to be "true" in his book was, in fact, fiction. In the wake of Frey's national humiliation—Oprah's public chastisement and harsh rebukes from creative nonfiction gurus like Lee Gutkind—I asked my contributors what aspect of the personal essay, if any, it was permissible to fictionalize.

"I guess I believe in truth in advertising," Gil Allen responded. "If you call something a memoir, or if you write a 'personal political essay' like my own in *Living Blue*, then you're obliged to respect the facts. You're free to select from them, emphasize them, and reconstruct them according to your own conscience, but you can't write as if they don't exist."

John Lane agrees, though he places a caveat on the reliability of memory:

> I don't make things up, but I work from and trust memory, my memory, and I'm sure my dead aunt (or other relatives of mine) would re/member our shared lives (what I write about) with different details. They'd come to different conclusions about what situations mean as well. I see "the personal essay" as a literary mode more akin to the short story than the news article, so I think, in the end, the James Frey mess is important only as an argument about style. If Frey had written a better book, he would have a better argument for his grand fabrication. (Think of Annie Dillard with *Pilgrim at Tinker Creek*; she's admitted the visit from her cat that begins the tale so powerfully never happened to her either.) After all, literary writing is textile work— weaving a fabric!

David Romtvedt is more forgiving of Frey's genre transgressions, arguing that "if the lesson is there, I don't care whether the events actually happened or happened in the realm of imagination":

> *A Million Little Pieces* would not have been a problem if the book were simply marketed as a work of fiction dealing with our pro-

pensity to be self-destructive and our need for some kind of redemption. If a work of literature is meant to offer me a lesson, that lesson need not come in the form of "Oh, my god, that happened to the author." Our struggle over fiction and nonfiction is in some ways a battle about the dignity of the imagination. It is through imagination that we create the material world and it is imagination that can help us to understand and recreate the world we've made.

Sherry Simpson's comment was echoed by several contributors: "James Frey? There's a place for his kind of writing. It's in the section titled 'Fiction.' I love fiction. I just don't want to be tricked into thinking I'm reading someone's true story."

Whatever one might say about Frey and his book, he obviously had a clear sense of his audience and how to connect with it. One of the issues that rankled so many devotees of *A Million Little Pieces*—especially recovering addicts—was that they felt they'd come to know the *real* James Frey. He had connected with them; something about his presentation of the authorial self rang true. Of course candid revelation of an author's limitations is often a strategy to win sympathy for his or her point of view. Even if personal essayists relentlessly expose their own faults, foibles, and blind spots, we must ultimately find ourselves cheering for them, and Frey's tactic was to heap guilt upon himself for all the bad things he'd done. (How ironic, then, that so much criticism was directed toward him because he wasn't the malefactor he'd made himself out to be!)

Frey presented himself as the prodigal son returned; it was relatively easy for his audience to follow protocol and forgive him. However, the issue of audience is a more vexing question for the contributors to this book. Are they simply preaching to the converted, the "true blue"? Are they trying to reach moderate Republicans, those who might be swayed by a reasoned argument for progressive values? Or are they squarely addressing a foe who is likely to disagree with almost everything they have to say? No matter how the essayists approach the task of garnering support for their points of view, some readers are bound to be affronted.

"Although I suspect that most of my readers will be blue rather than red," Gil Allen says, "I would hope that a reflective Republican could find something of value in my essay." Fellow South Carolinian John Lane, writing out of "a sense of isolation that stops way short of a sense of persecution," is similarly optimistic about reaching those who don't necessarily share his politics:

> In Spartanburg I never feel as if I'm floating on a sea of like-minded support but I'm not drowning in the community's dismissal either. I'm always in my lifeboat, the minority position, but I do feel I have a position, bobbing on the surface of their certainty. This is a good place for a writer to be. I write for those majority people who in the end will listen, and there are more who listen than you'd think, even in a place as politically conservative as this red corner of South Carolina. I try to listen to them as well.

Other contributors have a more personal sense of audience. Lee Martin notes, "I always think of myself as an audience because I'm talking to myself, trying to figure something out, trying to make sense of a curiosity or a confusion. I try to establish that conversational tone of the self talking to the self, and, if I'm successful, I'll hit that intimacy that will allow others to participate in the conversation." Jonis Agee similarly considers the personal essay a kind of dialogue: "My audience then would be people who are interested in exploring the questions that I am raising in my writing."

Tone is a crucial element of this conversation. The author must think carefully about how he presents himself to his auditors. "The biggest challenge is not to go on a rant," says Robin Hemley. "The only way I could write this piece was to inject some humor, though the humor is perhaps in the tradition of Mark Twain and more recently Stephen Colbert. In other words, the subtext of the humor is a scream at the top of one's lungs: 'You idiots!'"

Sherry Simpson admits that she may have chosen journalism early in her writing career because reporters are generally told to eliminate themselves from their story. As much as possible, their tone is supposed to be "objective," the authorial self invisible. "Now I'm trying to stand up more," she says. Simpson recalls recently pitching a story to a magazine:

> When the editors said, "ok, but you'll have to be objective," I thought it over and said, "Never mind. I don't want to be." Nor do I want to beat a drum, because I don't think most people will read what they don't already agree with, unless it's approached in a thoughtful way. So the authorial self, I hope, is someone who's trying to ask questions on behalf of others, and presenting some answers, but not always trying to persuade. Let people persuade themselves; then they'll believe. Crack open the door and hope they'll walk through it.

Finally, what about topicality, an issue I had fretted over from the start? What details from current events were necessary to bring the essays to life? What references to news items would tend to make the pieces obsolete? Angus Woodward, whose essay on the aftermath of Hurricane Katrina is perhaps the piece closest to traditional political reporting, is blunt:

> I worry that my essay will get "stale" more quickly than others, that between the time I finished it in December 2005 and its publication, Louisiana/Katrina politics will change drastically (that's one reason I put "December 2005" at the end of the essay, a feature I hope will be preserved in publication). So my target readers live in 2007 and beyond. The essay is a snapshot of the political situation at that moment. I suppose that's true of all political essays—all we can do is report on the situation up to the moment in which we write.

As he wrote his essay, Sidney Burris sometimes found himself overwhelmed by topicality—"the continual political rhetoric that spills into my living room from the cable news channels." Burris contrasts the safe, election-friendly "pabulum" coming from politicians with the intentionally inflammatory "histrionics" from cable news commentators:

> Of course, they're working with the brief amount of time allotted to them by their commercial sponsors—who seem to be

gobbling up more and more time each hour—so these celebrity anchors don't have the time to develop an authentic opinion and have to settle for: 1) shallowness; 2) entertainment, or "news-er-tainment," as I recently heard; or 3) cynicism (I'm thinking of Keith Olbermann). This kind of reportage influenced my essay because I found myself gradually narrowing my notion of political action until it became almost uncomfortably situated within my living room. Once every four years a group of people whom I know nothing about begins to harass me into voting. In a good year, half of the country drags itself to the poll, and half of that diminished group, on an average year, puts someone in office, at which we point we go back to our regular lives, until harassed again, four years later. If I was going to find a political life, I couldn't find it as traditionally defined within the national arena—that had become an abstraction to me. I had to find it elsewhere, and that's what I was trying to do in the essay.

The difficulty of "finding a political life" is at the heart of *Living Blue in the Red States*. One of the most important functions of this book is that it shows those of us who consider ourselves progressive or liberals how important it is to move beyond anger ("seeing red") and depression ("feeling blue") toward a thoughtful, reasoned response to the political situation we find so troubling. If we are to make a difference in the America of the new millennium, we must channel our passion into work that presents us as the reflective, concerned, honest and generous people that, at our best, I believe we are.

Contributors

Jonis Agee is the author of eleven books, including four novels, *Sweet Eyes, Strange Angels, South of Resurrection,* and *The Weight of Dreams* and five collections of short fiction, *Pretend We've Never Met, Bend This Heart, A .38 Special and a Broken Heart, Taking the Wall,* and *Acts of Love on Indigo Road.* Her newest novel, *The Riverman's Wife,* will be published by Random House in the summer of 2007. Among her awards are a National Endowment for the Arts Fellowship, two Loft-McKnight Fellowships for fiction, two Minnesota State Arts Board grants in fiction, and the Nebraska Book Award. She teaches creative writing at the University of Nebraska–Lincoln, where she directs the Nebraska Summer Writers' Conference. She is currently at work on a collection of essays.

Gilbert Allen has published four collections of poems: *In Everything, Second Chances, Commandments at Eleven,* and *Driving to Distraction,* which was featured on Garrison Keillor's *The Writer's Almanac.* He received the South Carolina Literary Arts Fellowship in 2002–3, and he is a five-time winner of the South Carolina Fiction Project Prize. He coedited the anthology *A Millennial Sampler of South Carolina Poetry* (Ninety-Six Press, 2005). Since 1977 he has lived in upstate South Carolina with his wife, Barbara. She is a lifelong Democrat with a Rolodex memory.

Sidney Burris is currently completing a memoir of reading. Portions of it have appeared in AGNI *Magazine, The Georgia Review, The South-*

ern Review, *Five Points*, and *Studies in the Literary Imagination*. Another section is forthcoming in *The Southwest Review*. Two of these pieces were selected in 2003 and 2005 as a "Notable Essay" in *Best American Essays*. He has also written two volumes of poetry—one with the University of Utah Press (*A Day at the Races*, 1989) and the other with Louisiana State University Press (*Doing Lucretius*, 2000). These poems originally appeared in *The Atlantic*, *Poetry*, *The Kenyon Review*, *The Virginia Quarterly Review*, *The Southern Review*, *Prairie Schooner*, and other journals. His work was also included in *Best American Poetry, 1996*.

David Case teaches English at Los Angeles City College and plays piano for the Amphion Quartet. He has published poems, reviews, and articles in the usual variety of places—several of them in the South, no less—and has a novel called "Poison Cures" ready for publication, or at least ready for perusal. David also helps edit *King Log* poetry magazine: poets, please take note of www.angelfire.com/il/kinglog.

Stephen Corey, born in Buffalo, New York, and reared in nearby Jamestown, was educated at Harpur College/Binghamton University (BA, MA) and the University of Florida (PhD). He has published ten poetry collections since 1981, most recently *There Is No Finished World* (White Pine Press, 2003). His essays have appeared in such periodicals as *Shenandoah*, *The Laurel Review*, *Poets & Writers*, and *Connecticut Review*. Corey was cofounder, coeditor, and editor of *The Devil's Millhopper*, an independent poetry journal, from 1976 to 1983. Since 1983 he has been on the editorial staff of *The Georgia Review*, for which he is currently acting editor.

Steve Heller is professor and chair of the MFA in Creative Writing Program at Antioch University–Los Angeles. He grew up in the wheat country of central Oklahoma, where much of "Here Was Johnny" is set. Steve is best known for his novel *The Automotive History of Lucky Kellerman* (Anchor, 1989) and his book of short stories, *The Man Who Drank a Thousand Beers* (Chariton Review, 1984). His essays, nonfiction narratives, and short stories have appeared in numerous magazines and anthologies, including *New Letters, Colorado Review, Fourth Genre, Southern California Anthology, Manoa, American Cowboy,* and *In Brief: Short Takes on the Personal.* He is currently working on a new novel called *Return of the Ghost Killer.*

Robin Hemley is the director of the Nonfiction Writing Program at the University of Iowa. He is the author of seven books of fiction and nonfiction, including *The Last Studebaker, The Big Ear* and *Nola: A Memoir of Faith, Art and Madness.* His most recent books are *Turning Life into Fiction* (Graywolf, 2006) and *Invented Eden* (Bison Books, 2006).

John Lane's books include *Against Information and Other Poems, Weed Time: Essays from the Edge of a Country Yard, Waist Deep in Black Water, The Dead Father Poems,* and, most recently, *Chattooga: Descending into the Myth of Deliverance River.* He teaches at Wofford College in Spartanburg sc, where is is writes a weekly environmental column, The Kudzu Telegraph. He is also one of the cofounders of Spartanburg's Hub City Writers Project, a national model for community publishing and literary life. He lives and writes deep within the "Red" territory. In the last presidential election his precinct voted almost 70 percent Republican.

Anthony Kellman was born in Barbados and has lived in the South for the past twenty years, first in Louisiana, where he was a graduate student at Louisiana State University, and then in Georgia, where he is a professor of creative writing at Augusta State University. He has published four books of poetry, most recently *Limestone,* and two novels, most recently, *The Houses of Alphonso.* He is the editor of the first full-length U.S. anthology of English-language Caribbean poetry, *Crossing Water,* and is a recipient of a National Endowment for the Arts poetry award.

Lee Martin is the author of the novel *The Bright Forever,* a finalist for the 2006 Pulitzer Prize in Fiction; two memoirs, *From Our House* and *Turning Bones;* another novel, *Quakertown;* and a short story collection, *The Least You Need to Know*. He is the winner of the Mary McCarthy Prize in Short Fiction and fellowships from the National Endowment for the Arts and the Ohio Arts Council. Since 2001 he has taught in the MFA program at The Ohio State University where he is now a professor of English and the director of creative writing.

Donald Morrill is the author of three books of nonfiction, *The Untouched Minutes, Sounding for Cool*, and *A Stranger's Neighborhood*, as well as two volumes of poetry, *At the Bottom of the Sky* and *With Your Back to Half the Day*. He is currently an editor of *Tampa Review* and the University of Tampa Press Poetry Series, and he is the 2006 Bedell Visiting Writer at the University of Iowa.

Jim Peterson is associate professor and coordinator of creative writing at Randolph-Macon Woman's College. He has published one novel, *Paper Crown* (Red Hen Press, 2005), and four poetry collections, including *The Owning Stone* in 2000 and *The Bob & Weave* in 2006 (both from Red Hen Press). His poetry has won the Benjamin Saltman Award and a 2002–3 fellowship from the Virginia Commission for the Arts. Several of his plays have been produced in regional and college theaters. He lives in Lynchburg, Virginia, with his wife, Harriet, and their left-wing Welsh Corgi, Dylan Thomas.

David Romtvedt lives in Buffalo, Wyoming, and serves as the poet laureate for the state of Wyoming. His most recent book of poems is *Some Church* (Milkweed Editions, 2005). His essays have appeared in the collection *Windmill: Essays from Four Mile Ranch* (Red Crane, 1997) as well as in *The Sun, Poets and Writers*, and *Orion* magazines. He loves languages, and, since he is a musician as well as a writer, he is currently working on making a multilingual arrangement of the U.S. national anthem.

Michael J. Rosen has published some sixty books of poetry, children's books, cookbooks, and fiction. As an editor he has worked with over a thousand authors, illustrators, photographers, and chefs to create more than fifteen volumes that benefit Share Our Strength's fight to create a hunger-free generation and various animal welfare efforts across the country. Recent titles include three volumes of the humor biennial *Mirth of a Nation, The 60-Second Encyclopedia* and *ChaseR: A Novel in E-mail.* He lives on one hundred forested acres in central Ohio.

Mona Lisa Saloy, New Orleans native and folklorist, is currently Visiting Associate Professor in American Ethnic Studies at the University of Washington. She is the author of a love song to New Orleans, *Red Beans and Ricely Yours: Poems* (Truman State University Press), selected by Ishmael Reed as the winner of the 2005 T. S. Eliot Prize.

Sherry Simpson is the author of *The Way Winter Comes: Alaska Stories* (Sasquatch Books, 1998) and is writing a book about bears and people for the University Press of Kansas. She frequently writes about wilderness and wildlife for anthologies, journals, and magazines. She teaches creative nonfiction writing at the University of Alaska–Anchorage. She grew up in Juneau.

Jennifer Sinor is an associate professor of English at Utah State University. Selected work has appeared or is forthcoming in *Fourth Genre, The Bellingham Review, Ecotone,* and *Green Mountains Review.* She lives with her husband and two sons on the southeastern edge of Idaho.

Frank Soos is the author of two collections of short stories, *Early Yet* and *Unified Field Theory*, which won the Flannery O'Connor Award for Short Fiction in 1997. His collection of essays, *Bamboo Fly Rod Suite,* has just been reissued in paperback by the University of Georgia Press. He has lived, fished, and skied in Fairbanks, Alaska, for twenty wonderful years.

David Starkey's essays have appeared in *American Literary Review, Barrelhouse, Cimarron Review, Gulf Stream Magazine, Santa Clara Review, Tampa Review,* and elsewhere. He teaches at Santa Barbara City College and is the author of a textbook, *Poetry Writing: Theme and Variations* (McGraw-Hill, 1999), as well as several collections of poems from small presses, most recently *Ways of Being Dead: New and Selected Poems* (Artamo Press, 2006). With Paul Willis, he coedited *In a Fine Frenzy: Poets Respond to Shakespeare* (University of Iowa Press, 2005), and with Wendy Bishop he cowrote *Keywords in Creative Writing* (Utah State University Press, 2006). He is currently at work on an introductory creative writing textbook for Bedford/St. Martin's.

Deb Olin Unferth's work has appeared in *Harper's*, *Conjunctions*, *McSweeney's*, the Pushcart Prize anthologies, and other publications. She lives in Lawrence, Kansas, and teaches at the University of Kansas.

Angus Woodward has lived in Louisiana since 1987. His fiction, poetry, and nonfiction have appeared in numerous journals, including *Alimentum*, *Xavier Review*, *Iowa Review*, *Prairie Schooner*, *Laurel Review*, *King Log*, *Bellingham Review*, *The Writer's Chronicle*, and others. He lives in Baton Rouge with his wife and two daughters and teaches at Our Lady of the Lake College.